TEXT IN
CONTEXT

OTHER RECENT VOLUMES IN THE
SAGE FOCUS EDITIONS

TEXT IN CONTEXT

Contributions to Ethnomethodology

Graham Watson
Robert M. Seiler
editors

SAGE PUBLICATIONS
The International Professional Publishers
Newbury Park   London   New Delhi

For information address:

SAGE Publications, Inc.
2455 Teller Road
Newbury Park, California 91320

SAGE Publications Ltd.
6 Bonhill Street
London EC2A 4PU
United Kingdom

SAGE Publications India Pvt. Ltd.
M-32 Market
Greater Kailash I
New Delhi 110 048 India

Printed in the United States of America

Library of Congress Cataloging-in-Publication Data

Main entry under title:

Text in context : contributions to ethnomethodology / edited by Graham
    Watson and Robert M. Seiler.
            p.   cm. — (Sage focus editions ; v. 132)
    Includes bibliographical references and index.
    ISBN 0-8039-4253-2. — ISBN 0-8039-4254-0 (pbk.)
    1. Ethnomethodology.   2. Discourse analysis.   I. Watson, Graham
II. Seiler, Robert M.
HM24.T458   1991
305.8'001—dc20   91-2619
                                                                      CIP

FIRST PRINTING, 1992

Sage Production Editor: Astrid Virding

For Harold Garfinkel

Contents

Transcript Notations

The notational conventions employed in this volume—and in conversation-analytic research generally—are taken from a set of conventions that were devised by Gail Jefferson. Understandably, this system continues to develop in response to the interests of researchers (see Psathas & Anderson, 1990). The version employed here derives from a version found in Atkinson and Heritage (1984, pp. ix-xvi). The symbols are designed to capture the verbal as well as the prosodic details of speech as it naturally occurs.

(word)	Parentheses surrounding a word indicate uncertainty about the transcription.
(.)	A dot enclosed in parentheses marks a micropause (i.e., less than one-tenth of a second).
(0.8)	Parentheses around a number on a line or between lines indicate silence, in tenths of a second.
((cough))	Items in double parentheses provide characterizations of events not fully transcribed.
[	Open brackets indicate the onset of simultaneous talk between utterances.

]	Closed brackets indicate the ending of simultaneous talk between utterances.
//	A double slash marks the onset of overlapped talk.
=	Equal signs indicate the "latching" of utterances or words with no intervening silence.
-	A hyphen indicates a cutoff.
,?.	Punctuation marks indicate intonation contours. They do not indicate grammatical status, such as a question. A comma indicates upward intonation at the end of a word. A question mark indicates upward intonation on the whole word. A period indicates downward intonation at the end of or over the course of a word.
<u>out</u>	Underlining indicates emphasis.
WORD	Upper case indicates especially loud sounds relative to the surrounding talk.
::	Colons mark the prolongation of the preceding sound.
.h	The letter *h* preceded by a period indicates aspiration in the course of a word, commonly laughter. Without the period, the *h* indicates outbreath.
→	A right-hand arrow marks an utterance to which the author refers in the text.
[WJS/11]	Codes in square brackets designate parts of the author's collection of tape recordings or a published source for datum in question. For obvious reasons, the names of the speakers have been changed.

Preface

This volume emerges from the First International Conference of the Discourse Analysis Research Group (DARG), which was held at the University of Calgary, August 23-26, 1989. We organized this interdisciplinary conference primarily to celebrate the group's tenth anniversary. Judging by the accounts that reached us, it was a huge success. We issue this volume with the hope it has captured the essential features of the deliberations that took place.

The Discourse Analysis Research Group dates from 1979, when Richard D. Heyman brought together a small group of University of Calgary scholars to form an association for the purpose of promoting the study of language as it is used in everyday life. This group of like-minded people met informally to present papers and to discuss the latest developments in their research areas. Aaron Cicourel and the late Erving Goffman were among the speakers who addressed the group in the early days.

The organization quickly expanded to include scholars from other institutions. Since 1985, when the *Discourse Analysis Research Group Newsletter* (edited by Robert M. Seiler) first appeared, the organization has become a network in the true sense of the word; that is, it comprises researchers around the world whose interests encompass a wide range of problems in the area of language and communication, such as conversation and textual analysis, interpersonal and cross-cultural communication, human/machine discourse, interviewing, classroom discourse, medical and legal discourse, philosophy of language, reading, rhetoric, semiotics, sociolinguistics, and other specialized discourses. The newsletter prints accounts of work in progress; commentary on issues arising out of new publications; discussion of innovative courses; news of conferences, seminars, and workshops; and reviews of recent publications.

But to return to the conference (and the volume at hand): We are pleased to say that more than 100 scholars, representing a variety of disciplines and working at no fewer than 42 institutions, gathered in Calgary late in August of 1989 to discuss the issues involved in "understanding language use in everyday life." These scholars gathered in Calgary to attend the keynote addresses that were presented by such ordinary-language experts as Rodney Watson (Manchester), Michael Moerman (University of California, Los Angeles), Fr. Edward Murray (Duquesne), Jeff Coulter (Boston), Deirdre Boden (Washington), and Don H. Zimmerman (University of California, Santa Barbara). Three of these presentations are included in this volume.

These scholars gathered to attend as well the 30 paper sessions on such topics as educational discourse, conversation, face-to-face interaction, rhetoric/argument/persuasion, philosophical issues, human-machine-mediated interaction, textual analysis, and everyday language concerns, and to take part in research workshops on such topics as analyzing machine-mediated interaction, Newton's and Goethe's experiments on color, gender issues, and cohesion in everyday English. Six of these presentations are included in this volume.

Above all, these scholars gathered in Calgary to hear our guest of honor, Harold Garfinkel (UCLA), deliver a presentation titled "Finding the Radical Sense and Relevance of Detail and Structure." We include a slightly altered version of Garfinkel's presentation here.

Heartfelt thanks are due to the Organizing Committee, which included Geoff Cragg, Sue Ditchburn, the editors of this volume, Rod Evans, Richard D. Heyman, David Fisher, George Labercane, Gerry Wilson, and Judith Gingrich and Ruellen Gunhold (administrative assistants), for ensuring that the conference ran smoothly.

We would also like to thank the Social Sciences and Humanities Research Council of Canada, the Province of Alberta, the University of Calgary Endowment Special Projects Fund, the University of Calgary

Research Policy and Grants Committee, and the Departments of Anthropology, Educational Curriculum and Instruction, Educational Policy and Administrative Studies, English, Political Science, Psychology, Religious Studies, and Teacher Education and Supervision, University of Calgary, for their financial assistance.

We have made every effort to ensure that this collection transcends the genre of "conference proceedings." Only a few of the many presentations made at the conference are collected here.

A great many people have contributed to this volume, directly and indirectly. For obvious reasons, we have acknowledged just a few of them. We would like to conclude these remarks by extending special thanks to Augustine Brannigan, Rom Harré, Paul ten Have, Richard D. Heyman (who continues to act as director of DARG), Leslie Miller, and our anonymous referees for (among other things) giving us the benefit of their observations.

—Robert M. Seiler

Introduction

GRAHAM WATSON

This is a mischievous collection of papers, each of which contributes, directly or indirectly, to the question: How far is extratextual material necessary to the carrying on of analysis at the level of concreteness common to ethnomethodology, conversation analysis, and contemporary language-oriented social constructionism? The question emerged, unforeseen, as the theme of the First International Conference on Understanding Language Use in Everyday Life, held at the University of Calgary in August of 1989. It provoked varied and sometimes incompatible responses from among the anthropologists, psychologists, linguists, philosophers, and sociologists present. That has proved fortunate, for it is our intention, in putting together this selection of responses, to highlight disagreements and to stimulate debate, rather than to express a unified point of view.

Our contributors are not invariably at loggerheads. In the first place, they agree that people, through their talk and other actions, produce and reproduce features of social life, such as "deviance," "mishearings," and "the organization."

Social scientists in (and around) ethnomethodology insist that social facts are not encountered, as Durkheim would have it, but rather are continuously constructed. This insistence has given rise to some wildly inaccurate characterizations of ethnomethodology. Bourdieu (1989), for example, has misinformed a generation of anthropologists by tarring ethnomethodology with the brush of voluntarism and subjectivism. Nothing could be more misleading. As Sharrock and Watson (1988)

point out, ethnomethodologists are interested neither in individuals as such nor in reading people's minds, but, rather, in describing the methods people use when *together* (but not necessarily consensually) they work up an account of what, for the purposes at hand, and until further notice, will count as "the way things really are." Which is to say, ethnomethodologists focus exclusively on *social* phenomena.

A related popular misconception, exemplified by Alexander and Giesen's (1987) claim that Garfinkel "continues to advocate a radically micro program" (p. 36), is that ethnomethodology is to be placed at the "micro" end of a dualism that ethnomethodologists find problematic and that is squarely the product of the very orthodox social scientific thinking that ethnomethodologists have abandoned.

A second characteristic shared by our contributors is that they agree that linguistic resources are crucial to the production and reproduction of the social order. All agree, too, that language has a socially organized character. The issue that divides them is how social organizational considerations are to be taken on board. Should attention be confined to recorded materials, or should an ethnographic context be taken into consideration?

The relationship of text to context has long been a focal point of interest among language-oriented ethnographers (Ardener, 1971; Bauman & Sherzer, 1974; Gumpertz & Hymes, 1972; Moerman, 1988). Some have been dismayed by the fact that Lévi-Strauss's structuralism has encouraged their colleagues to think of language as merely the embodiment of intellectual signification (Grillo, 1989, p. 5). Others have been even more dismayed to see Chomsky's "transformational" revolution become the dominant paradigm in mainstream linguistics, for that paradigm, too, marginalizes the social. However, even those who account themselves dismayed and who have challenged Chomskian hegemony have largely taken it for granted that language and society are mutually independent entities. They have failed to appreciate sufficiently the properties of conversation as a process of social interaction (Moerman, 1988, p. 12). That is a charge that cannot be laid at the door of any of our contributors.

It is by invoking ethnographic context that most contributors to this volume resolve the predicament that, while there is nothing but the text, not everything needed for its analysis is in the text. Of all our contributors, it is perhaps Tony Hak who makes the most explicit use of that context. In Chapter 8, he focuses on a psychiatric report based on a visit paid by a member of the Dutch Service for Emergency Psychiatry to an agitated young woman. What is absent from the text of this report is (a) the patient's behavior and the psychiatric procedures adopted by the visitor, that is, the "reality"; (b) the background expectancies and the rules for writing by means of which this reality was transformed into another reality, the psychiatric report; and (c) the rules for competent reading, that is, the meaning of the report. The solution that Hak offers to problems posed by these absences is that the transcription of the tape recording of the conversation that occurred during the consultation between the young woman and the psychiatric worker be treated as "reality," that the transformation process from this reality into the report be analyzed by means of a detailed comparison of the two texts, and that the institutional meaning of the report be discovered by consulting psychiatric textbooks or other texts that represent idealized professional knowledge. Hak, then, has no misgivings about interpreting his text in the light of what he sees as its ethnographic context.

In Chapter 1, Rodney Watson adopts a more cautious approach to context. He warns against treating "ethnography" as a monolith when in fact it consists of a diversity of ironic and nonironic approaches. In ironic ethnography, the analyst substitutes his or her interpretation for that of informants—hence (in orthodox social science) references to "latent functions," "false consciousness," and the like. In nonironic ethnography, informants are treated not as people who do not know what is really going on but as practical ethnographers who build ethnographic knowledge into their discourse (Zimmerman & Pollner, 1970). So, while it might be agreed that background knowledge is necessary in order to understand discourse, the question, for Watson, remains: What background knowledge? That which the analyst brings with him or her and imposes by fiat? Or that which we can show informants using?

The third characteristic our contributors share (and one that they demonstrate to the extent that space allows) is a respect for the virtual requirement of ethnomethodology and conversation analysis that we work from "texts" (records/representations) of behavior so that we do not engage in sophistry: argument borne solely on the wings of language. This insistence on anchoring analysis in the text of behavior has prompted the taunt that ethnomethodology is the new empiricism. (The irony of this taunt will not be lost on those who have for so long had to fend off the ubiquitous complaint that they engage in navel gazing.) "New empiricist" is a sobriquet some of our contributors would embrace more gladly than would others. Perhaps most would profess that they wish to be neither empiricists nor sophists and that they wish, rather, to work within the tension between what can be publicly shown and what can be intelligibly said. This, in turn, could provoke the counterclaim that they are thereby in danger of perpetuating an out-moded distinction between an observable behavioral part of an action and an unobservable mental part. The matter remains unresolved.

Though our contributors all think of themselves as ethnomethod-ologists or something close to that, few, if any, would recognize all of their fellow contributors as (so to speak) coreligionists, for while ethnomethodology/conversation analysis is a broad church, it encom-passes many persuasions, some of which are incompatible with others. Moreover, the question of how ethnomethodology might be related to conversation analysis, and of how these might be related to discourse analysis and language-oriented social constructivism, remains unre-solved. Rodney Watson (in this volume) couples ethnomethodology and conversation analysis, while Paul Atkinson (1988) sees them growing apart. Bilmes (1986) goes further than Atkinson in asserting that the two are based on fundamentally different assumptions: "For conversa-tion analysis, order is not there only by *ex post facto* interpretation; it is actually present in the phenomenon, and the conversation analyst tries to explain, by positing rules and procedures, how it gets there" (p. 166). In this volume, Garfinkel and Wieder (Chapter 10) argue to the contrary, that, as far as ethnomethodology is concerned, "order is already complete in the concrete." So a subtext of this volume concerns disputes about emerging disciplinary boundaries.

We begin with chapters programmatic in intent or effect. Rodney Watson asks if it would be possible to integrate in some complemen-tary or additive way the various approaches to the study of language in everyday life. He considers two cases of attempted integration: the conflation of Erving Goffman's work with that of conversation ana-lysts and ethnomethodologists, and the conflation of micro and macro approaches to social phenomena. He claims that such attempts neces-sarily fail as each approach constitutes phenomena differently, so that the set of phenomena available to one approach is invisible or irrelevant to another. By the same token, he argues, the move from one discipline to another involves a gestalt switch; hence we are naive to conceive of the interrelationship of the various social sciences in terms of a cozy complementarity of perspectives. Our attempts to conflate approaches are as absurd as would be the attempt to conflate the games of football and tennis to produce a supergame. This uncompromising stance has implications for the way we think of the interrelationships of *any* discipline, and, henceforth, it is one that only the disingenuous will be able to ignore.

The stance raises a number of questions about the nature of disciplines and gestalt switches. If a gestalt switch is what is involved in the move from one discipline to another, and if disciplines are to be identified by the fact that movement from one to another involves a gestalt switch, then disciplines and gestalt switches are mutually constitutive and we are no nearer than ever to answering such questions as, Do ethnomethodology and conversation analysis constitute a single discipline?

Another question: If a gestalt switch is involved when orthodox social sciences take on the concerns of ethnomethodology, then how are we to account for the fact(?) that the notion of reflexivity has been employed to great effect in the researches of Mulkay, Woolgar, Latour, and others who make up the European constructivist school of the sociology of scientific knowledge? The notion has enabled them to argue convincingly that scientists actively engage in the construction of scientific truths. While they have not consistently employed the notion of reflexivity in the sense Garfinkel intended (see Lynch, 1982), a case could be made (which Halfpenny, 1988, vigorously disputes) that they are now getting it right (consider Woolgar, 1988). Whether they are right or not, they have at least not abandoned reflexivity as an issue, as most contributors appear to have done. Is this not a worry? Not, perhaps, if Wes Sharrock (personal communication) is correct in asserting that good ethnomethodological work invariably and unfussily treats describing as a socially organized matter, as an otherwise unremarkable feature of phenomena, and not as a source of methodological angst. He cites Bjelic and Lynch's chapter in this volume as one that instantiates treatment of the topic of reflexivity without talking about it or agonizing over it.

In Chapter 2, Michael Moerman searches for common grounds to the study of language in everyday life. He finds it in (a) the investigation of specific occasions rather than of some glossed or generalized characterization of behavior, and (b) the concept of action as continuously created rather than as structurally released or constrained. He goes on to tell how his fieldwork in Thailand led to his involvement with conversation analysis, and how conversation analysis thereafter informed his ethnographic research. Conversation analysis and ethnography need each other, he concludes. Conversation analysis can help ethnography reach its goal of discovering how abstract rules are invoked, enforced, and disputed in the course of everyday life; to do this conversation analysis must take on board ethnographic knowledge of the sort that enables it to recognize actions for what they are—commands, boasts, jokes, and so on. For Moerman, the text of talk is not enough to analyze lived experience. He wants to enlarge the text with ethnography while anchoring ethnography with the text.

Clearly, ethnomethodology has implications for anthropology, as it has for other forms of orthodox social science. One of these implications is the idea that both native and ethnographer are in the business of constituting meaning; another is that culture, far from being a given framework that lies behind and is expressed in action, is, rather, a flexible repertoire of interpretive resources drawn upon by participants in accounting for action. But what of conversation analysis per se? It could be argued that, if we mentally eliminate from Moerman's work his highly developed and phenomenologically informed sensitivity to the reality work his informants unceasingly engage in, what we are left with looks far more like conversation analysis than it does anthropology: transcripts of tape recordings of minute segments of naturally occurring talk. But it must be conceded that the close examination of naturally occurring talk constitutes an obstacle to any tendency to substitute imagined scenarios for what informants actually do and say. Hence the force of Moerman's (1988) complaint that "ethnographers of speaking do not provide or refer to transcripts or other public records, and have largely concentrated on special sorts of speech events other than everyday conversations" (p. 11).

Moerman touched on the matter of the moral basis of ethnomethodology by characterizing conversation analysis as barren, as about turns, adjacency pairs, and so on, and by contrasting it unfavorably with the early work of Sacks, which, he says, is about "lived experience" and is filled with "searing compassion." Such humanistic concerns were dismissed by some floor speakers as a hangover from early and problematic affiliations with phenomenology. In Rodney Watson's account, they would entail yet another analyst's interest imposed on the *in situ* specifics of everyday discourse.

One speaker threw fat on the fire by urging that ethnomethodology should adopt some of the moral concerns of continental European approaches to discourse. Others rejected the implied accusation that ethnomethodologists and conversation analysts are so imbued with the dominant ideology that they are guilty of moral dereliction. Rodney

Watson characterized moralizing approaches not only as radically incompatible with ethnomethodology but also as a retreat to stipulative and absolutist forms of theorizing that ethnomethodology and conversation analysis have forsworn. "Who cares what Foucault says," he added, "he's just another member!"

Don H. Zimmerman, in Chapter 3, shuns both the aridity of adjacency-pair analysis and the vacuity of imagined scenarios. In a detailed empirical study of interaction in an emergency answering service, he addresses the vexing question of the relationship of behavior to institutionalized contexts. For him, participants constitute organizations through their discourse and then orient their behavior to what they have constituted.

Zimmerman's chapter has massive implications for the current search for the much-vaunted micro/macro linkage (see, e.g., Alexander et al., 1987; Knorr-Cetina & Cicourel, 1981). Structures, systems, cultures, and so on are "occasioned" phenomena, which exist only in the practices of participants. They exist nowhere else. Particular participants at particular moments, in particular strips of discourse, constitute what they refer to as "the system." And they do so collectively; not just anything goes. As Stanley Fish (1980, p. 356) has observed, it is a mistake to think of interpretation as an activity in need of constraint; interpretation is a structure of constraints. (Actually, Rodney Watson reminds us, it is a complex of constraining and enabling features. Orthodox social scientists devote a disproportionate amount of time to constraints.) Having constituted "the system," participants then orient themselves to it as if it had an objective existence prior to and independent of their discourse. Thus constraints are to be found not in such reified entities as rules, structures, or class interests, but in the practices of participants. Since constraints are to be found in the very practices of participants, the macro/micro dichotomy is false (or, rather, it is an artifact of conventional social scientific reasoning), and the search for the link between macro and micro, the preoccupation of the social sciences throughout the 1980s, is a futile quest.

In his comments on Zimmerman's paper, Arthur W. Frank (1990) seizes upon the observation that conversation does not stand alone—that conversation not only makes sense of settings, it makes sense only in settings—as evidence that ethnomethodology is being assimilated into mainstream sociology. He proposes that this assimilation be recognized "once and for all" and, further, that ethnomethodologists embrace Anthony Giddens's structuration theory. Structuration theory would bring back the organizational context and the voluntaristic action that conversation analysis has left out.

In pursuing this line, Frank ignores ethnomethodologists' pleas that their subject originated in opposition to the kind of speculative theorizing that, arguably, Giddens's work exemplifies.

Giddens's structuration theory has the merit of recognizing explicitly that interaction involves not only meaning but also power. Some conference participants lamented what they identified as the neglect of this variable, especially in conversation analysis. They complained that while Deirdre Boden, in her keynote address, considered the transcripts of telephone conversations between President Kennedy and the governor of Mississippi concerning the civil rights riots of 1962, she did not address the question of what it was that made these conversations ones between a president and a governor rather than ones between two housewives at the laundromat. In response, Boden protested that talk assumes context; talk and context elaborate each other; power is part and parcel of that context. Sharrock and Watson (1988, p. 64) implicitly endorse her stand, for they reject the analytical distinction between talk and the ethnography that lends sense to that talk. For them, ethnographic context is a constituent part of talk.

In Chapter 4, Dusan Bjelic and Michael Lynch's principal concern—one they share with Watson and Garfinkel—is to demonstrate, *contra* Art Frank, that ethnomethodology is "not just another sociology." They claim that their chapter exemplifies "a distinctive ethnomethodological approach" to the study of work in the sciences (see Heritage, 1984a, pp. 293-311). By this they mean that they seek to explicate the situated reasoning that makes up actual laboratory practices and that they refuse to ironicize such reasoning by subsuming it under conventional social scientific concerns. (For Lynch, 1982, the use of a term such as *construction* has inescapable connotations of fabricating.) They set out to respecify Goethe's rereading of Newton's experiments in color. Their method comprises not the analysis of written text, but the manipulation of physical objects and an emphasis on the sequential arrangement of observable *activity* (rather than on *action* in the Weberian sense). Their chapter is intended to act as an "installation" (in the artist's sense of the term: an interactive exhibit); rather than describing a social activity, they provide a material base for exhibiting the order of an activity in progress. The reader (that is, the reader who takes the trouble to get a prism) is placed in the position of examining how a "scientific" argument is produced *in situ*.

Bjelic and Lynch explain that for Newton the prism opens up white light, disclosing its objective components, while for Goethe the prism provides a way of displaying the interaction between light and darkness in a substantive field. Goethe respecifies Newton's spectrum by leading us to see it not as the natural rainbow, but as an artifact of Newton's having produced a narrow slit for his beam of light. They, in turn, respecify Goethe's "primal phenomena" as phenomena inseparable from his method of exposition and demonstration. However, their intention is not Goethean; it is not to debunk anybody. It is, rather, to demonstrate how the embodied and sequential practices enjoined by Goethe's text generate facticity. The figures and cards in the chapter are arranged both to recover Goethe's demonstration and to enable the reader to struggle with the work of following the demonstration. Both the structure of the demonstration (the order of the cards and so on) presented and described in the text and the reader's work in coming to terms with that order *are* the phenomenon.

The chapter is designed to be unsatisfying in at least one sense: It does not provide an elaborate account of the actions of performing a scientific demonstration. Instead, it involves the reader, prism in hand. The ambivalence expressed in a proposed title for this collection, *Not Everything Is in the Text, but There Is Nothing but the Text*, formulates the essential incompleteness of the presentation on paper.

Bjelic and Lynch's insistence on the distinctiveness of ethnomethodology has its epiphany in Garfinkel and Sacks's (1970) famous paper on formal structures. While Bjelic and Lynch may join with Watson in their admiration for that paper, they part company with him in their estimation of the merits of conversation analysis. "The currently established program in conversation analysis," they declare, "disregards a vast array of . . . phenomena that simply do not take the form of sequential structures of talk," and the result is "an absurd account of situated competencies."

Bjelic and Lynch's characterization of conversation analysis is a popular one (see Cicourel, 1973, p. 56; echoed in Torode, 1989, p. xiii), but it is indignantly rejected by Schegloff (1987a):

> Indeed, it is ironic to find some critics insistently taking conversation analysis to task for not setting its findings into context or for not incorporating context into its inquiries. For much of this work can be viewed as an extended effort to elaborate just what a context is and what its explication or description might entail. (p. 221)

Conversation analysis is reproached by Paul Atkinson (1988) for having "an unduly restricted perspective" that is "behaviorist and empiricist, and which does not reflect the interpretive origins that inspired ethnomethodology" (p. 441). His strictures may be telling, but they hardly apply to Bilmes's and Psathas's chapters in this collection, for both Bilmes and Psathas give due weight to interpretation and rebuke those (straw men?) who are still wholly preoccupied with adjacency pairs, turn-taking, and so on.

In Chapter 6, George Psathas argues that concentrating on restricted sets of utterances or turns fails to capture either what a conversation is about or even whether or not it constitutes an activity system, such as a lesson in which a blind student is taught how to orient himself. To capture such features, extended sequences in interaction need to be considered as whole units. To know what such units are, the analyst must do more than examine transcripts; the study of extended sequences is not to be thought of as merely an expansion of the adjacency-pair structure into longer and longer strings. The analyst must go beyond talk to consult ethnographic knowledge. The ethnographic knowledge that Psathas draws on is knowledge acquired in the course of years of study of instructional activities. Psathas knows more than is said in the lines quoted.

In a similar vein, Jack Bilmes argues in Chapter 5 that when a recipient gives an utterance a hearing, we must make a judgment as to whether that hearing is an acceptable reflection of what we had in mind or wanted to be heard as having had in mind. This judgment is far more than a mechanical matter of matching meaning and hearing, for a "mishearing" is something that can be claimed and disputed or agreed on, rather than an objective phenomenon existing independently of participants' claims.

From the point of view of orthodox conversation analysis (as opposed to that of, say, interpretive discourse analysis), both a "lesson" and "mishearings" refer not to abstract (nonsituated) meanings but to meanings as they are demonstrably oriented to by participants. Thus the orthodox conversation analyst's selection of contextual (ethnographic) details depends on what aspects of the context are "used" by participants in the course of interaction.

James L. Heap is primarily concerned with sequences of actions other than utterances. In Chapter 7, he sets out to establish how normative order is brought to bear on particular instances of observed behavior

(text) by investigating the actions of two children engaged in collaborative computer editing. He argues that each child has grounds for
believing that the other is oriented to a specific normative order, that
he or she acts upon those beliefs, and that the resultant action, in turn,
provides the other with grounds for beliefs on which to base his or her
actions. A sense of normative order is thus built up through sequences
of actions, which resemble the turn-taking machinery of talk described
by Sacks, Schegloff, and Jefferson (1974).

Heap shows that, while all the children can see and hear are behavioral displays and their artifacts, they are nevertheless able to produce
for each other, and for the analyst, a sense of a stable social order. While
the text of behavior is not self-interpreting, it does provide participants
grounds for ascribing beliefs, purposes, and concerns to each other.
Heap uses the visible, behavioral resources that members have in
building their sequences of interaction as a resource for making claims
about how these behaviors and artifacts could be interpreted and used
by participants. For him, the text of behavior furnishes material for
interpretation, but such material is not enough: The text must be connected to normative order. Normative order is not in the text, but renders
the text intelligible.

In Chapter 8, Tony Hak adopts an ethnomethodological approach to
the study of psychiatric records; he regards these records neither as
reflecting reality nor as distorting it, but as constitutive of psychiatric
practice. His model, which he devises in the course of a comparative
analysis of the field notes written by a psychiatric worker and the
worked-up version of those notes, suggests that psychiatric interpretation can be described as a transformation of raw material (the field
notes) into a description (the worked-up version) under the auspices
both of common sense and of an idealized version of psychiatry, such
as one finds in psychiatric textbooks. The raw material may have
undergone many transformations before it reaches the psychiatrist and
may undergo many after it leaves him. So any interpretation is represented as a transformational link in a chain without beginning or end.

In Chapter 9, Stephen Hester performs a membership categorization
analysis of transcripts of meetings between educational psychologists
and teachers with problem pupils in order to discover the methods by
means of which references to "deviance" are produced and recognized.
For him, a text is best understood as an "indexical expression" inseparable from the "knowing" subject or "reader." His emphasis on how
such references are produced and recognized is to be contrasted with

the emphasis other researchers have placed on the kind of deviance pointed to. The significance of these methods, he argues, is that the intelligibility of references to deviance, and therefore the intelligibility of the sociology of deviance as a subdiscipline of sociology, depends upon them. Unless speakers are able to produce recognizable references to deviance and unless hearers (in turn) can recognize them as references to deviance, intelligible talk about such a subject is impossible.

Harold Garfinkel, to whom we dedicate our book, outranks even Schutz and Wittgenstein in importance to ethnomethodology. It is fitting that the last word should be his. In his conference address, Garfinkel insisted that ethnomethodology has no quarrel with conventional social science. Ethnomethodology and conventional social science, he said, differ so profoundly that they do not find themselves competing for the same ecological niche. Nevertheless, this chapter may be read as, in part, an extended critique of conventional social science.

Conventional social scientists, as ethnomethodology sees them, are preoccupied with producing explanations rather than descriptions, typifications rather than particularities, "studies about" rather than "studies of." Their task, says Garfinkel, is "finding and reading signs," or, as Heritage (1984a) puts it, transmuting lived realities "into objects suitable for treatment within the accounting practices of professional social science" (p. 300). The kind of social order they are predisposed to discover is the kind that is available only upon analysis. They are systematically blind to the kind of mutely self-explanatory order that is "evidently, really, actually" built, skillfully and unremarkably, into events and things by members of society in the course of their everyday lives. In dismissing this as uninteresting, conventional social scientists stand condemned as "eyeless in Gaza."

But neither Garfinkel nor any of the other contributors to our collection is concerned principally with revealing the deficiencies of normal social science. Garfinkel, like the other contributors, is more interested in demonstrating what ethnomethodology alone can do, which is to display "just how vulgarly competent members concert their activities to produce and to show . . . order [and] meaning in the haecceities of their ordinary lives together."

For Garfinkel, haecceity (the specifics, the peculiarities—the "thisness") is of central importance. Order (for him) is locally produced "just here, just now, with just what is at hand, with just who is here, in the time that just this local gang of us have." Order is thus "an assemblage of unavoidable haecceities" (unavoidable because "every attempt to remedy or to avoid the haecceity of whatever matter haecceity modifies . . . preserves . . . the identical matters that were the cause for complaint"). It is this concerted production of order from among and out of haecceity that makes society "a wondrous thing."

1

The Understanding of
Language Use in Everyday Life

Is There a Common Ground?

RODNEY WATSON

I want to suggest that the search for an analytic common ground among
the various disciplines and "perspectives" that bear upon "discourse
analysis" is a search for a chimera, and that claims that a common
ground has been, or can be, established are misconceived. The two cases
I shall examine are chosen for no better reason than that I happen to be
fairly familiar with them. They will be examined for their interior logic
and the issue of integration will, briefly, be considered in that light. I
shall consider the issue of integration not at the level of substantive
content but at the procedural level, the level that addresses the organizational properties of the approaches concerned. My plan in this chapter
is to look—after some prefatory remarks—at two sets of approaches.
First, I shall consider Goffman's analytic work on communicative
conduct and consider it in relation to (some) ethnomethodological and
conversation-analytic studies. The issue of combining these approaches
will also be discussed, given that, to general sociologists, the approaches of Goffman and the ethnomethodologists and conversation
analysts are often seen as cognate, if not identical. Then I shall examine,
far more briefly and schematically, some selected issues concerning the
characterization of sociological approaches to language use and social

action around the "agency/structure"-"micro/macro" distinction, together with the attempts to bridge the opposition thus generated.

In general terms, I shall attempt to show that the Goffman/ethnomethodology-conversation analysis pairing is, despite well-intentioned attempts to treat it as being of a piece, composed of approaches that are, in terms of their inner reasoning, quite distinct and indeed irreconcilable. Concerning the second pairing, the agency/structure distinction, I shall argue that it and its derivations are a radically misleading way of locating (say) ethnomethodological and conversation-analytic work in the first place. I recognize that the impetus toward such attempts at integration is, sometimes, morally toned, connoting the values of openness, flexibility, and the like, and that voting against these would be a little like a Bible Belt politician voting against motherhood. Far be it from me to challenge the values of openness and flexibility; indeed, I suppose my aim here could be conceived as preventing them from falling into a desuetude born of promiscuous espousal.

Language is important to members and analysts alike simply because in one way or another it is the instrument of all social life and because a vast number of the interchanges that make up social life are *linguistic* interchanges. The world we live in is "language saturated" in all kinds of respects and pervasively involves the mastery of ordinary language; we encounter the world in this way. Thus as analysts of social life we are, whether we wish to acknowledge it or not, always encountering linguistic transactions in our data gathering. Discourse analysts treat their communicative character as their primary data. Some who choose to do so may examine language in a self-contained way, as itself constituting a set of generic social practices jointly deployed. Others may seek to treat social institutions (such as religion, science, or medicine), as well as their reproduction and transformation, as ways of talking. Sociologists, social anthropologists, linguists, and others may seek to inquire into what can be learned about these institutions by treating them as oral phenomena, and, reflexively, into how such talk comes to be seen on this or that occasion as specifically religious speaking, scientific speaking, and so on. We may then inquire into what we can learn about religious or scientific work from these linguistic materials.

There is no "time-out" from all this for sociology and the other discourse-analytic disciplines. Graham Watson (1984) has described how we may see anthropology as ways of (talking and) writing, and has shown some of the persuasive and other rhetorical devices that construct the internal and external boundaries of the discipline. This and the other discourse-analytic disciplines conduct their inquiries, produce their reports, give their lectures, and so on through some natural language or other, although they are sometimes far from appreciating this point, as Sacks (1963) has shown, in an early paper, by reference to Durkheim's putatively sociological study of suicide. This is a pity, since by and large the unacknowledged descriptive and other resources of the language shape the activity of doing sociology or the other discourse-analytic disciplines. (By *shaping* I mean the "enabling" as well as the "constraining" properties of the language; I find the virtually exclusive focus by some sociolinguists, sociologists, and others on the constraints set by some forms of language unfortunate and obscure, to say the least.) Sacks (1963) has observed—with Durkheim's work on suicide in mind—that the investigation of how we talk of an object such as suicide, and how we assign cases to that class, is a prior task that sociology must address: "Having [analytically] generated procedural descriptions of the assembling of a suicide classification it may turn out that it is the category and the methodology for applying it that constitutes the interesting sociological problem" (p. 8). Certainly, I suggest, this might tell us how sociologists talk and write about suicide.

This conception of sociology as ways of talking and writing brings us conveniently to Goffman, whose work on communicative conduct is treated as a resource in many disciplines and whose textual devices are particularly vivid. It is not entirely clear how we can arrive at the right level for the analytic characterization of these devices; certainly, one cannot do this simply by assigning Goffman's work to a school of thought, a sociological perspective, or whatever, in the usual sense of those terms.

It is clear that Goffman's textual work involves a variety of extraordinarily extended metaphors and similes that are brilliantly employed in order to force into visibility features of "communicative conduct" usually left in the half-light. He derives this imagery from a number of language games—the theater, team games, confidence tricks, espionage, and the like—and also from sources that do not derive from conventional arenas, such as ethology. His approach often combines various images (e.g., the "confidence trick" and "dramaturgical" metaphors) so that we get a complex and composite view, and very often he seems to start over and tread very much the same ground—information transmission, control, and "leakage"—in terms of a new metaphor (espionage, say, rather than dramaturgy). The question is: How are we to characterize these particular textual devices, these ways of sociological writing?

A first move is to note that Goffman's work is pattern-elaborative: It involves the subsuming of a huge variety of seemingly discrete phenomena under the aegis of, initially, a single metaphor. His work thus establishes a homologous pattern in an immense range of images. This approach capitalizes on an element of surprise and on the capacities of readers as active pattern detectors, in order to achieve a fresh view of what typically are overfamiliar phenomena. Through the imposition and great extension of a given metaphor, what Crews (1986) calls a "master transcoding device" is mobilized. In this way, as Anderson and Sharrock (1982) put it, apparently disparate phenomena can be treated as versions of each other; metaphors can thus serve as "order-enhancing procedures." Observe, for instance, the first position of descriptions in establishing the master transcoding device in the following passage:

> A second technique for counteracting the development of affective ties between performers and audience is to change audiences periodically. Thus filling station managers used to be shifted periodically to prevent the formation of strong personal ties with particular clients. It was found that when such ties were allowed to form, the manager sometimes placed the interests of a friend who needed credit before the interests of the social establishment. Bank managers and Ministers have been routinely shifted for similar reasons as have certain colonial administrators. Some female professionals provide another illustration, as the following reference to organized prostitution suggests. (Goffman, 1959, p. 215)

Basically, we can see that a diverse range of phenomena is subjected to a "reproducible theme" (Anderson & Sharrock, 1982), contained within the space of the "performer-audience" metaphor: *multum in parvo*.

A correlative move that is intended to mobilize this order-enhancing procedure is the utilization of what Burke (1935/1954) calls "planned misnomers," that is, the methodical misnaming of objects that already have more familiar names (which Goffman also provides) in the attitude of everyday life. This is integral to Goffman's project of sociological redescription, where primordial terms given in the natural attitude are replaced by terms that, although derived from a familiar and conventional area, are transplanted and appropriated for analysis in the form of an extended metaphor. It *de*contextualizes these primordial terms and adventitiously *re*contextualizes them.

Burke (1935/1954) calls these analytic tactics a "perspective by incongruity," since the imposition of a sensible order through planned misnomer establishes incongruous applications of terms through "violating" their *conventional* applications. This, Burke says, produces "new alignments incongruous with the alignments flowing from other modes of classification" (p. 102), especially, we might add, those modes located in the natural attitude. This assists in Goffman's devising of a culturally indigenous sociology/anthropology of communication conduct,[1] in that the textual devices that establish such a redescription operate to occasion a "look-again technique," so that we may vividly see these virtually unremarked communicative activities with fresh eyes, even though it is through and through an *instructed* seeing. The frequent building of subsidiary metaphors upon the initial one occasions yet another shift, another realignment. Multiple laminations of incongruity are built up, so that what we have is a constant perspectival shift, even if each shift is only one of nuance. If, through these devices, Goffman turns us to some extent into foreign travelers in our own land, he does so in a remarkably multiplex way.

It might be noted in passing that Goffman's work is not unique, as is often claimed, in using a perspective of incongruity for sociological/anthropological purposes. Long (1958), for instance, has used the game analogy to characterize the interplay of institutions in a local community, and Miner (1956) has written a well-known parody of anthropological writing, "Body Ritual Among the Nacirema," using planned misnomers.

This approach, then, renders familiar things exotic and works parallel to those that focus on real-world exotic phenomena as somehow standing for or casting light on mundane phenomena (see Schwartz, n.d.). Goffman himself employs such a focus when examining confidence tricks for what they tell us about the interactional nature of the adjustment to failure in general. Like Goffman, the writers in question use textual resources as persuasive devices to accomplish their task. As Graham Watson (1984) points out, these rhetorical or stylistic devices do not constitute "empty flourishes and the evasion of real issues." To point out such devices is not to relativize them in any sort of "knockdown" way, nor is it to discredit them in any moral sense. Compare such approaches now with the analytic styles of ethnomethodology and conversation(al) analysis. The initial analytic issue in these styles has to do with the social orderliness of conduct, settings, or the like as recognizable states of affairs for members. For researchers, the orderliness of the social world is recognizable in the first instance in terms of the *commonsense* understandings that operate from within the settings concerned (Watson, 1984, p. 360). Members have, then, understandings born of and constituted by inhabitation. The problem of social order, for researchers, becomes: How is order produced as a visible and recognizable matter? How are "transparency arrangements" (arrangements that render objects perspicuous not only as orderly in some general sense of that term but also, specifically, as just what they are in themselves) built into actions, interactions, and settings?

The inspection of these endogenous arrangements brings us to the examination of the procedural knowledge and practices whereby "orderly properties" such as regularity and recurrence are rendered identifiable in highly specific determinations. We may simply refer to these practices as the self-describing and self-reporting features of a setting, which in turn are built into its self-organizing and self-renewing character.[2] The analysis of a course of action or setting, then, *necessarily* involves the analysis of how the action or setting renders itself recognizable as what it is.

Clearly, for ethnomethodologists, the mastery of ordinary language is, in a huge variety of ways, a central, ubiquitous, and indispensable feature in the interior detection, display, and elaboration of a pattern in the course of action or in a setting. Talk is centrally involved in establishing the accountable features of settings, in constituting settings.

For ethnomethodologists, talk is an inseparable, constituent feature of settings and the activities that compose them; it gives settings and activities their recognizable character, or appearance, as (for example) normal, familiar, typical instances of what is observed. Not only is talk a routinely expected feature of most settings, but it also serves, reflexively, as an "inner guide" to the setting.

This approach allows ethnomethodologists to avoid the kind of position adopted by those types of sociolinguistics in which ordinary language styles or whatever are examined for their correspondence with some separately conceptualized phenomenon, such as social class, region, or ethnicity, and in which the talk may be examined not in and of itself but for what it tells us about that "other" phenomenon. In sociolinguistics, talk is treated more or less as a transparent conduit to the phenomenon, or as standing on behalf of the phenomenon in some way. Sidestepping such issues, ethnomethodologists are freed from making Bernsteinlike stipulations about differential perceptual complexity or flexibility or from making, for instance, imputations of differential rationality, truth value, and the like, in relation to those "forms" of talk. Instead of seeing language as some kind of lens through which we see social reality, ethnomethodologists treat social reality as something that is self-explicating, that "talks about itself," as it were.

This capacity of talk to "fold back" upon itself and its setting (as Cicourel put it) has been described by Garfinkel and Sacks (1970) when referring to conversational formulations:

> A member may treat some part of the conversation as an occasion to describe that conversation, to explain it, or characterize it, or explicate, or translate, or summarize, or furnish the gist of it, or take note of its accordance with rules, or remark on its departure from rules. That is to say, a member may use some part of the conversation as an occasion to *formulate* the conversation. (p. 350)

This clearly indicates the procedure of rendering a conversation self-descriptive; it also raises the issue of what there is in common between conversation(al) analysis and ethnomethodology. One construction of this commonality has been given by Sacks, who differentiates *his* position from the approaches taken by classic thinkers such as Socrates, Freud, and Darwin by avowing an interest in *what* people know and *how* they use that knowledge (see Heritage, 1984a, p. 233). He formulates a nonironic stance, a set of analytic auspices that do not incorporate the stipulations of a competitive or subversive attitude vis-à-vis lay members' knowledge.

The knowledge involved is shared procedural knowledge, although substantive knowledge is, of course, involved; indeed, Sacks presents the issue in terms of the questions: "How do members know that?" and "Why that now?" As Heritage (1984a) points out, conversation analysts espouse the same procedural "symmetry proposal," which is derived from Garfinkel's observation that "procedural knowledge is involved in the production, reception, monitoring and interpretation of items of conduct." The sense of an utterance is assembled by members with reference to the utterance's position in a sequence of utterances; the interlocutor's understanding of an utterance is exhibited in the next utterance, just as the producer of the prior utterance can monitor the next one in terms of that prior utterance. Indeed, a complex back-and-forth process pertains whereby interlocutors check out each other's understanding, a process that is built into the alternation of turns at talk. Thus what Heritage terms an "architecture of intersubjectivity" is established in conversation, which involves constantly updated states of knowledge and understanding occurring in real time.

Typically, these states of knowledge and understanding are treated by members as more or less background features of the talk. Only in limited spheres, such as in understanding checks and formulations, are knowledge and understanding, to varying and limited degrees, treated as matters for attention on their own behalf. We can cite formulations in conversation as examples of the achievement of understanding and knowledge as interactional (and, more specifically, as turn-taking) matters, operating at different levels of conversational organization.

Regarding the utterance-by-utterance level of formulations, we can note that those formulations where a recipient is formulating matters delivered by an interlocutor are typically adjacency paired.

[excerpt from a British Radio *Slimmer of the Year* interview]

Slimmer: And I was completely alone one weekend and I got to this stage where I almost jumped in the river. I just felt life wasn't worth it any more—it hadn't anything to offer and if this was living, I had had enough.

F *Interviewer:* You really were prepared to commit suicide because you were a big fatty.

D+ *Slimmer:* Yes, because I(:) I just didn't see anything in life that I had to look forward to . . .

(F = formulation; D = decision)

Here, the formulation as a candidate understanding is adjacency paired with a confirming decision (+) of the formulation as a "proper gloss" or adequate gist/upshot of the interview so far. Other formulations occasion disconfirming decisions:

[excerpt from a British ITN *News at Ten* interview on December 8, 1977, with Yorkshire Area Miners' Union president, Mr. Arthur Scargill, concerning a new national-level agreement between the government and the Miners' Union, which allowed local pay deals and differentials based on local productivity bonuses]

Scargill: . . . but you can rest assured that I will not sit idly by, and nor will my area council, and allow any other mineworker in Britain (.) to earn more money than those that I represent.

	Interviewer:	Well will you
	Scargill:	We will i (.) ensure that those we represent (.) get the same amount of payment (.) that others (.) are going to be fact they are (.) anywhere else in Britain.
F	*Interviewer:*	So i (.) so pits in your area will be allowed to go for productivity schemes
D–	*Scargill:*	I didn't say that at all that at all (.) I said very clearly that my members <u>w</u>ould not accept a p<u>o</u>sition (.) where <u>o</u>ther mineworkers were going to be paid <u>more</u> money for <u>coal</u>mining activity. . . .

Here, the candidate understanding proposed by the interviewer in the formulating utterance is accorded an upgraded or intensified disconfirmation (–) by Scargill, linked to a reformulation, a differing proposed understanding, of the foregoing talk.

This formulation-decision pair can, as I have indicated, operate at superordinate levels of conversational organization (Heritage & Watson, 1979). They may operate particularly powerfully at the level of topic, as Heyman (1986) has pointed out in a paper on classroom talk in a science lesson, where, for example, confirmations may realign and proliferate talk-to-topic and disconfirmations may redirect the topic of talk. Similarly, formulations may work as part of preclosing sequences in closing down the conversation as a whole (Heyman, 1986).

It is in this way that conversation analysis furnishes an approach to understanding the methods whereby formulations are built into talk and whereby they exhibit, for interlocutors, the self-explicating features of the talk.

We can now briefly compare Goffman's approach on the one hand and ethnomethodology and conversation analysis on the other. It will be possible to sketch out only a very few of the many differences in what, ironically, have often been seen as cognate and even complementary analytic stances.

Insofar as ethnomethodology and conversation analysis seek to explicate members' understandings, they may be said to preserve what Schwartz (n.d.) has termed the "phenomenological intactness" of the phenomenon observed (so far as the deployment of analytic relevances allows). Ethnomethodology and conversation analysis seek to adopt not a competitive stance vis-à-vis members' understandings, but a nonironic stance. They seek not to stipulate in advance members' orientations.

By contrast, Goffman's analyses contain several stipulative and ironic elements. Insofar as he mobilizes a "perspective by incongruity," his analyses contain a built-in feature of irony, namely, what Burke terms "downward conversion." To present *all* actions as, say, forms of "playacting," espionage, or whatever, is at the level of membership to downgrade or ironicize them.

This may lead us to Louch's (1966) observation that Goffman stands accused of stretching a metaphor beyond its ordinary occasioning contexts so that it loses its pointedness. Treating some item of conduct as playacting ordinarily relies for its impact on those instances of conduct that, for members, are quite clearly *not* "merely playacting." Analysts have reported that, when inmates of mental hospitals feel they have to perform in this way all the time, they see this as unnatural, as an interruption or disruption of their normal orientation to their social world (Messenger, 1962).

The use of planned misnomers basically ensures and transacts this ironic cast in Goffman's analysis. Redescriptions of admissions procedures and other complex instances of communicative conduct in terms of "betrayal funnels," "mortifications of the self," "civil death," and the like would seem to bear at least a problematic or (often self-avowed) *parti pris* relation to members' constructions. And what G. W. H. Smith (1989a, 1989b) has termed "incongruous juxtapositions" carry a similar ironic cast. Mental hospitals are adjacently gathered with concentration camps, and mental patients with prison inmates, in order to make a particular analytic point. Communicative activities such as therapy are accorded what may (in the natural attitude) be incongruous predicates such as "serviceability to the institution."

On top of this, Goffman's redescriptions seem designed to supplant what for members is the point of the interaction with a focal and ever-exclusive emphasis on impression management, performance, and so on, as Blumer (1972) observes in an early critique. In this regard, Goffman seems to subsume (for members) a whole range of substantively differing communicative encounters under a single and exogenous standard. It may thus be apposite to inquire whether Goffman's work can properly be considered "naturalistic" at all, let alone "radically naturalistic," as Jary and Smith (1976) have characterized it. It seems to me, in fact, that Goffman's work contains many elements of what Crews (1986) terms "theoreticism," something more usually associated with so-called macro approaches.

I do not think it is useful to treat the approaches I have been discussing as ossified and reified "perspectives," with all the implications of "tunnel vision" on the "same" phenomena, such that they may complement each other in some kind of additive way so as to produce a "fuller" or "total" view with a shared problematic and shared objectives. Instead, we might choose to treat them as discrete arrays of analytic practices or sets of moves, more or less skillfully put together, as Anderson, Hughes, and Sharrock (1985) have put it. These "sets of activities" are self-contained with regard to objectives, proper moves, rules mobilized in appropriate contexts—rules that enable and constrain legitimate analytic conduct and that describe and circumscribe that conduct, the implementation of *standards* of conduct, and so on. These sets of analytic practices cannot be conflated any more than can the games of football and tennis be conflated to produce a "supergame." Nor is there a single standard, master problematic or transcendent objective in terms of which these sets of analytic moves can be synthesized (indeed, to treat football and tennis as ball games is to employ a gloss that forestalls the specification of difference).

The focus, then, may be placed more profitably upon the interior moves that gain their specific sense as members of the figurational work of the set concerned. Moves are "figurational" in that they are dynamic constituents of the particular gestaltlike configuration of analytic practices; they cannot be transplanted into other configurations any more than the configurations themselves can be conflated.

A highly truncated illustration of how this figurational work involves radical incompatibilities when considered in the above light can be given in the respective treatment accorded by Goffman and conversation analysis to utterances such as "Good God!" or a sudden laugh. In giving this illustration, I am refashioning for my own purposes an observation originally made in a most insightful review by Helm (1982).

In accordance with his usual imagery, Goffman calls such utterances "floor cues," a subclass of self-talk, and characterizes them according to his self-presentation-cum-dramaturgy frame of reference. Thus he says that a speaker who does not want to be seen as egocentric, intrusive, and the like, and who does not want to request a hearing openly may command the attention of a listener by means of floor cues. Floor cues let hearers in on our experience. In this characterization, Goffman again concerns himself with the nonconversational aspects of certain conversational utterances (see Goffman, 1978/1984b, pp. 106, 119).

This approach differs markedly from that of conversation analysts, who might see what Goffman calls these "blurted vocalizations" as (minimal) preannouncement sequences. "Good God!" thus serves as a first part of an adjacency-paired presequence that may usher in an announcement such as "X has died!" Here, the analysis would be a self-contained one, conducted without reference to what Schegloff has termed the "psychological motivations" of speakers or to any putative orientational feature extrinsic to the serial organization of the utterances. Goffman, however, treats these motivational features as the core phenomena and he typically characterizes them in dramaturgical terms. Given that Goffman seldom resorts to "retrievable" data (audio or video recordings and transcripts thereof), any reference he does make to sequence is given by type concepts appealing to native intuition. Here again, the two sets of analytic practices generate incommensurate kinds or orders of documentation (Atkinson & Heritage, 1984; Drew & Wootton, 1988). As Schegloff (1988b) remarks, Goffman seems more interested in the individual than in the syntax of interaction, although I far prefer the term *performing self* over *the individual.* Indeed, as Edward Rose suggested at the DARG meetings at the University of Calgary, the critical difference is that between *self* and *member.* We cannot properly understand the former in terms of the latter or vice versa. These terms constitute moves in different language games.

These differences in core and peripheral concerns may go some way toward accounting for why Goffman often seems to rename phenomena that conversation analysts have already named, something that clearly causes Helm much anguish and puzzlement.

To adapt Ryle's (1966) phrase to my own purposes, the concepts that "Goffmanians" and ethnomethodologists/conversation analysts, respectively, use have a "logical geography," which forms their relations with other concepts of similar and dissimilar logical types (p. 10). I have argued that conflating the two conceptual configurations breaks this logical geography and involves logically illegitimate operations. It involves the transplantation of concepts to logical types to which they do not belong, that is, within which they lose their specificity of sense and application. Within their own conceptual configurations or fields of moves, we shall find strong conjunctive propositions between concepts, whereas the "relations" between concepts derived from different sets (logical types) are disjunctive or senseless, as in "She came home in a flood of tears and a sedan chair." [3] This surely applies to the ironic sets of Goffman's analyses and the nonironic conversation-analytic sets.

To attempt to conjoin concepts from different sets is to create what Ryle calls "category mistakes." While such mistakes may well on occasion have their pragmatic uses, my argument is that, at the analytic level, they create conceptual congeries. It seems more sensible to preserve the distinctiveness and respective inner logic than to conflate them.

An interesting example of such conflation is to be found in Manning's (1989) publication "Ritual Talk," where, in his attempt to integrate a Goffmanian notion of ritual constraints and varieties of interactional participation with a conversation-analytic notion of sequencing in conversation, he observes: "Slightly more newsworthy is the methodological point that C.A.'s forward lurch can be fuelled by *both* observation *and* by the sharp conceptual work of which Goffman is sociology's finest exponent" (p. 381). This, I suggest, commits the classic faux pas of treating concepts as though they were neutral vis-à-vis the different analytic "language games" I have delineated above, and as such is amenable to the kind of critique potentiated by Ryle. One major consequence of this is that Manning glosses over the radically differing means whereby Goffman and conversation analysts, respectively, make their phenomena available (see my comments above on irony in the characterization of phenomena). Also, in a paper that is (with a couple of possibly passable exceptions) notably light on anything but invented or "just so" examples, there is little by way of thoroughgoing empirical demonstration of how sequential analysis might conceivably mesh with the Goffmanian analyses of, say, differentially "honored" participator status. By and large, the examples are, perhaps necessarily for Manning's purposes, slanted and formatted in terms of the family of analytic moves deployed by the Goffmanians. If these examples are not neutral, what faith can we have in the neutral or transposable nature of the concepts that yield them? The "integration" Manning proposes is seductive but spurious. It strikes me that in fact his proposal is more vampirical than empirical, sucking new life into a sadly flagging Goffmanian scene from another source. Goffmanville is a ghost town; only tourists go there.[4]

Harper (1989) has recently indicated, in Chapters 3 and 4 of an ethnographic study of accountancy, the nature of the analytic senselessness such integrative attempts can create, despite their tempting plausibility. Indeed, Chapters 6 and 7 of Harper's study serve to show the incommensurable nature of the ethnomethodological and dramaturgical language games.

I do not mean to suggest that there can be *no* transaction between two distinct arrays of analytic practices; I simply call for caution in specifying the precise *nature* of such transactions. *Dialogues* between two or more sets may cast light on them, without *synthesizing* them; such dialogues will likely generate more of the same of each set.

I shall now indicate that the early conversation-analytic description of the ordinary use of "membership categorization" procedures can give us considerable purchase on the quotation from Goffman I cited earlier.

Membership categories—that is, commonsense identifications for persons—are, in a given culture, organized into conventionally given collections that Sacks (1972a) terms "membership categorization devices" (MCDs); for example, mother, father, and daughter can be collected into the device *family*. These MCDs provide one locus for the deriving of "standardized relational pairs" (Sacks, 1972b), and single categories (and pairs and devices) provide a locus for the accountable imputation of rights and obligations and for associated predicates such as "category-bound activities."

Sacks describes a *consistency* rule for the coselection of membership categories, which, broadly paraphrased, states: If two or more membership categories are introduced proximately into a single conversation, and if these categories can be heard as coming from the same MCD, then hear them that way. This, then, is a procedural rule for "making sense" of the cooccurrence of two or more categories, to see them as *relevantly* cooccurring or coselected. It has been observed by Sacks and others, including Cuff and Francis (1978), that membership categories provide one basis for the organization of a huge amount of commonsense knowledge of social structures.

In the example of Goffman's text I gave earlier, we see that a considerable number of membership categories are introduced proximately, the first of which takes the form of a standardized relational pair, "performer(s)"-"audience," followed by "filling station manager," "clients," "friend," "bank managers," "ministers," "colonial administrators," "female professionals," and so on.

We can also observe that the total list of membership categories cannot readily be treated as coming from a *single* device/collection. Thus "filling station manager" and "friend" (as opposed to the supplied pairing category "customer") may not easily be seen as coming from the same MCD. The vivid diversity of the list is itself a significant resource for Goffman, since it permits him to find a compelling unity in the diversity, a unity that allows him to lay claim to having effected an analysis.

What Goffman does, in effect, is set up the first two categorizations, "performer"-"audience," as a master transcoding device (Crews, 1986), which predisposes us toward supplying a relationally paired counterpart category for "bank manager," "minister," and so on, presumably "customer" and "congregation member," respectively, such that the category "friend," mentioned immediately after "bank manager," may appear anomalous in terms of the relational pairing and consistency rule. Goffman gets us to perform a "category-mapping exercise," whereby we map the subsequently introduced categories onto the performer-audience pairing. The first positioning of the performer-audience pair is crucial in that it provides instructions to the reader, as a pattern detector, for what operations to perform on the subsequent categories.

In this way, Goffman sets up a "preferred reading" so that we find a homologous pattern in this apparently internally heterogeneous list of categories. We pull the rabbit out of the hat, so to speak, except that he provides the rabbit first. The above procedural apparatus is nowhere explicated by Goffman himself, nor does he need to do so for his purposes. What would this analysis add to his? This is the point. However, conversation analysts might argue that he relies upon the MCD apparatus in an entirely taken-for-granted way, in order to bring off his analytic effect. Goffman tacitly counts on a whole range of commonsense competencies on the part of his readers, including the category-mapping operations through which, for instance, we map "performer" onto "minister" in order to establish a planned misnomer, which in turn works to ironicize the commonsense competencies upon which in other respects Goffman's text counts. Put another way, Goffman depends upon our ability to establish very finely tuned congruities at the level of *procedural* knowledge in order to establish his perspective by incongruity at the level of *substantive* social definitions.

Goffman's reliance on his own and his readers' commonsense skills is nowhere more evident than when we conceive of his operations as exemplifying the working of the family of lay sense-making procedures that ethnomethodologists gather together under the title "the documentary method of interpretation" (Garfinkel, 1967/1984, pp. 76-102)—the reciprocal, back-and-forth determination of particulars and underlying pattern, in which the particulars are taken as pointing to the pattern, which in turn gives coherence to the particulars. This hermeneutic process operates flexibly over time. McHoul (1982, pp. 17-33) has most cogently shown the importance of analyzing a "course of reading" in terms of the retrospective and prospective features of the process. Nowhere is the appositeness of McHoul's comments more apparent than in the passage I have cited from Goffman, where, quite characteristically, Goffman provides the pattern first so that the subsequently introduced particulars can readily be seen, individually and collectively, as an *ensemble* of pattern elements. The solution comes before the puzzle, as Anderson and Sharrock (1982) have put it in another context. We are enjoined to see the subsequent list of categories (e.g., "minister," "filling station manager") as instances of the initially provided performer-audience pattern.

It should be observed, however, that the appropriate interest in applying such an ethnomethodological/conversation-analytic approach to Goffman's work is not to integrate the analyses into each other. Indeed, I suggest that the above analysis points up the distinctiveness of the two approaches, since it takes Goffman's approach as "incarnate" in his textual work, as an *object* of study. When one is performing this kind of analytic operation one is really proliferating ethnomethodological/conversation-analytic studies of Goffmanian phenomena. An example of such proliferation is Zimmerman's (1990) study of "footing," which instead of providing a framework for integration runs parallel to Goffman's analysis. Zimmerman gives primacy to footing as an organized interactional matter within a speech exchange system rather than to "individual" acts of self-presentation.

The advantages of such a nonadditive approach are, I believe, evidenced when we consider a frequently found move both in sociology and in the field of discourse analysis, namely, the attempted welding of so-called microanalysis and so-called macroanalysis. This kind of exercise is intended to render complementary the two modes of analysis so that they become a purportedly more "comprehensive" and "exhaustive" analysis. Such a micro/macro conception seems to work on the assumption that macro- and microanalyses, considered as separate and autonomous approaches, constitute narrow and perspectival views focusing on some phenomena at the expense of others and that need to be supplemented by the other. Ethnomethodology is frequently characterized in just such a way, as microanalysis, with a focus only on agency.

Ethnomethodologists, however, might respond that attaching ethnomethodology to a macro or "structural" approach would be based on a misconception. Ethnomethodology, as we have said, constitutes an inquiry into how members make sense of their society from within, into how they describe that society in their everyday activities. So-called structuralist sociologies claim privilege for a view putatively from outside society, more or less irrespective of members' conceptions.[5] Further, those who espouse the micro/macro distinction tend to resolve at the level of theory what, for ethnomethodologists, are empirical matters. This is another major incompatibility.

Two points may be made here. First, even if we accept the agency/structure-micro/macro distinction and slot ethnomethodology into the agency-micro side, any additive exercise would be incoherent, for it weds a set of nonironic analytic practices to a set that is essentially and necessarily ironic, and that self-avowedly sets up a competitive attitude to members' own conceptions of society (hence "latent functions/dysfunctions," "false consciousness," and so on). This additive exercise runs the risk of incorporating a whole domain of a priorism into (say) the characterization of agency (as Giddens's notion of "structuration" appears to me to risk), in which the initial framework for the characterization of action is tailored to incorporate the characterization of structure. This a priorism often locates, for instance, social constraint as operating at and deriving from the macro level. It often seems as though macroanalysis is utterly preoccupied with constraint, and a particular analytic version of constraint at that. The characterization of action at the micro level typically incorporates this so-called framework of constraint, whether the constraint is presented as straightforwardly prior to the action or whether it is part of a hermeneutic, as in "Marxist ethnographies." The concern for constraint seems to have as much to do with a *morally* enforceable topic agenda as with anything else. Rather than simply attending to the standard(s) that members themselves employ as intrinsic or endogenous to the actions they produce, this imposes at least one external standard for the analysis of agency. Thus for ethnomethodology to accept the terms of such a dualism is to risk analytic incoherence.

Second, the rejection of the agency/structure-micro/macro distinction as an *analytic* distinction allows us to focus upon the crucial point that, of course, ethnomethodology, symbolic interactionism, and the other purportedly micro approaches do indeed carry a conception of constraint. This is evident in even a cursory reading of, say, Wieder's (1974a) study of the inmate code in a parole institution or Bittner's (1965) paper on members' orientations to and deployment of the terms and determinations of formal organizations, even though these studies do not address constraint in terms that are recognizable and admissible to constructive analysts. Such rejection allows of a notion of comprehensiveness and exhaustiveness that is not an additive one but one that is worked out in a self-contained way "within" the terms of a given set of analytic practices. In this way we can begin to treat ethnomethodology as containing in itself all the elements necessary to the understandings it yields. This recognition renders unnecessary what is known at the Woolworth candy counter as the "pick 'n' mix" approach, where elements of diverse theories are wrenched from the frameworks that give them sense and are recontextualized to form a composite, as Crews (1986) has pointed out. So ethnomethodologists had better eschew the undoubted seductions of theorizing in and for itself. An endogenous view of comprehensiveness may well work to forestall the prior stipulation of topics (which at bottom is a moral agenda). There is no reason anything and everything substantive cannot be addressed in this self-contained, self-sufficient way.[6]

This view may help us in other ways too. With regard to ethnomethodology, for instance, it may help us to see that the agency/structure distinction may, at bottom, be one that is established by members' practical purposes rather than simply being generically problematic at the analytic level. Indeed, in a couple of papers, we have begun an analysis of members' orientation to oppositions as evinced in their conversational work (Sharrock & Watson, 1988; R. Watson, 1978). It then becomes possible to examine what this dualism does when used in occasioned ways by members, for instance, in claiming *force majeure*. In terms of the concerns I listed at the beginning of this chapter, perhaps such an approach can tell us something about how commonsense ways of talking about micro and macro issues might tacitly shape the ways in which constructive analysts talk about those issues.

I have been arguing for the preservation and proliferation of distinctions between sets of moves in the analysis of ordinary language or communicative conduct. The illustrations have no special status; other illustrations would have done just as well. I have suggested that any search by discourse analysts for an overarching theory, or any attempt by them to accord privilege to some single approach, or to devise a criterial feature or "Occam's razor" technique for the analysis of language use, is based upon a most dubious premise, a premise that will saddle us with a great many problems. A healthy diversity in ordinary language use, based on a proper regard for the irreconcilability of the approaches taken, will surely obviate these problems.

Notes

1. However, there is one sense in which Goffman's work is, from the standpoint of some analytic perspectives, not culturally indigenous enough, as we shall see later, when we consider the issue of members' understandings.

2. For another version of this argument, geared more extensively to the notion of "accounts," see Watson and Sharrock (in press).

3. Similarly, as Ryle (1966) puts it, we can logically say, "He brought a right-hand glove and a left-hand glove but not a right-hand glove and a left-hand glove and a pair of gloves" (p. 23).

4. While much is written about Goffman, it is a regrettably rare thing to find anyone actually conducting empirical research purely and simply in the terms Goffman set. His line has far more advocates than practitioners. His approach is also all too often spuriously used to corroborate very different approaches.

5. For a penetrating discussion of these issues, see Garfinkel (1987).

6. This view is more extensively (and rather differently) argued and illustrated by conversational data in Sharrock and Watson (1988).

2

Life After C. A.

An Ethnographer's Autobiography

MICHAEL MOERMAN

Who You Are

Being part of a conference sponsored and organized by the Discourse Analysis Research Group raises some questions for me. Who are we as a "group"? What is this "discourse" that our research is said to analyze? What sort of "research"? What kind of "analysis"?

We are, severally, sociologists, rhetoricians, philosophers, psychologists, anthropologists. Our various substantive interests are in such diverse topics as persuasion, educational discourse, human-computer interaction, conversation, power, gender, the language of protest, and how language connects to thought and reality. The materials we study range from philosophical treatises through textbooks and consumer warnings to classroom talk and everyday conversation.

But we are nevertheless not merely an assemblage of persons, but a "group," one with something of a common culture. Indeed, I am testing that culture right now. In Southeast Asia—a culture that in some ways (albeit merely statable ones) I know rather better than I know ours— proper reasoning and public talk are etymological in form. They start, conclude, and sometimes seem to consist of no more than examining the origins and the correct meanings of words and phrases. This group's common culture is not Southeast Asian, but I expect that we are never-theless a group for whom it should not have seemed odd to begin by attending to the actual words of a specific text: "the Discourse Analysis Research Group."

One strong bond that unites us—and that probably separates most of us from our official colleagues in academic departments and profes-sional associations—is a reverence for and an insistence upon the actual, in all appropriate detail and in the relevant contexts of its oc-currence. This is not to deny difficulties and the disputes about how much detail—and of what kind—is appropriate, and about which con-texts are relevant. But all of us are the sort who want to hear not "the gist" of what J. L. Austin meant, but what he actually wrote (Vaida, 1989); not the "tendencies" in psychiatric writing, but real case records; not Goethe's theory, but how he looked through his prism and what he saw. Insistence on the details of actual contexted occurrences pervades and helps to define our group of conferring persons.

For some of us, this insistence on the actual and contexted has aes-thetic or moral nourishment and sustenance. For all of us, its justifi-cation is empirical, observational, experiential: We have found that whatever it is that we study and experience—language, knowledge, interaction—is not something "'release[d]' under certain structural con-ditions" (Preston, 1988, p. 4). It is not governed, produced, described, or analyzed by abstract rules. We see, hear, and understand our phe-nomena to be "continuously created and recreated through . . . situated *praxis*" (Pollner, 1979, p. 249); to be processes, not products; verbs, not nouns; to be socially negotiated, not given. What we study and what we experience are living things in motion: situated, consequential, used, and constantly under construction. And so are we.

Another theme I detect, or hope for, in our common culture is awareness that we are parts of the natural world, that we cannot stand outside it to inspect it, that we resonate with what we study, affect it, and are affected by it.

Who I Am

In fealty to our common culture, I will honor the present occasion by trying to tell you, in appropriate detail, how I came to be here, who I am here, and what I think I am supposed to be doing here and now, giving a "keynote address" at the "First International Conference on

Understanding Language Use in Everyday Life." That telling, like every telling and every writing, must inescapably be my telling for a particular occasion as I understand it. This, too, is something that we all know and expect.

I came to this conference in Calgary by means of an airplane. The ticket was provided by the Conference Organizing Committee, whom I hereby, performatively and yet sincerely, thank. The ticket was preceded by a phone call in which a woman's voice ascertained, early on, that I was Michael Moerman, the anthropologist who had studied the Lue and written a paper (1968a) about their ethnicity. To my ears, a relevant identity of Michael Moerman—that he was the author of a recent book (1988) called *Talking Culture: Ethnography and Conversation Analysis*—was significantly absent. Over the course of the telephone conversation that initiated my presence here, I noticed the absence of this descriptor of Michael Moerman and reacted to it emotionally. I commented on it when reporting the conversation in subsequent interactions. The absence informs my notion of who the Michael Moerman invited, *this* Michael Moerman, talking to you now, should be.

One of the great contributions of the conversation analysis that Harvey Sacks founded, and that no few of us here pursue, is its capacity to recognize an absence that is significant for the interaction and to its participants, to discriminate such a "significant absence" from the cabbages and kings, the myriad extrinsic things that are simply not present. So I note as a challenge to the conversation analysis that I practice that this consequential absence would not be discernible from a transcript of the conversation in which it occurred.

I asked my co-conversant for suggestions of what I should talk about. The response was deferred to a "human-computer interaction" that also informs this presentation. The promised E-mail message read, in part, "It would be appropriate to address . . . the actual and potential impact of discourse analysis and relat[ed] studies on ethnographic field research, and *vice versa*." A subsequent electronic message suggested:

> Your address should in some way try to explicate the ways in which we study or understand language use in everyday life . . . from the perspective of your life and research. . . . bring in the work of those . . . who have illuminated your thoughts and work.

A proper member of our group's culture, and a loyal participant in this "human-computer interaction," the I for this occasion will tell my notion of you how my version of ethnography lead to my version of "discourse analysis," and who helped me along the way.

Ethnography

I begin with ethnography, my primary professional identification. The ethnographer's job, as I understand it, is to live among some other people in order to learn their way of life, and then return to his or her[1] own people and try to communicate that understanding. The mythic ethnographer is a science fiction character, an interpreter and emissary between alien worlds. Bad ethnographers—and there are some—are propagandists who champion their peoples, pornographers who use some theoretical obsession to bleed all human meaning from what their peoples do, or lying gossips. The competent ethnographer is an honest reporter. A good one is an indiscrete but articulate lover.

Januslike, facing two ways at once, talking out of both sides of his mouth, split brained, perhaps schizophrenic—it is not surprising that some strains or inconsistencies pervade the practice of ethnography.

The Ethnographer's Mind

One strain is that there are two kinds of sense that an ethnographer tries to make of what he learns. They do not sit together easily. The ethnographer's main goal is to find out how the events he observes and experiences in the alien world make sense to the aliens, how their way of life coheres and has meaning and value for the people who live it. The ethnographer's other goal is to use theory so as to understand what he has observed as an instance of some general type (such as peasant society), phenomenon (such as ritual), or process (such as modernization). But these concerns may not be the natives' concerns. Indeed, they often distort and sometimes demean native knowledge.

I received my professional training at Yale, where I—like many ethnographers of my generation—was much influenced by George Peter Murdock, the author of *Social Structure* (1949), and by Floyd Lounsbury, the originator of "componential analysis" (Lounsbury, 1951). Their breadth of knowledge and intellectual rigor were inspiring. But I was young, and only a student. So what I brought to the field were the tools and techniques, the tricks of the trade, that I thought would make me—whatever my own passions and concerns—into a professional anthropologist. I am glad that I never tried to publish "Componential Analysis of Tai-Lue Kinship Terminology," which absorbed no little of my limited field time and of the villagers' abundant patience.[2] The paper had a lot to do with what I learned in graduate school, but precious little to do with how villagers understand kinship, *kan pin pii-nøønq*. For them, kinship is only partially and sometimes only incidentally a matter of genealogical position. It often has more to do with having lived in the same household, or having been ordained together, or otherwise having forged and come to feel a bond of close fellowship (Moerman, 1966a, 1966b). A few energetic and cooperative informants strained to answer my obsessive questions about "What do you call your father's mother's elder brother's daughter's son?" But most were merely amused, or bored, and rightly so.

I take comfort that these silly questions did not demean my Lue hosts, as an alien's questions and suppositions can so easily do. More recently than I like to admit, a UCLA graduate student came to me with the following complaint. During her two summers at the field school in which our department took pride, she had been required to assist the instructor in his research. An "economic" and "development" anthropologist, he was interested in these Guatemalan peasants' "need to achieve" and "propensity to save." She recognized that participating in professionally respectable, peer-reviewed, foundation-funded, readily publishable research was a valuable part of her training, but she was disturbed by how the instructor and "principal investigator" (this is the language of our American grant proposals) reacted to her report of the responses she was sometimes given to the questionnaire item: "Would you rather get one automobile this year or two next year?" On at least two occasions, the peasants she interviewed said something like: "Here we have neither roads nor gasoline. A car would only require space on my small farm. So, if I had to have any, I would rather have one than two. It would use up less space." The instructor told her that the questionnaire was scientific. It had been standardized and tested throughout the world. There was no place on it for respondents' statements. "One car now is one car now, and that means a low propensity to save!"

This true story is an extreme instance, I hope. But what it is an instance of is a universal feature of ethnographic research. Our professional concerns and suppositions are just that: our own professional concerns and suppositions, inescapably the products of the ethnographer's own culture, of his position in a particular society, of the organization and distribution of power, money, and official "knowledge" in a world that educates and feeds us, that furnishes our cameras, our air tickets, and our tenure. Of course, ethnographers can, and often do, mystify themselves with an infantile fantasy of omnipotence that says: "Except for me and the other members of my professional association, the viewpoints, values, and understandings of all human beings are the products of their biographies, cultures, and social positions." But I do not think that any serious ethnographer can hold this view, or hear it without embarrassment. What is sometimes said to be ethnomethodology's special twist, that all ways of making sense—including the "scientific" way of making sense—are equally and unprivilegedly social and cultural constructions, is every ethnographer's birthright. Like many birthrights, it can be bitter and unwelcome. I, for one, refused it for quite a while.

For a long and awkward time, my professional self-regard was hampered by my persistent inability to readily align anthropology's concerns with what I felt and observed in the field. My first paper on ethnicity (Moerman, 1965) confesses that its stimulus was how hard it was for me to answer the simple question, Whom did you study in the field?

We ethnographers rarely see each others' field notes. They are our "magic bundles," our *churingas*, as sacred and private as those of any Blackfoot Indian or Native Australian. But a fellow predoctoral student and I were unusually trusting. We visited each other's field sites in 1960, taking and sharing notes. It was his fourth year in Thailand; it was my first. Cornell had given him field training; I had none. Where I had written "Toward the end of the headman's speech, *maj nø* [household 36] slowly stood up, stretched, and yawned," he was able to record that "a middle-aged man exerted informal leadership." I chuckle with comfortable superiority now, but how envious I was then.

The Ethnographer's Body

If belief in the acultural objective truth of our theories is grandiose, another ethnographic fantasy is more endearing, because childlike: We pretend to be invisible, and sometimes believe that we are. Quite a few of the ethnographer's disparate procedures are herded together under the slogan of "participant observation." Like many appealing slogans—"guided democracy," "unity in diversity," "people's capitalism"—"participant observation" is something of an oxymoron.

When working at the observational edge of his procedures, the ethnographer tries to just "hang out," to be there like the proverbial "fly on the wall." But the creature weighs over a hundred pounds. The ethnographer fly on the wall is much like the fly in the film *Brazil* (1985). It falls into a computer, so kicking off the whole bizarre plot.

To hold oneself back in the name of science is an unnatural posture.[3] It is also an incoherent confusion of perspectives. Goffman has noted that one cannot be present without giving off information. If I go to a party in order to observe it, others will see me as shy, standoffish, or a wallflower. The scientist's white coat is not a cloak of invisibility. The ethnographer is always a human among fellow humans whom he thereby affects and is affected by. The paper that motivated the phone call that resulted in the ticket that brought me here pointed out how my presence as someone interested in ethnicity altered native consciousness and presentations of ethnicity (Moerman, 1968a, p. 165).

When working at the participant edge of our enterprise, the ethnographer does things along with the natives. His joining in inescapably changes what is being done. This is not a reason for being aloof. Our effects on the scene are not errors to be compensated for magically or embarrassments to be denied, but part of the phenomenon to be studied (Moerman, 1988, pp. 71-86). Our participation always makes something happen. The ethnographer must study that something.

In 1959 I plowed with the villagers because I wanted to know what it felt like (although I knew it would feel different to my body than to their practiced ones), because that is what real ethnographers—Indiana Jones ethnographers—do, and because I wanted them to think I was a "regular guy." As plowing, it didn't quite work. *Khwaj lun, thaj hak*— "The water buffalo ran away, the plow broke"—is how the amused villagers talked about it then, and 20, and still some 30 years later.

To the degree that I distance myself from embarrassment, the episode provides material for ethnography. We learn what *khwaj* are like: They look back, sniff at footprints, and frighten easily at the unaccustomed. We learn what could be said to my face about what made me different: height and sunglasses.[4] We learn what's funny: that a plow breaking, a valuable animal having to be chased, some rice getting trampled are all things to laugh about, without anger or worry. And we learn how stories are made and how they last, how reputations are made and kept.

Much of what an ethnographer does is neither participation nor simply observation. We write notes, take photographs, and ask questions. Asking questions provides the satisfaction of getting something done, of finding something out. I certainly could not have written about farming decisions (1968b) or temple careers (1966a) without censuses, inventories, and questionnaires. But in undertaking them, I always felt the same discomfort as I had when selling magazine subscriptions while an undergraduate.

Like "hanging out" and "joining in," there is nothing intrinsically wrong with asking questions. But it must be done with awareness of its consequences, for the power of a question is also its weakness. Universally and without recourse, if you ask someone a question, you require that person to put his or her mind where your mind is, to accept and address *your* relevancies, *your* issues, *your* concerns, *your* ways of connecting topics. How, then, could an ethnographer work? It was clear that if he wanted to learn and report what is important and relevant in *native* thought and life, wanted to learn and report how the natives make sense of things, organize them, think about them, he could not ask questions and guide discussions. It was clear that an ethnographer who recognizes his own corporeality, who recognizes that he is a human among other humans, a person, and therefore someone whose presence and activities affect others, must have ways for recording and studying his presence and its consequences. The ways in which an acknowledgedly encultured, embodied, visible ethnographer could work were among the many things that I learned from Harvey Sacks. To talk, as my E-mail instructions proposed that I do, about those "who have illuminated [my] thoughts and work" is to talk, above all, about Harvey.

Help Along the Way

Harvey and I were contemporaries at Columbia College and then at Yale. At both places we had friends in common through whom we shared books and ideas, but we did not meet until I came to UCLA in 1964. From then until his tragic and untimely death some 10 years later, he was my mentor and my closest friend. For me, as for everyone who knew him, there can be no successor.

The undergraduate instructors Harvey spoke of were C. Wright Mills and Lionel Trilling; the graduate ones, Talcott Parsons and Erving Goffman. The greatest current influence, of course, was Harold Garfinkel.

Among the books that Harvey talked about and had me read were ethnographies, such as Gluckman's *The Judicial Process Among the*

Barotse of Northern Rhodesia (1955), and Evans-Pritchard's *Witchcraft, Oracles, and Magic Among the Azande* (1950); monographs on behavioral ethology, such as Schaller's *The Mountain Gorilla* (1963); biblical studies, such as Tur-Sinai's *The Book of Job* (1957); literary criticism, including Bakhtian, I. A. Richards, and Auerbach's *Mimesis* (1953); classical studies such as Havelock's *Preface to Plato* (1963) and Jones's *On Aristotle and Greek Tragedy* (1962); analytic philosophy, such as Nelson Goodman's *Fact, Fiction, and Forecast* (1954); the *Oxford English Dictionary*, works of Franz Kafka, and the novels and prefaces of Henry James. I list them with some happy sense that this group, our assembled conference, is the first I have encountered who might hear this set of readings as having coherence, mutual resonances, and some common thrusts; who might, therefore, be just the sort of group that Harvey would have liked to talk to.

Toward a Science of Society

Harvey's central research enterprise was to look for culture and society in what people do with and to one another as they go about their business of experiencing and creating their society and culture. Harvey had a naturalist's ear and eye, and a scientist's standards and aspirations. He saw no established method for studying human society that he would call a science. He would build one. To quote from a now published lecture he delivered many years ago:

> I figured that sociology could not be an actual science unless it was able to handle the details of actual events, handle them formally, and . . . be informative about them in the direct ways in which primitive sciences tend to be informative, that is, that anyone else can go and see whether what was said was so. (Sacks, 1967/1984, p. 26)

Ethology may have helped to nourish his conviction that—because humans live, survive, and reproduce in a social world—the actual, encountered, experienced social world must itself have a close-grained natural order. As a *social* world, a *human* world, it is a world of meanings, feelings, interpretations, moral significance. For him, as for many of us here, the way to show the relations—perhaps the identity—between the natural and the human worlds was illuminated by Garfinkel's (1967/1984) research and insight into how the natural, taken-for-granted, everyday world is an ongoing, mutual, continuous, socially organized, and socially enforced creation; was Garfinkel's insistence that "stable social organization is . . . the product of . . . empirically discoverable set[s] of locally managed and implemented procedures through which organized courses of . . . [inter]actions are produced and recognized" (Heritage, 1984a, p. 132).

Such abstract language can be a lulling litany. Better for me to describe how Harvey pantomimed it to Parsons, his former teacher. For Harvey, close inspection of actual social events could show how they were ordered. For Parsons—and here Harvey began to flail his arms wildly and jerk his body first in one direction, then another—actual society was a clumsy Rube Goldberg device, a sort of spastic elephant. Parsons's professional social scientist developed special methods—and here Harvey bent over, his head close to the ground, and moved one hand as if slowly pulling something from the closed fist of the other—developed special methods for discerning and extracting the golden chain of social structure hidden in the accidental droppings, in the shit, of the elephant.

Conversation

The program was not yet what would become known as "conversation analysis." While it did use talk as its data, "it was," to quote again from Harvey's lecture,

> not from any large interest in language or from some theoretical formulation of what should be studied that I started with tape-recorded conversation, but simply because I could get my hands on it and I could study it again and again . . . and because others could look at what I had studied and make of it what they could, [and so would] be able to disagree with me. (p. 26)

But this is really somewhat disingenuous. It was not merely that talk was available for capture and study. It is that talk is a central part of social interaction, and social interaction is the core and enforcer, the arena and the teacher, the experienced context of social life.

Harvey was a passionate and sensitive person, not a cold scientific observer. He knew and felt deeply that

> in every moment of talk, people are experiencing and producing their cultures, their roles, their personalities. Not just "the natives," but you and I live lives of talk, experience the social world as motivated talkers and listeners, as

tongued creatures of the social order; each with our own bursts of pleasure and pain, each with our own proud differences of personal style. (in Moerman, 1988, p. xi)

His papers on "The baby cried, the mommy picked it up" (1972b), said in a child's story; on "You want to find out if anybody really does care" (1987), said in a call to a suicide prevention center; and on "the course of a joke's telling in conversation" (1974) are instances of this concern. They examine the organization and the substance of talk for the social actions that the talkers work to accomplish; for the cultural knowledge that they assume, reveal, interpret, and manipulate; and for the structure of the ideas that form their consciousness and assign their pleasures and pains. The papers are informed, even motivated, by a searing compassion for the anonymous persons—adolescents, the aged, the lonely, the suicidal—whose talk they overhear.

Button and Lee (1987) observe that what has come to be called "conversation analysis . . . takes the social organization of talk as its topic of inquiry" (p. 1). In papers such as those cited, as also in many of the papers collected by Button and Lee (1987), the social organization of talk is not an object of study in its own right. Talk is, rather, the locus, accomplice, and accomplisher of social organization. Harvey used recordings of real talk as material for a radical ethnography of our own culture. The substance and social organization of talk furnished him with resources for what was once called "philosophical anthropology," an inquiry into abstract structures of human consciousness and experience.

These early papers preceded and led to contemporary conversation analysis. But to view them as mere precursors, as "prefigurings" that later events "fulfilled," is to adopt unthinkingly the "figural interpretation of history" that Auerbach (1953, pp. 64ff.) shows the church fathers to have imposed upon the Old Testament. Let me propose *topoi* from a different tradition.

The Buddhist *topos* of the hut, the temporary discarded station along the way, is an old one.[5] In *The Karma of Words*, William LaFleur (1983, pp. 60-79, 107-115) depicts the profound and generative use that Japanese thought makes of the *topos* of the hut. The classic text—one that every cultivated Japanese should know, at least know about—is Kamo no Chōmei's (1156-1216) *Hōjōki* (*An Account of My Hut*). The hut is not a way station to be used on the journey to a more durable mansion. It is built, rather, in rejection of mansions, palaces, and permanent settlements. They are the opposing *topos*. Their claims of grandeur and durability—like all claims of grandeur and durability—are always false, stultifying, and misleading. Instead of a permanent edifice, Kamo no Chōmei "fashioned . . . a hut where, perhaps, a traveller might spend a single night; it is like the cocoon spun by an aged silkworm" (LaFleur, 1983, p. 63).

Ethology and the Bible, literature and ethnology, Parsons and Trilling, science and compassion, Bach cantatas and country rock: There were and must be strains and tensions in Harvey's work, and in his legacy. Harvey's intellectual career was a progress of challenges and changes. The hut and the palace are *topoi* and images that I think he would have liked and accepted.

Harvey's path was too rudely shortened for us to know where it would have led. But—as it should be for us all—each point along it was but a hut, a temporary way station. This is no less true of the enterprise that examines the social organization of talk than it is of the work that examines the social actions and formal understandings accomplished *in* talk, that delineates the coherence not of conversation per se, but of lived experience.[6] For both, as for Harvey's short life, Saigyó's (1118-1190) poem:[7]

> Nowhere is there place
> To stop and live, so only
> Everywhere will do:
> Each and every grass-made hut soon leaves
> Its place within this withering world.

Discourse Analysis

Obedient to my electronic directives, I have talked about "ethnographic fieldwork" and about who "has illuminated [my] work." But I have yet to mention "discourse analysis." In part this is because that term is usually understood in the linguists' sense of "language beyond the sentence," a sense that is not appropriate for "conversation analysis," then or now, or for the other kinds of work that most of us do. But this is not the occasion for elaborating on the differences between *language*, as linguists, psychologists, educators, and philosophers use that word, and the living, embodied, contexted things that we all deal with (see Moerman, 1990).

Conversation analysis is a way of studying the organization of face-to-face social interaction. From 1964 to 1968, when I went into the field, I trained with Harvey to become an ethnographer-consumer of conversation and its analysis. I tried to do with Tai materials (Moerman, 1972, 1973) what Harvey was doing and teaching me to do with American ones. The procedure was quite simple, but how few ethnographers seem to have learned it! [8] Let the natives talk among themselves, record that talk, and then find out how the natives made, negotiated, and enforced their sense of it. Examine recorded scenes of native life for what their native participants oriented to and used in organizing and interpreting those scenes. If this does not play to standard disciplinary interests, then so much the worse for those interests. The new information and relevancies could reform them.

While I was in the field, conversation analysis progressed and changed immensely. It discovered its fundamental unit, the turn; its minimal actors, speaker and recipient; and its basic procedure, making collections of isolated instances of a phenomenon. The collective effort of Sacks, Schegloff, Jefferson, and then of their students had produced a new science that progressively discovers the fine reticulate sequential structures and processes by means of which conversation is demonstrably organized.

I have elsewhere described my surprise, excitement, and distress at finding that the Tai villagers whose conversations I had recorded ordered their talk just as conversation analysis said they should (see Moerman, 1988, chap. 3). Surprise and excitement are proper researcher's responses. The distress is perhaps more personal, but I expect that my fellow ethnographers would share it.

Ruth Benedict, the American Museum of Natural History, and *Kim* (both the book and the movie) had inspired me to become an ethnographer, an emissary to alien worlds, an explorer in remote northern Thailand searching for the exotic, hoping for experiences that would stretch my sense of what it means to be human. But there on the tapes and transcripts were *mai khamping*, and *mai kham*, and even *thaw món*, talking like so many Bronx teenagers or Orange County housewives.

The anthropologist, as comparativist and natural historian, was bound to want to find out how general, transcultural, or universal these regularities were. This is serious work that I prefer to leave to others. My own concern is to use the regularities of conversational organization as tools for ethnography.

For an ethnographer, Tai conversation is not principally a locus for testing conversation analysis. It is a component of Tai face-to-face interaction, and interaction, in turn, is the living, vital, experienced component of Tai culture and society, of Tai life and thought. Neither, of course, is American conversation principally a locus for exchanging turns, doing repair, or making announcements. It is how the Americans do and suffer their social business with one another.

The conversational analysis of records of interaction enables the ethnographer, the therapist—the policeman, I suppose—to discover how participants use the tools, rules, and machinery of conversation to accomplish their purposes, and to expose and test their mutual understanding. It therein can make ethnography a public and verifiable "primitive science" in the sense that Harvey had promised: "Anyone else [could] . . . see whether what was said was so." It can also permit the investigator to track the consequences of his own presence.

Ethnography begins—and conversation analysis does not end— with finding abstract rules and regularities. Its goal lies in discovering how those rules and principles are invoked, made relevant, enforced, and disputed in the rough and tumble, the felt and fought over, course of everyday life. For conversation analysis to help do this, it must take on board ethnographic (or members') knowledge of the sort that can recognize such actions as jokes or boasts, that can note the social significance of types of occasions, that can react to the statement or hint of cultural themes, that can clothe those robots—speaker and recipient—with their invoked and enlivened roles. I tried to do this in *Talking Culture*.

I would like to end on terrain that is less familiar to me, by listing some of the ways in which *Talking Culture* should be amended. One is to honor the fact that interactants have—*are* would be better—visible, mobile, clothed bodies (see Nomura, 1990) that occupy and move in space. Another is to investigate the extent to which the importance of conversation to interaction, and of language to conversation, can vary from community to community. If the Tai, for example, do not converse much, or if they use means other than conversation for accomplishing significant social actions, that they converse as we do becomes less important for understanding their society and their lives. And the easy salience of such cultural labels as "the Tai" or "the Americans" must be questioned. The interactional patterns of the people we study may have more to do with the kinds of physical work they are doing together or with how well they know each other than with their culture, gender, class, or citizenship. The rounds of repetitions and the silences that I remember hearing from ranchers in La Junta, Colorado, sound a good deal like Tai village talk.

But the orientation and suppositions of *Talking Culture* may need reforms more fundamental than these, for, like conversational analysis, and most Western social science, its model of social life seems linear, step by step, stimulus-response, back and forth, exchange based—located in separate signaling actors rather than system centered. It leaves little room for the unsaid and the unsayable, and none for the communion of common focus and feeling that sometimes wordlessly and wondrously unites us (see Kitamura, 1990).

Notes

1. With apology to half the world, I will hereafter use my own gender, and so write *he* and *him* and *his* as neutral terms for all of us.

2. My overly belated thanks to J. M. Brown and F. K. Lehman, whose painstaking comments on that 1960 manuscript demonstrated its irrelevance to how the Lue understood and organized their kinship terminology.

3. Its consequent pain is eloquently described by Rabinow (1977).

4. By 1986, the villagers, too, had both.

5. LaFleur (1983, pp. 108ff.) finds its scriptural source in the *Vimalakirti Nirdesa Sutra*.

6. I am indebted to Doug Macbeth for this distinction.

7. This is Poem 2175 in *Sanka-shū*, as translated and published in LaFleur (1983, pp. 66-67).

8. It has recently become common for ethnographers of such varied topics as law, ethnicity, power, or ritual to praise, demand, and then fail to produce accurate records of real talk. Goldman (1983) is a salutary exception.

3

Achieving Context

Openings in Emergency Calls

DON H. ZIMMERMAN

The major focus of conversation analysis has been on the organization of talk-in-interaction as such and, in particular, on the analysis of sequential organization. The machinery of sequential organization (e.g., the turn-taking system, sequences for organizing entry into and exit from conversation, the repair of trouble, and the doing of invitations, requests, assessments, and the like) provides structure for conversational encounters and for talk-in-interaction more generally. As a consequence, the sequential environment of talk provides the indispensable context for participants' understanding, appreciation, and use of what is being said, meant, and, most important, done in and through the talk (Schegloff & Sacks, 1973).

The primacy of sequential organization in conversation-analytic accounts of the orderliness of social interaction runs against the grain of the received view of social structure, which holds that, when it comes to social behavior, large-scale structural and institutional contexts are what matter sociologically. In this view, interaction is of interest only insofar as it reflects societal features writ small, a micro focus for macro

AUTHOR'S NOTE: I would like to thank Tim Halkowsky, Robin Lloyd, Wayne Mellinger, and Thomas P. Wilson for their helpful comments on various drafts of this chapter.

forces. Juxtaposed to this is the stance taken by conversation analysis toward its subject matter: Talk-in-interaction is an autonomously organized domain (see Goffman, 1983), the "primordial site of sociality" (Schegloff, 1987a, p. 208) that must be a topic of study in its own right (Heritage, 1984a; Schegloff, in press; Zimmerman & Boden, in press). Whatever "context" is required to organize a particular interaction, it is locally activated and interactionally achieved and sustained.

The fundamental question for conversation analysis is: What is the nature of the organization of talk-in-interaction? A derivative (but still important) question is: Within the limits of what we know about the organization of talk-in-interaction, how does this organization "enable" (Schegloff, 1987a, p. 208) the production of observable (which is to say, accountable) scenes and settings of ordinary activity, including those activities occurring "in" and informed "by" institutional contexts?

As a point of departure, recall Schegloff's (1987a, p. 219) observation that just because talk is occurring "in" some formal setting (e.g., a hospital) between parties who can be correctly identified as occupants of endogenous roles (e.g., doctor, patient) does not in itself warrant treating that talk as "institutional" in character. The "doctor" and "patient" have other identities that could organize their interaction, and, given this, must have some way of mutually displaying and recognizing just which identities are relevant to their current talk (see also Sacks, 1972a, 1987). We must look to the shape and placement of the talk itself for evidence of the relevance and consequentiality of institutional "context," for, in the first instance, this is what the participants must do if they are to bring off an interaction, institutional or mundane.

The principle here is straightforward: Since context functions to foreground and activate pertinent knowledge and skills and to provide the situated sense and relevance of activities, it must in some sense be "available" to participants in these activities, then and there. The availability of context is found precisely in the ways in which participants make locally observable and accountable for one another such features of their current activities. That is, insofar as context "beyond" the immediate interactional situation influences conduct, it does so only insofar as it is oriented to in some fashion by participants who hold each other accountable (see Wilson, in press) for exhibiting contextually sensitive actions. Thus conduct situated in formal settings or occasions and oriented to institutional aims can be understood as "institutional" (as opposed to "mundane") interaction only in terms of the deployment of general conversational resources activated and configured not only

opening/identification/acknowledgment

request

interrogative series

closing

Figure 3.1. The Constituent Sequences of Calls to the Police

to produce but to provide the relevance and recognizability of specific types of activity.

Accordingly, I will not view talk-in-interaction that does "institutional" work to be "dependent on" institutional setting in the sense that the latter is somehow constituted and recognized entirely independently of those actions that, in being undertaken "in" and being "oriented to" the setting, constitute it. Indeed, measurement of "institutional setting" as the "independent" variable is irremediably confounded with measurement of "configuration of talk" as the dependent variable.[1]

I will explore these proposals by reference to analyses of an extensive corpus of telephone calls to a centralized community emergency service in a Midwest U.S. city and a 911 dispatch center on the Pacific Coast. The sequential organization of these encounters creates the locally shaped interactional space within which identities are aligned, expectations tested, requests for service advanced, information transferred, and service provided.[2] The phases of emergency calls have elsewhere (Whalen & Zimmerman, 1987; Whalen, Zimmerman, & Whalen, 1988; Zimmerman, 1984) been represented as a sequence of five sequences that calls to Mid-City Emergency routinely (but by no means invariantly) exhibited (see Figure 3.1).[3]

My focus will be the organization of the opening/identification/acknowledgment sequence in these calls. I will examine the notion that the achievement of an entry into an encounter mutually understood to be "institutional" is a situated, turn-by-turn accomplishment of participants focusing general interactional skills and specific knowledge on issues posed by the exigencies of the call as an interaction and a service encounter (Whalen et al., 1988, p. 344). I begin not at the beginning, but at a point prior to the commencement of vocal interaction: the prebeginning.

Prebeginnings

In face-to-face conversations, one may speak of processes occurring prior to a conversational opening—"prebeginnings," in Schegloff's (1979, p. 27) terminology (see Schiffrin, 1977). Since the activities of selecting and dialing a telephone number and the readiness to respond to the summons ordinarily are not visually available to the parties involved, the notion of prebeginnings for telephone encounters is more problematic. For casual calls, answerers usually do not know who is calling or for what reasons, although they may be oriented to a set of possible callers, such as friends and relatives (Schegloff, 1979, pp. 32-33). Callers, of course, cannot be certain of reaching the right number, or of who will answer. Nevertheless, in initiating a summons for someone to answer, they have undertaken an act for which they are accountable, for example, for having some purpose (however vague) in mind.[4] It is the accountability of callers that provides one of the keys to the telephone call prebeginnings, particularly in the case of the service call.

Consider the following Central County calls reported in Whalen and Zimmerman (1987, p. 179).

[6] [CDV5-B/017]

```
01  D:   County Emergency
02       ((Caller hangs up))
03       ((Phone being dialed and ringing))
04  A:   Hello?
05  D:   Yes, this is nine one=one emergency calling back,
→ 06       do you have an emergency?
07  A:   No we don't
```

[7] [County Dispatch field notes]

```
01  D:   Nine one emergency
02       ((Loud voices in the background—screaming
03       and arguing))
04       ((Click))
05  D:   Oo:::ps! Sounds like a domestic
06       ((Dispatcher calls phone number from which call
07       originated))
08  D:   This is thuh Sheriff's Department. Is there
09       a problem?
```

Callers sometimes hang up upon hearing the answering identification, as in example 6. In Central County, the telephone number and address of callers dialing the 911 number appear on a computer screen, permitting the dispatcher to recontact a caller (or to dispatch assistance if warranted). The utilization of this technological enhancement displays the dispatchers' presumption that emergency assistance is the purpose of the call until determined to be otherwise. In call 6 the callback "disconfirms" the assumption of need. Background sounds serve to frame call 7 as a request for assistance in a domestic dispute, which the dispatcher seeks to confirm in the callback.

These observations extend the analysis of sequential context even further, for the opening sequence itself is embedded in a presumptive prior sequence of actions that establishes the subsequent accountability of talk cum action in the call: Dialing the number projects need prior to the alignment ordinarily achieved by the identification/acknowledgment portion of opening sequence. The issuance of the telephone summons itself projects a virtual identity, although subject to disconfirmation in the callback. In a similar fashion, the alignment initially achieved in the opening/acknowledgment sequence may prove precarious.

[8] [MCE:21:3a:3]

```
01  CT:   Mid-City Emergency:
02  C:    Hi
03  C:    Um I don' think this is really emer┐
04  CT:                                        └Well then hold
05        on please ((click))
```

[9] [MCE:21:18:25]

```
01  CT:   Mid-City Emergency
02  C:    Oops
03  C:    I didn' need thee emergency number=I: ih need uh my car
          was towed (.) an I uh n-need tuh find out where it was
          towed to,=
04  CT:               =Hold on please.
```

As the two fragments above suggest, the issue for caller is: Is the service sought provided by this service port? And as displayed in the following fragments, the issue for answerer is: Does this caller seek the kind of service that this service port provides?

[10] [CDV31B-A/080]

```
01  D:   Nine one one emer:gency.
02       (0.6)
03  C:   Yes, I need a towing tru:ck for one car away
04       (    ) they di:d park in my parking spa:ce the
05       who:le day and overni:ght (0.6) 'n they won't
06       mo:ve.
07       (0.5)
→ 08  D:   I'm I'm sarry?
09       (1.2)
10  C:   Okay, I need a towing truck (0.6) for towing.
→ 11  D:   You need a TOW TRUCK?
12  C:   Yes.
→ 13  D:   Then call a tow company.
```

As has been established earlier, dispatchers are sensitive to silence on the line and other ambient events as indicators of possible trouble. Moreover, it is the sequential organization of prebeginnings and openings that provides the resources for doing this interpretive work—for hearing what occurs in just that slot in just that way. Any alignment thus achieved is, of course, provisional, subject to revision over the course of the interaction (Zimmerman, 1990).

Thus the openings of these calls, as in service calls in general (Zimmerman & Boden, 1985), announce an identity selected to deal with the general interactional issue of contact between anonymous parties who must be sorted out into particular types of callers and answerers with typified interests and competencies. The fundamental "institutional" connection between a server and a client, generically, and, in this case, emergency dispatching organizations and the public (i.e., citizen complainants, victims, and so on) is found in the initiation and completion of the telephone connection between caller and answerer.

Moving to Respond

The summons/answer sequence involves a summons item, the ring, as the first interactional move. As Schegloff (1986, pp. 122-123) notes, the summons raises the question of who shall respond when entitled and nonentitled potential answerers are present, as well as the issue of how to respond relevantly. The act of replying to the summons as well as issuing it implicates issues of identification and recognition and, thereby, the activation of context.[5] I want now to consider more closely the activity of placing, and responding to, a telephone call to an emergency number, using both recordings and transcripts of actual calls and ethnographic observations derived from County Dispatch Center in Central County.

One set of institutional elements relevant here are found in embodied action in the setting in question—here, Central County Dispatch. First, some ethnographic detail. County Dispatch is staffed by five to six dispatchers (including at least one supervisor) per 10-hour shift. These personnel sit at stations dedicated to the three types of emergency service dispatched: two stations for Sheriff, one each for Medic and Fire. Each station has basically the same telephone lines, so that a dispatcher at any station can answer any incoming call. Calls are ordinarily taken in order first by dispatcher staffing Medic, then by Fire, then Sheriff Two, and last by Sheriff One (ordinarily the busiest of the stations). The calls announce themselves with either a gong (a call coming in on the 911 lines) or a buzzer (a call coming in on one of several six-digit telephone numbers). The radio equipment at each station is tuned to the frequencies appropriate to the workstation, that is, for contact with patrol cars, ambulances, or fire equipment in the station or in the field.

The workstations are arrayed along an L-shaped counter occupying two walls of the room. Dispatchers are capable of eye contact with each other, and can converse across the room. Conversation between dispatchers, and with the many visitors to the center, is virtually constant except in moments of peak work demand or in the early morning hours of a shift. It is important to note here that while conversation could and did take place with a dispatcher facing her or his workstation (e.g., while engaged in filling out an "incident" card on the details of a particular call), a common practice was for dispatchers to turn on their swivel chairs toward the center of the room and hence position themselves for face-to-face interaction with their colleagues.

Let me make several rather prosaic observations. First, talk occurring in Central County Dispatch, including some of the telephone talk, ranges from interactions that are demonstrably "institutional" in character to talk that is casual or mundane. Put another way, these vocal activities range from talk *as* work (e.g., processing a 911 call) to talk *at* work (e.g., organizing a softball practice). Thus participants face the task of managing possibly competing relevancies in the course of a shift, that is, maintaining the boundaries between talking that may be done when there is no work at hand and talk as an activity that constitutes their major task involvement.

Second, then, whatever the nature of the conversation taking place in the County Dispatch, it is interruptible upon the occurrence of a gong or buzzer. Movement from involvement in talk at work with colleagues to involvement in talk as work in managing a call traces an easily observed trajectory, usually entailing gross change in bodily orientation, such as turning away from coparticipant toward the console.

Third, this movement often exhibits a transition between two types of activity, two sets of relevancies, a transition occasioned by an organizationally relevant event.[6] It is oriented to by others in the setting as a transparent act: answering the phone (and not just any phone at that, but one with a possible emergency at the other end). Coparticipants will self-interrupt or pause in their talk upon the occurrence of a summons, sometimes even anticipating dispatcher's movement toward the console.

Fourth, movement toward the workstation entails picking up a handset and positioning a finger on the appropriate button on the console to connect to the incoming call. In one I have on videotape, a dispatcher on Fire swivels in response to a gong, reaching out to connect. The dispatcher on Medic has also disengaged from conversation and turned to the console, but more slowly. Fire, who has "beaten" Medic to the call, waits, finger on button, until Medic has positioned herself so as to connect[7] no sooner than simultaneously with her colleague who, by the organizational policy mentioned earlier, should take the call.

The foregoing conduct could be glossed from a commonsense viewpoint as role performance ("doing one's job") or as action prescribed by organizational rule ("going by the book"). I suggest that such glosses point to the natural—that is, *in situ*—accountability of the break-off of ongoing conversation, movement to the console, positioning to connect, and so on, as a transparent exhibition of the dispatcher's orientation to her or his work undertaken under the auspices of their identities as dispatchers.

It is important to note, nevertheless, that the activity of responding is an act organized by the more general machinery of summons/answer sequences and adjacency pair organization. In a fundamental sense, the activity of responding to a telephone summons, including withdrawal

from interaction in progress, is interactionally no different in Central
County than in anyone's private residence, although the configuration
of the telephone technology involved differs. Nevertheless, 911 is not
a private telephone line; more to the point, it is not *treated* as such, as
subsequent discussion will make clear.

Responding to the Summons

In the case of mundane telephone calls in the United States
(Steenstra-Houtkoop, in press), answerers' "Hello" (or some similar
token) is designed for *recognition*; that is, the as-yet-unknown caller is
projected to be one who can (or should be able) to recognize answerer
from the voice sample provided. Caller's return "Hello" is similarly
designed.[8] If mutual recognition is not achieved in this manner, other
procedures are available to address the issue (see Schegloff, 1979, pp.
33-45; 1986).[9]

For institutional calls, the selection of categorical—or better—situated self-identification,[10] such as "911" or "Mid-City Emergency,"
exhibits answerers' orientation to essentially anonymous callers' interest in having reached the intended service port. And, in dialing the
advertised number of the police or fire department, callers expect to
connect with an answerer acting in the capacity of an agent of that
organization, an identity that the answerer's self-identification confirms.[11] Equally routinely, callers acknowledge the offered identification as the initial component of their first turn, and follow it with a
second component projecting an up-and-coming strip of interaction
appropriate to this kind of call:

[11] [CDA30A:315:3]

01 *D:*   County dispatch
→ 02 *C:*   Yea:h
→ 03 *C:*   I'm callin ta report a wre:ck on Melanie Road about three mi:les
          north of uh York Avenue.

[12] [MCE:17:8:72]

01 *D:*   Mid-City police and FIre
→ 02 *C:*   Uh: yeah
→ 03 *C:*   Can you send thuh police tuh twunty three ninety South
04   Forest? Avenue.

[13] [CDA30A:185:15]

01 *D:*   Nine One One Emergency
→ 02 *C:*   Yes
→ 03 *C:*   Uh: I need help at' uh (.) uh residence. My two sons are fighting,
            and I think one has a broken nose, and sumpin doesn't (.) .h
            happen now to stop them, somebody's gonna be hurt badly.

[14] [MCE:21:4a:4]

01 *D:*   Mid-City Emergenc<u>y</u>:
→ 02 *C:*   Yes
→ 03 *C:*   Uh I need thuh paramedics please?

The selectional issues posed here, and their mode of resolution, highlight the fact that callers and answerers exhibit the accountability of their choices in initiating and pursuing the call. Through the accountability of talk, participants display for each other so-called social structural aspects in ways that are organizationally and motivationally transparent to each other (Zimmerman, 1970). In short, they align for an interaction of a particular sort.

Alignment

Alignment refers to participants' mutual orientation to the set of articulated identities they have projected or assumed in the local strip of interaction. Procedurally, alignment of situated identities involves the display and coordination of "who" it is that is calling and "who" is answering, and hence "what" these parties are (or might be) up to in the current situation; for instance, in what capacity and for what reason is the call placed and in what capacities are the caller and answerer prepared to participate in the interaction projected by the call.

As we have seen in the discussion of prebeginnings above, an incipient alignment of identities relevant to the up-and-coming call appears to be under way *prior* to the commencement of the vocally realized opening section. An initial alignment of identities is thus possible, along with some preliminary sense of the character of the encounter about to begin prior to the occurrence of talk.

For both answerer and caller, the achievement of the recognition or identification provides for an alignment of the identities of the parties beyond what is given in the fundamental organization of speech exchange—that is, *speaker* and *hearer*—and of the telephone encounter itself—that is, *caller* and *answerer* or *caller* and *called* (Schegloff, 1968; Schegloff & Sacks, 1973). These may be termed discourse identities, that is, identities internal to, and projected by, the organization of conversational sequences or types.

Discourse identities can be allocated in relation to another type of identity assumed by the parties as they enter the call, namely, *situated identities*. For example, Mid-City's *complaint taker* and Central County's *dispatcher* (both of which are service providers) are also the *answerers* of calls for emergency assistance, (and consequently) the *request recipients*, and, frequently, the *interrogators*. The complainant (or service seeker) is the *caller*, the *request initiator*, and, as the case may be, *interrogatee*. Who is who *when* is a matter of interactional collaboration that marks specific ways in which context, so called, is made relevant as a temporally and sequentially activated feature of interaction.

In this regard, consider the following. Callers identify themselves by name only rarely in our corpus; somewhat more frequently, they provide self-identification on a par with complaint taker's opening, for example, "This is thuh Knight's uv Columbus Hall." Most commonly, there is no explicit identification at all (see Zimmerman, in press). Nevertheless, it is possible to demonstrate that the situated identity of callers is oriented to and used by complaint takers or dispatchers, and that it is similarly oriented to and employed by callers. Consider the following call:

[15] [MCE:21:5:6]

```
01  CT:   Mid-City emergency
02  CT:   Uh: yes. I would like tuh speak with someone abou'
03        havin'uh car come out to thuh Andrews Hotel please
04        hh=
05
06  CT:        =Hold on sir. ( ) Ah- thuh Andrews
07        hotel?
08  C:    Right.
09  CT:   In thuh lobby? ←
```

```
10  C:    Correct.
11  CT:   What's thuh=problum there.
12  C:    Thuh problum iz, that we have ←
13        a tendent here that uh didn't pay thuh rent We
14        went up to her room tuh askt her tuh either leave
15        or (whatza callu,) .hh an whan thee uh security
16        guard knocked on the door tuh tell ur (.) she
17        threatened tuh (tow) thuh security ta guards heads
18        off wif a gun.
19  CT:   O:kay will get somebod=there right away.=
20  C:                                              =Okay
21        thank you
22  CT:   Thank you.
```

In this call, caller does not provide an identification of the usual form, such as "This is the Andrews Hotel calling," although a request to come to an establishment is something that is routinely done by persons calling "on behalf of" such places. Note complaint taker's query: "In thuh lobby?" While this appears to be a question, it also formulates not only a place where contact between the responding officers and the complainant could be made, but also a location where a particular sort of employee—namely, the desk clerk—has her or his post. Here, I suggest that the complaint taker's query concerning where to send the responding officers is formulated in such a way as to display her understanding of who, organizationally speaking, is calling, without having been explicitly informed.

The caller, in response to complaint taker's probe for the nature of the problem, uses the "we have" format, characteristic of callers who present themselves as agents of some establishment. Thus, while callers who call "on behalf of" an organization typically identify themselves in such terms, this call suggests that callers assume such identities without announcement and that complaint takers can detect the nature of the call and the relevant situated identity of the caller without the use of such explicit forms. The request for dispatch of a "car" to a named establishment, the use of the "we have" locution, and the nature of the reported trouble may logically establish sufficient context for complaint taker to recognize "who" she is talking to. That she did so in this case is evident from inspecting the dispatch to a patrol unit:

[16]

24th St. S/Andrews Hotel   theft   p1
→   see desk clerk. . . . they have been threatened by tenant in
bldg. tenant has threatened to shoot security guard

This dispatch is interesting in several ways. Recall that complaint taker's query was "In thuh lobby?" while the instruction to the responding officers is "see desk clerk." While it may seem obvious that "desk clerks" are found in "hotel lobbies," the point is that there is a connection between situated identities and settings such that one can move from the one to the other in a warranted fashion. This movement is exhibited in talk through presenting one side of the relationship, as in "In thuh lobby?" and, finding that affirmed, subsequently employing the other side, "see desk clerk."

Thus the "who" and "what" and "why" of the "situation" are mutually informative and mutually elaborative. Identity, for example, can project the frame for subsequent activities, while these activities can also shape identity (see Maynard & Wilson, 1980; Wilson, in press).

The Reduction of Opening Sequences

Elsewhere, Whalen and Zimmerman (1987) have noted that reduction of the "core opening sequence" (Schegloff, 1986) plays an important role in achieving the institutionally constrained focus characteristic of service talk.[12] This reduction promotes first topic slot to caller's first turn, which is the second turn of the call. The main work of the caller in turn two is thus the delivery of "first topic" or "reason-for-call."

In mundane telephone calls, first topic can be placed earlier in the opening by a preemptive move shifting the opportunity to produce first topic from caller to answerer. Preemption of other elements of the opening sequence may also be employed to mark a topic as important or urgent. Thus the modifications in the "canonical order" of core opening sequences can furnish options for dealing with a variety of interactional contingencies (Schegloff, 1986, pp. 116-117, 133-144).

In contrast, once alignment has been achieved in "institutional" calls, the slot for first topic is firmly allocated to caller. It is not that other elements of the core opening sequence have been preempted; they are simply not relevant. What is relevant is the business of the call.

Caller's first turn (turn two of the call) may, of course, not be the site of first topic or a statement of the "business at hand" (Button & Casey, 1988-1989). Identification or alignment issues may be addressed in this space:

[17] [MCE/21-25/35]

```
   01 D:   Mid-City Emergency
→  02 C:   Can I 've thuh police=please=
   03 D:                              =This is police.
→  04 C:   O:h uh there's .hh suh lou' music over on . . .
```

The delivery of first topic can also be deferred by second turn components that are hearably prefatory to delivery of reason-for-call, such as caller self-identification (Zimmerman, in press):

[18] [MCE/21-20/27]

```
   01 D:   Mid-City Emergency
   02 C:   .hh Hi we gotuh:
→  03 C:   This iz security atthuh bus
   04 C:   depot=Greyhound bus depot?=
   05 D:                              =Umhm
→  06 C:   An we gotuh guy down here that's uh: over intoxicated
```

The routine fact of "reduced" opening sequences in institutional calls and the anchoring of reason for call in caller's first turn are characteristic of calls to 911 emergency and presumably other service numbers. Recognitionals, greetings, and "howareyous" are routinely absent in emergency and other types of service calls. Such calls move directly from the completion of the summons/answer/acknowledgment sequence to the issue of the (legitimate) reason for the call.[13]

Yet, as Whalen and Zimmerman (1987, pp. 176-178) have shown, calls to emergency numbers can display a range of elements approaching the full core opening sequence. When mutual recognition becomes an issue, for instance, in dealings with organizational colleagues, the core opening sequence may "reappear" in what are otherwise "business calls."[14]

The emergence of issues of recognition rather than identification and the consequent exchange of greetings (or greeting substitutes) and "howareyous" change the footing (Goffman, 1984a) of such calls, at least initially. Whalen and Zimmerman (1987) write:

> Parties who have a joint biography broader in scope than that required to conduct the business of the call may conduct their instrumental relations in light of the issues that prior acquaintanceship might pose. Note also that the attempt at or movement into the fuller opening sequence proposes the relevance of recognition, and the interactional consequences such recognition entails. In a phrase, the relevance of recognition is a key feature of talk at work versus talk as work, at least where the latter involves emergency calls. (p. 177)

Moreover, the accountably impersonal and instrumental character of the service encounter is in part exhibited by the fact that recognition is not a relevant issue (see J. M. Atkinson, 1982; Jefferson & Lee, 1981). The reduction of the opening sequence (summons/answer/acknowledgment) displays an orientation to the contingencies of activity under way: seeking and providing assistance. The sequential arrangements for achieving prompt attention to urgent need not only exhibit for participants the institutional features of the interaction, they constitute the locally achieved institutional "context" of the encounter.

Conclusion

The local accomplishment of telephone service transactions brings to "focal consciousness," for both callers and answerers, the knowledge and skills relevant for the management of the encounter, and hence for the production and recognition of sequentially fitted utterances addressed to the contingencies posed by the task at hand. The openings of calls for help thus put in play relevant identities and initiate (as well as withhold) sequences of interaction that enable participants to manage the interactional issues involved in contact between anonymous parties seeking and providing help.

The trajectory of the call is thus anticipated in its opening, which projects a framework—the shell of a particular kind of activity—within which structurally and substantively relevant understandings of subsequent utterances can be achieved. The opening turns of the call, and in particular the components of the first turns of answerer and caller, regularly establish an identity set implicative for the nature of the business to follow. For caller, transacting the "business" of the call is contingent upon the availability of not just any answerer, but upon a recipient prepared to receive and to deal with that business.

The resource by which talk and setting are joined is the sequentially organized mechanisms for managing the recurrent issues that any telephone opening involving a public service port confronts. In so doing, participants exhibit for one another (and for the analyst) their appreciation of who, situationally speaking, they are, and what, situationally speaking, they are up to. And doing this involves the local display, however adumbrated, of the social and organizational circumstances that bear upon the encounter that are accountably accomplished as relevant to the service task at hand.

Notes

1. Consequently, the relationship between the two is, from a structural-equation point of view, entirely circular, and any model involving it is hopelessly underidentified. In short, from an ethnomethodological point of view, the relation is essentially *reflexive*.

2. Strictly speaking, service is merely promised, since the dispatch of a police car or other emergency unit often occurs subsequent to the call.

3. As this chapter focuses on the openings of emergency calls, I should point out that some dispatch operations employ a different opening by call taker that has definite consequences for the organization of the call. See Zimmerman (in press) for a critical reassessment and elaboration of the five-part sequence representing the organization of emergency calls.

4. Whalen and Zimmerman (1987, p. 180, n. 12) note that the accountability that attends caller's selection of a number perhaps figures in apologies for wrong numbers. Caller, in addition to owning responsibility for the selection, can by use of an apology token project the cancellation of the summons issued by the selection in the first place, with cancellation occurring upon provision of the account, "wrong number."

5. Schegloff (1979) suggests that identification is "generically relevant in interaction [with] its recognitional variant especially important among humans" (pp. 25-26). That is, given that parties to an incipient interaction can come to recognize or identify each other, they can and do design their subsequent conduct accordingly.

6. Work activities are also interruptible, of course. The point here is that dispatchers exhibit the relevance of their occupational identity by treating the summons as "directed" to them and responding to it in a specialized fashion, for example, by a situated self-identification (see below).

7. It is routine for two (or even more) to connect with incoming calls, although only one will "answer" a call. Dispatchers listening in on a call can initiate actions, such as sending assistance, while the dispatcher answering the call gathers information from the caller.

8. Note also that answerers of mundane calls need not select "recognitional" items (see Steenstra-Houtkoop, in press). Moreover, personal identity can also perform an indexing function; that is, it provides a linkage between a particular person and some

other identity he or she has assumed (or been assigned)—for instance, in the case of emergency calls, complainant, victim, witness, or whatever—a point to be considered below. Thus the provision of a name, or knowing another by name, does not per se establish a personal relation (see Zimmerman, in press).

9. Recognition entails bringing to bear previously acquired knowledge of, or familiarity with, the other party as a person (her or his "personal identity"). One consequence of mutual recognition is the ability to render relevant and accessible shared biographical knowledge, including some understanding and appreciation of each other's concerns, plans, sensitivities, and so on (see Maynard & Zimmerman, 1984).

10. The term *categorical identity* should be reserved for those identities that are potentially usable across all social situations, such as age, sex, or race (see Sacks, 1972a, 1987). This type of identity will not be a direct concern to this analysis.

11. The response can be characterized as *specialized*, that is, selected and focused for a particular, defined purpose (Heritage, 1984a, pp. 238-240; Whalen & Zimmerman, 1987, p. 175).

12. The discussion of reduced opening sequences is drawn from, and is heavily dependent on, Whalen and Zimmerman (1987, pp. 175-178).

13. Ordinary calls involving prearrangement (and thus recipient awareness of caller's identity) can exhibit this shape (Schegloff, 1986, pp. 121-122).

14. Consider the following fragments reported in Whalen and Zimmerman (1987, p. 177):

[19] [CDV6-B/010]

```
01  D:  Coun'y ^dispatch
02  C:  Hi Myrna?
03  D:  Yeah?
04  C:  Kin I have (Sheriff)side please?
05  D:  Sure . . .
```

Briefly, Whalen and Zimmerman observe that a candidate recognition item follows caller's acknowledgment of the dispatcher's self-identification. The dispatcher acknowledges her identity but withholds reciprocal recognition, transferring the turn back to caller (line 03). Thus, however transitory, recognitional issues do emerge and receive some minimum attention. In the next example, mutual recognition is achieved and "howareyous" exchanged:

[20] [D30-A/011]

```
01  D:  County Dis:patch
02      (0.4)
03  C:  Hi.
04      (1.0)
05  D:  Hi! (0.2) How are you?
06  C:  .hh Fine howyadoin'
07  D:  (Fine      me a minute)
08      (0.3)
09  C:  Yeahu:p
10  D:  What's up?
11      (0.6)
12  C:  Uh::oh, I jus'called f'r times:.
```

4

The Work of a
(Scientific) Demonstration

Respecifying Newton's and Goethe's
Theories of Prismatic Color

DUSAN BJELIC
MICHAEL LYNCH

Instructions for Use

This chapter is a demonstration of Newton's and Goethe's experiments with prismatic color. It was initially developed for a workshop in which the audience participated in the enactment of the experiments.[1] The present version is designed as a textual installation, where the text's instructions, figures, and arguments furnish materials for readers to use while working through the demonstration. The theme of our demonstration is Goethe's *respecification* of Newton's experiments on color. Goethe attempted to delegitimate Newton's observations on color by reconfiguring and recontextualizing an arrangement of materials described in Newton's *Opticks* (1704/1952). Here we shall respecify

AUTHORS' NOTE: We are very grateful to Harold Garfinkel for his extensive and illuminating comments on an earlier draft of this chapter. We would also like to thank Guido Sandri for reading the manuscript and sharing his reflections on it, and Lou Rossi for showing us some of Newton's and Goethe's optical demonstrations.

Goethe's treatment, not in order to cast it into ironic relief, but to make perspicuous the embodied work of a (scientific) demonstration.[2] Our aim is not only to demonstrate Goethe's theory of color but to exemplify a distinctive ethnomethodological approach to studies of work in the sciences (Garfinkel, 1988; Garfinkel, Livingston, Lynch, Macbeth, & Robillard, 1989; Livingston, 1986; Lynch, Livingston, & Garfinkel, 1983; Morrison, 1990).

To bring off this demonstration we will need to accomplish an "alchemistic" task: to extract colors from this text, and to do so in accord with the text's argument. The work of respecification is the "philosopher's stone" for ethnomethodological studies of work (Eglin, 1986). By this we mean that respecification is the practical origin of a methodic chain of metamorphoses reflexively constituting its point and preoccupation, its motivating task, its indispensable material, and its central theme. We have no interest here in explaining how the term *respecifying* is used in Garfinkel's texts. Instead, the term identifies our problem at hand. In this study, prismatic colors will be our "potter's object" (Garfinkel, Lynch, & Livingston, 1981, p. 137), an "object" whose accountable configurations will exhibit the present state of the argument *in its course*. If we succeed in systematically extracting colors from this text by devising an order of "color games," that is, if we succeed in exhibiting Newton's color spectrum as Goethe's demonstrable achievement, we will have *shown* our readers an ethnomethodological phenomenon. But to do so we will need to impose an essential requirement in addition to the usual demands on our readers' patience: To read this text clearly you will need to look through a prism. Otherwise, our text will provide only a virtual demonstration, an order of words *about* the demonstration rather than an installation of materials *in and as* the demonstration. We will give further instructions about this requirement after further explaining why we impose it.

Foundational Phenomena

Readers of this volume may wonder why we do not opt for a conversation-analytic approach to scientists' discourse. Why not study scientific work by collecting tape recordings of scientists at the bench, and then treating transcripts of these recordings as instances of institutionally situated conversation with distinctive limitations on turn type, turn allocation, turn distribution, and, perhaps, specialized preferences for reaching agreement? For a variety of reasons we do not figure there is very much to show distinctively *about* scientific shop talk. Among other things, there is little basis for treating scientists' discourse as a distinctive species of speech exchange system (see Lynch, 1985a, pp. 167ff.). Scientists play innumerable language games, and these are inseparable from such embodied activities as preparing specimens, setting up and handling equipment, making experiments work, recording and analyzing results, and writing them up.

Even if we grant that while they go about such activities, parties evidently orient to the categorical types and orderly distributions of conversational turns described by conversation analysts (Sacks, Schegloff, & Jefferson, 1974), we are not ready to say that "talk" acts as the *foundation* of those activities. Conversation analysts have begun to assign a foundational role to "mundane" conversational sequencing in the codification and analysis of diverse activities (see Boden & Zimmerman, in press; Heritage, 1984a, p. 238; Schegloff, 1988a). Although we agree that tape-recorded and transcribed records may offer a convenient *indexical surface* for addressing the situated organization of practical actions, we do not think the analysis of "talk *qua* talk" can adequately come to terms with the disciplinary activities out of which "talk" arises. This is not to deny that scientists (or, for that matter, doctors, lawyers, mathematicians, musicians, and truck drivers) talk in well-formed adjacency-pair sequences, rely upon others to do so, and do so while conducting diverse tasks. It is only to say that the currently established program of conversation analysis disregards a vast array of practical and temporally organized *phenomena* that simply do not take the form of sequential structures of "talk," "talk-in-interaction," or even "institutionally specific talk-in-interaction." Garfinkel also speaks of "foundations," but these are *ethnomethodological* foundations, that is, locally produced, used, and recognized contextures of embodied activity that organize the sense and coherence of any constituent movement, utterance, text, or "analysis." [3]

When we speak of contextures of embodied action we mean something more than gestures occurring in conversation; more than the capacities, movements, and postures of the human flesh; more, even, than the phenomenologists' transparent body-in-the-world. The "body" in embodied action shows up *scenically*, in and through actions with others; it is the body disclosed in the midst of constellations of equipment and text; it is the body in the midst of coherent games and courses of play (Garfinkel, 1967/1984, pp. 165ff.; Macbeth, 1989; Sudnow, 1978). It is not a naked "actor" through which perception and agency emanate, nor is it a "discourse" about the body. It does not array itself on a photograph, videotape, or transcript of talk's body, except and insofar as such textual materials find their places as objects in-and-as organized contextures of activity. In our demonstration, embodied work will include a prism, a prism handled according to instructions, a series of textual figures viewed through the handled prism, a methodic chain of metamorphoses shown in and through the series of figures viewed through the handled prism, and a demonstrable "point" made via the methodic chain of metamorphoses shown in and through the series of figures viewed through the handled prism.

So, instead of elaborating upon an order of talk believed to act as a "foundation" for innumerable situated competencies, we shall try to demonstrate an order of things (Foucault, 1970), a discursively instructed and embodiedly elucidated order of witnessing. We take it that Goethe's "color games" (*Farbenspiel*) are the heart of the matter, that they act as locally accomplished and textually demonstrable grounds for his arguments.[4] To see what Goethe is saying, one needs to look through a prism, and not the "mundane colored glasses" (Schegloff, 1988a, p. 218) worn by conversation analysts.

Demonstrating a Competence

Following Garfinkel's (1988) suggestions, our initial task is to exhibit a competence, but any attempt to demonstrate an organized constellation of (scientific) activity confronts at least two rather daunting problems: first, how to bring the audience (or, in a written version, the readers) into the presence of activities using complex equipment, mathematics, technical skills, and vocabularies; and, second, how to organize a demonstration of those activities given limitations in our own training, the probable lack of technical competence by the social science audience, and the limited time (or number of pages) available for instructing the audience on how to master the relevant techniques.

To deal with these problems, we designed this demonstration as a primitive (scientific) argument using a simple and readily purchased item of equipment, a series of figures that can be reproduced in a text, and a readily grasped argumentative "point." [5] Goethe's *Farbenspiel* lend themselves to this purpose, although they have one rather interesting drawback: Many physicists and philosophers of science treat Goethe's "theory" of color as a scandal.[6] We have no immediate interest in vindicating or debunking Goethe. What interests us is that his demonstration converts Newton's spectrum into a textual artifact and then respecifies it in terms of an entirely different account of color. We are not arguing that Goethe's demonstration closes the issue; we are more interested in showing how it works. The strangeness of Goethe's treatment of color actually works to our advantage, since it is unlikely to be familiar to most readers and it instructs a surprising and even startling way to *see* colors. Newton's approach is far more established, and is more likely to be ascribed to a natural ordering of colors. It thus provides an apt precondition for an apparent displacement and respecification in Goethe's demonstration. If in the end we are puzzled about the validity of Goethe's demonstration, so much the better.

How to Get Colors from This Text

The following is a set of preliminary instructions for obtaining a prism and using it appropriately to view Newton's and Goethe's demonstrations.

Prism. To read further and to follow the demonstration adequately, you will need to get an inexpensive item of equipment: a clear glass or plastic prism. Prisms can be purchased for less than $5.00 in toy stores, natural history museum shops, and various specialty "nature" shops. Prisms come in a variety of sizes and shapes. Newton and Goethe used prisms with 60° angles on the triangular faces, but a 90° × 45° × 45° prism will also work. The prism does not need to be especially large; one with 2-inch × 1-inch rectangular faces will be sufficient.

After finding a suitable prism, play with it for a while. Once you accommodate your hands and eyes to it you may discover that the prism offers two angles of view and that colorful fringes can be seen around particular edges in the field. You may also find angles of sight from which colors will not appear. One angle from which you can see colors, which we shall call "downward," passes through the lower angle of the prism. A second angle, which we shall call "upward," passes through the upper angle of the prism (see Figure 4.1).

Light. In order to intensify the appearance of colors, look at the text under relatively bright light. This can be accomplished by viewing the text near a window in daylight or under a lamp.

Distance. Changing the observational distance (from eye to prism to text) may modify the phenomena described in the demonstrations. For this reason, you should maintain the same distance (from 12 to 15

Downward Angle   Upward Angle

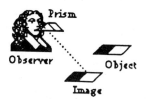   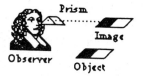

Figure 4.1. Angles of View Through Prism

inches) between the prism and the text unless required to do otherwise by specific instructions.

The following sections assume the reader will follow the above instructions. First, we will review the third experiment described in Newton's *Opticks*. We will present his account of refraction and the origin of colors as "instructed phenomena": systematic arrangements in the visible field made plausibly accountable through Newton's textual instructions and figures. After exhibiting the Newtonian spectrum, we shall then go through a longer series of demonstrations adapted from Goethe's experimental exercises. These will "respecify" the orderly relation between the Newtonian spectrum and the materials used in the demonstration, placing colors literally and figuratively in "a new light." We then conclude with some remarks about Goethe's *work* of respecification.

Newton's Demonstration

Newton began his prism experiments in 1666 in the course of constructing and testing the performance of telescopes (Whittaker, 1952, p. lxvi). Beginning with an instrument maker's practical concerns about chromatic aberration, Newton systematically tinkered with lenses and prisms to investigate the relation between color and refraction. Newton's *Opticks* presents the upshot of these investigations in a series of carefully constructed definitions, axioms, theorems, and experimental proofs. His text includes instructions and illustrations on how to perform the experiments, but these textual materials do not act to ground the experiments so much as to allude to them. Although Newton did describe some "subjective experiments" to be performed by peering through a prism and examining the visual field thereby revealed, his major concern was to describe and depict phenomena external to the relation between reader and text: an objective configuration of light source, light beam, prism, and projected spectrum. Although the *Opticks* provides instructions for reproducing the experiments, readers immediately are positioned as "virtual witnesses" (Shapin, 1984; Shapin & Schaffer, 1985) of Newton's achievement and not as coparticipants and cowitnesses. In other words, Newton's text presents an objectified performance and an objectified result, albeit an achievement grounded in a "tacit social physics" (Bjelic, 1989). This becomes significant when we compare Newton's text to Goethe's account.

Newton's Theory of Optics

Newton (1704/1952) opens his *Opticks* with the following passage: "My Design in this Book is not to explain the Properties of Light by Hypotheses, but to propose and prove them by Reason and Experiments: In order to which I shall premise the following Definitions and Axioms" (p. 1). His first definition is as follows:

> *By the Rays of Light I understand its least Parts, and those as well Successive in the same Lines, as Contemporary in several Lines.* For it is manifest that Light consists of Parts, both Successive and Contemporary; because in the same place you may stop that which comes one moment, and let pass that which comes presently after; and in the same time you may stop it in any one place, and let it pass in any other. For that part of Light which is stopp'd cannot be the same with that which is let pass. The least Light or part of Light, which may be stopp'd alone without the rest of the Light, or propagated alone, or do or suffer any thing alone, which the rest of the Light doth not or suffers not, I call a Ray of Light. (pp. 1-2)

His Definition VIII, concerning the appearance of colors, is as follows: "*The Colours of Homogeneal Light, I call Primary, Homogeneal and Simple; and those of Heterogeneal Lights, Heterogeneal and Compound.* For these are always compounded of the colours of Homogeneal Lights; as will appear in the following Discourse" (p. 4).

Newton then presents a series of theorems and experimental "proofs," in which he demonstrates the refractive properties of the "rays" of light defined above. For Newton, white light is compounded of all the other

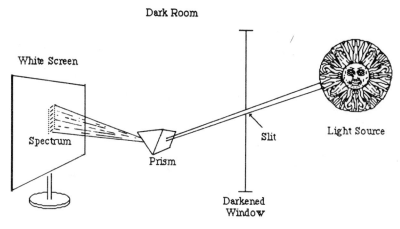

Figure 4.2. Generating the Newtonian Spectrum

colors, while black is the absence of color. He also argues that the different colored "lights" refract through a lens or prism at different angles. The best-known demonstration of this is his third experiment.

Newton's Third Experiment

Newton's third experiment was designed to prove Theorem II: "The Light of the Sun consists of Rays differently Refrangible." For this experiment Newton covered the window in his chamber to darken it. He then cut a small hole in the window shade to permit a bright beam of light to enter the dark chamber (a narrow slit in the shutters of a window also works for this). He positioned the prism so that the beam passed through the downward angle and projected a spectrum on the opposite white wall. Figure 4.2 is adapted from Newton's Figure 13 of Book One (p. 27).

Newton (1704/1952) concluded from his experiment:

This Image or Spectrum . . . was coloured, being red at its least refracted end . . . and violet at its most refracted end . . . and yellow green and blue in the intermediate Spaces. Which agrees with the first Proposition, that Lights which differ in Colour, do also differ in Refrangibility. The length of the Image in the foregoing Experiments, I measured from the faintest and outmost red at one end, to the faintest and outmost blue at the other end, excepting only a little Penumbra, whose breadth scarce exceeded a quarter of an Inch, as was said above. (pp. 32-33)

A   B

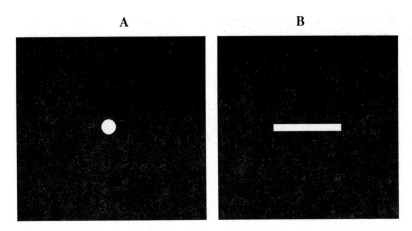

Figure 4.3. Virtual Specification of the Newtonian Spectrum

We can transpose this experiment by constructing a paper specimen that exhibits Newton's phenomenon. The specimen depicted in Figure 4.3, a white spot or slit against a black background, can exhibit Newton's spectrum (broken into discrete bands of homogeneous red, orange, yellow, green, blue, indigo, and violet) when viewed through a prism. (This is the classic spectrum that Newton constructed through his experiments; readers may of course see a somewhat different span of colors.) A small white patch against the black background provides an analogue for the beam of light framed by the darkened window of Newton's chamber. Instead of witnessing Newton's "real image" projected against a white wall, the viewer actively constitutes a "virtual image" by peering through the prism at the isolated white spot or slit.[7]

Observations. If you look at the white spot (Figure 4.3A), or the slit (4.3B), through the downward angle of the prism, you will see Newton's spectrum (starting from the bottom, and bounded by black): violet, indigo, blue, green, yellow, orange, red.[8] If you look through the upward angle of the prism, the same color sequence will appear, but in an opposite order from bottom to top.

In further experiments Newton isolated "homogeneal lights" in each of these bands. He did so by using a prism to project the spectrum for white light, and then projecting narrow bands of spectral color through another prism. He claimed that red, orange, yellow, green, blue, indigo, and violet did not decompose into other colors. Newton realized that orange, green, indigo, and violet could be produced by mixing other colors, but he distinguished (for example) green produced by mixing blue and yellow from "homogeneal green," which passes through a prism without separating into other colors.

Goethe's Demonstrations

Goethe borrowed prisms from a physicist colleague, Christian Wilhelm Büttner (at Jena University). Goethe initially intended to replicate Newton's experiments by setting up a darkroom with a small slit in the shutters in order to get a beam of light directed through a prism. Once he got the prisms, however, he did not get around to doing the experiments for a considerable length of time. Büttner asked him several times to return the instruments. Goethe kept delaying until, finally, Büttner sent a courier to pick them up. Goethe (1971) recalls this moment in the following passage:

> Since I could not count on occupying myself with these investigations soon, I decided to comply with the justified demand forthwith. I had already taken the box out to give to the courier when it occurred to me to look quickly through one of the prisms, something I had not done since earliest youth. I remembered well enough how everything had appeared variously colored, though in what way was no longer present to my mind. Being just then in a completely white room, I expected, as I raised the prism to my eyes, mindful of the Newtonian theory, to see the whole white wall colored in various hues, the light reflected back to my eye broken up into so many colored lights. But to my astonishment the white wall seen through the prism remained as white as before, and only when the white bordered on something darker did color appear more or less distinctly.
>
> The window-bars appeared the most vividly colored while the light grey sky outside showed no trace of color. It did not take much reflection to conclude that a boundary was necessary to produce colors and I at once exclaimed, as though by instinct, that the Newtonian theory was wrong. Now there was no longer any question of my sending back the prisms. (p. 242)

The reader can appreciate Goethe's experience by finding any homogeneous surface (white, gray, black, or other color) and looking through the prism at it. Colors will not be visible on this surface unless it is marked or shadowed. In other words, as long as the surface is homogeneous, other colors will not appear. (Contrary to Goethe's passage, this experience is not inconsistent with Newtonian theory, as Newton

[1704/1952, pp. 161ff.] accounts for this homogeneous field as a mixing of the prismatic light throughout the broad field of refracted rays. Nevertheless, this led Goethe to respecify Newton's theory over the subsequent years as he worked on his *Farbenlehre*.)

Colors may be found on the edges of the page, and beyond it on the edges of objects, lines, and wherever else a contrast between lighter and darker surfaces appears. Consistent with his initial observation, Goethe assumed that, for colors to arise through a prismatic viewpoint, light and dark surfaces must meet. Only at points of contrast between dark and light can colors be seen.

Goethe's Methodological Metamorphoses and Primal Phenomena

In what follows, we have arranged a series of figures to demonstrate Goethe's color games. In his various writings on color, Goethe (1840/ 1970, 1971) presents a much more extensive array of figures and a more elaborate set of arguments than we will be able to recover. For some of his illustrations, Goethe used color plates upon which he simulated the colored fringes appearing around the edges of the figures when viewed in prismatic light. At other times he presented just the specimens, inviting his readers to view these with prisms in order to see what he described. The latter specimens, which, after Goethe, we shall call "cards," along with the "methodological metamorphoses" produced through their serial arrangement, are of primary interest to us. We read Goethe's text to be inviting a kind of guided "play" with the cards it includes. Unlike Newton's, Goethe's argument is not "contained" by an assembly of definitions, axioms, theorems, objective facts, and empirical conclusions. Newton explained colors as sensations ultimately caused by the excitation of the viewer's eye by harmonic waves of essentially colorless rays of light. Building his theory of optics on the analogy of his earlier studies of sound, Newton treats color as the sensual effect of harmonic "music to the eye," where the "musical" arrangement occurs in an ontotheological space of purified physical relations. Goethe's readers are not invited to be virtual witnesses of the results of a finished project; instead, he produces a phenomenological condition for his arguments. His propositions efface themselves into "primal phenomena." This is not to say that Goethe's metamorphoses have no systematic basis. While presenting Goethe's respecification of Newton's experiments, we shall in turn respecify Goethe's

Card 4.1. Localization in an Irregular Figure

metamorphoses by pointing to the coherent arrangement of cards that gives rise to them. The card games are endogenous constituents of the *Farbenspiel.*

Again, we must emphasize the requirement of viewing the cards with a prism. To assure this, we have formulated our instructions and observations in a deliberately cryptic and incomplete fashion. These instructions and observations place a burden on the reader to find what we are saying through a prismatic inspection of the cards.

The initial card we shall present (Card 4.1) should be viewed as a "first" card only in the context of an already accomplished use of the prism to "see" colors in and around various surfaces in one's surrounding space. This card is an initial *textual localization* of the spatiality of prismatic colors.

Observations (looking through either downward or upward angle of the prism at a distance of 12-15 inches):

(1) Notice *where* colors emerge within the frame of the figure.
(2) Observe the *variations* in color along lines of different thickness and in the variable spaces between them.
(3) Rotate the page while maintaining the orientation of your prismatic gaze. Notice how colors simultaneously disappear in some regions and appear in others.

These observations are more readily made against this card's surface than in the spatial surround Goethe describes for his initial experience

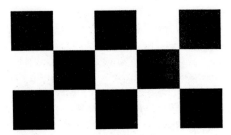

Card 4.2. Geometricized Rendering of Contrasts

with the prism. Although "irregular" in appearance, the arrangement of lines presents a demarcated contrast between dark and light, variations in line thickness and interval between lines, and a juxtaposition of these features within a closely confined two-dimensional space. Further, it is a space surrounded by the very instructions used for guiding the reader's inspection of its surface. The reader's observations thus emerge as a "natural" product of an informed gaze, compactly localized within the figural space. Note, however, that prismatic colors are as yet *merged* within the irregular arrangement of lines in the above figure. Subsequent cards systematically tease out an ordered set of relations retrospectively congruent with these initial observations.

A further metamorphosis can be exhibited through an inspection of Card 4.2, which builds upon the textual localization achieved in the first card by producing a simplified and geometricized rendering.

Observations (again looking through either downward or upward angle of the prism at a distance of 12-15 inches):

(1) Notice the orientation of prismatic colors and the black and white edges of the figure.

(2) Notice the differently colored fringes (red/yellow and blue/violet) at the upper and lower extremes of the black and white squares.

(3) Switch back and forth between viewing through the upward and downward angles of the prism, and observe the distribution of the red/yellow and blue/violet fringes with respect to the edges of the black and white squares.

(4) Rotate the page and observe how the colors hold their orientation with respect to the prism's position.

This card embodies a metamorphosis *in, of,* and *as* the visibly demonstrable prismatic colors. The observations listed for Card 4.1 have been selectively developed and reduced. Where colors were previously exhibited within the swirls of black and white, they are now arranged within a grid of black-white contrasts. And where colors were seen to appear and disappear in particular places of the irregular figure when it was rotated, they are now given an alignment and orientation. Colors appear and disappear with a vertical and horizontal alignment in relation to the prism's orientations. The card thus provides a geometricized ground for the appearance and disappearance of colors. The alignment of the figure with the horizontal/vertical orientation of the text provides a fourfold "graph" of possibilities: black over white and white over black along the horizontal axis, and black to the right of white and white to the right of black along the vertical axis. When viewed with the prism, the colors comply with this Cartesian arrangement: Red/yellow and blue/violet fringes hold discriminate places without mingling or mixing. Further, they show up differently according to the two possible horizontal contrasts (white above black or black above white) and the two angles of view through the prism (upward or downward).

Card 4.3 contains Goethe's (1840/1970, p. 82) "simplest object" (Card 4.3A), a light disk against a dark ground. (Note that this is a variation on Newton's narrow-beam experiment, only here Goethe devises a "subjective experiment" with a somewhat larger white circle than used in the "Newtonian" Figure 4.3A.) Next to this simplest object we have placed a quadrilateral version (Card 4.3B) that enables a clear demonstration of an oriented color phenomenon. This compares to Figure 4.3B.

Observations (looking through either the downward or upward angle of the prism at a distance of 12-15 inches):

(1) Hold the prism horizontally, and notice the orientation of the red/yellow and blue/violet fringes along the edges of the inscribed circle and rectangle.

(2) Switch back and forth between the upward and downward views through the prism, and notice the systematic reversals in the position of the red/yellow and blue/violet fringes.

(3) Vary the distance from which you view the cards, and observe how the color fringes will appear to broaden or narrow with changes in viewing distance.

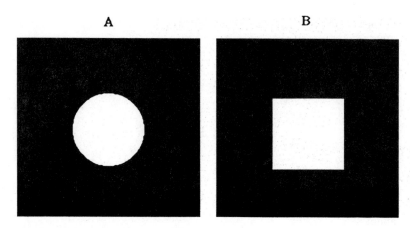

Card 4.3. Goethe's "Simplest Objects"

(4) Focus on the inscribed quadrilateral in Card 4.3B, and notice how one of the color fringes systematically projects into the white interior of the figure, while the other fringe projects beyond the edge and against the black background. A similar relation can be seen in Card 4.3A.

With this demonstration Goethe leads us to his conclusion that prismatic spreading of contrasting black and white edges creates colors *as a primal phenomenon*. The demonstration elucidates colors with respect to (a) contrasts between black and white, (b) the alignment of the prism and the contrasting fields, (c) whether white is placed above or below black, and (d) whether the prism is viewed through the downward or upward angle. He also demonstrates that the intensity and width of the fringe will depend upon available light and viewing distance. This set of relations can be represented in the following set of equations:

(1) downward angle + white/black = blue/violet

(2) downward angle + black/white = red/yellow

(3) upward angle + black/white = blue/violet

(4) upward angle + white/black = red/yellow

Each combination of prism angle, contrast, and orientation gives rise to *either* the blue/violet or the red/yellow color fringe. Goethe (1840/ 1970) treated this as an irreducible natural-perceptual phenomenon, a

"primal" phenomenon, in the sense that it is a law in and of itself, an
apodictic relation between color and seeing:

> To produce colour, an object must be so displaced that the light edges be
> apparently carried over a dark surface, the dark edges over a light surface, the
> figure over its boundary, the boundary over the figure. But if the rectilinear
> boundaries of a figure could be indefinitely extended by refraction, so that
> figure and background might only pursue their course next, but not over each
> other, no colour would appear, not even if they were prolonged to infinity.
> (pp. 85-86)

As we reconstruct Goethe's demonstration, we understand the primal
phenomenon to be an end point of the serial play of cards. From gazing
about a lighted room, to a localization via the "irregular" textual figure,
and then on to a geometricized and simplified rendering, our prismatic
wanderings have been led "home." The methodological metamorphoses
build upon each other, organizing, aligning, and bringing out the relation between figure and prismatic colors. By the time we reach the
"simplest figures," we have settled upon a set of contrasts beyond which
we cannot go without losing the phenomenon: a purified contrast
between black and white, aligned along horizontal axes.

Goethe's Respecification of Newton's Spectrum

Goethe's *Farbenlehre* contrasts remarkably with Newton's theoretical *Opticks*. Rather than treating colors as secondary phenomena generated through refraction or reflection of beams of white light, Goethe
embeds color within a primary system of relations between vision and
black-white contrast. For Newton, the prism opens up white light,
disclosing its objective components. For Goethe, the prism provides a
way of displaying the interaction between light and darkness in a substantive field. "Light" as such is not a package containing rays that
stimulate different sensations of color; rather, the prismatic colors are
attached to a sensuous field in which our actions observably forge their
attachment. Having devised the above metamorphoses to lead us to a
primal set of relations, Goethe respecifies Newton's spectrum. By this
we mean that he devises a further series of metamorphoses to lead us to
re-view Newton's spectrum not as the natural rainbow, but as an artifact
of particular textual arrangements. Goethe surrounds Newton's figures with systematic transformations of their tacitly configured textual

A   B

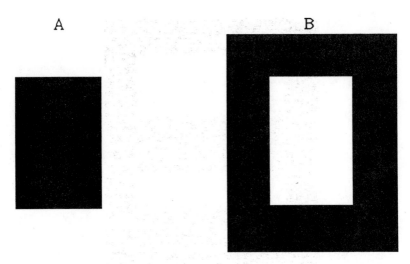

Card 4.4. Inverted Contrasts

formats (by *tacit* here we mean the "original" and "unmentioned" conditions for seeing Newton's spectrum that are thematized retrospectively in Goethe's demonstration). Cards 4.4-4.6 build upon the lesson embodied in the earlier metamorphoses (Cards 4.1-4.3).

Having found a simplest order of contrast, Goethe begins to build a color game that thematizes an inverse relation between black-white contrast and color fringes. The sense of this game will become clear only after we have succeeded in re-creating Newton's spectrum under systematically transformed conditions. A first set of observations will lead us in that direction.

Observations:

(1) Note that Card 4.4B is organized similarly to Goethe's "simplest object" in Card 4.3B. Card 4.4A is no less "simple," except that the relation between black and white has been inverted.

(2) Viewing through either the downward or upward angle of the prism and with the prism held horizontally, compare the relation between fringes on the upper and lower edges of the black rectangle in Card 4.4A and the inscribed white rectangle in Card 4.4B.

Card 4.5. Goethe's Respecification of Green

(3) Switch back and forth between the upward and downward views through the prism, and notice the systematic changes in the relation between color fringes and upper/lower edges of the rectangles.

This demonstration evidently extends what previously was observed, using the juxtaposition of Cards 4.4A and 4.4B systematically to inscribe an inverted relation between color fringes and black-white contrasts aligned horizontally. As noted, Card 4.4B is essentially similar to Card 4.3B, but, as we shall see, the structure of figure-ground inversion made perspicuous in Card 4.4 will be worked into a *critical* iteration of Newton's demonstration. The focus of this figural critique is the color green and its naturally analytic role in Goethe's color game (see Card 4.5).

Observations (either angle, distance 12-15 inches):

(1) First, examine the top of the three white rectangles inscribed within the black background of Card 4.5. Compare what you see to Cards 4.3B and 4.4B.

(2) Next, examine the middle of the three white rectangles. Notice the relation between the color fringe along the top edge of the rectangle and the fringe along the bottom.

(3) Examine the bottoms of the three rectangles. What has happened to the fringes? Have any colors emerged other than the blue/violet and red/yellow fringes described previously?

(4) Compare the colors emerging here to the Newtonian "spectrum" exhibited in Figure 4.3.

This card evidently builds upon the relations between color fringes and black-white contrasts established in the sequence of Cards 4.1-4.4. The juxtaposition of the three rectangles and their progressive narrowing produces a systematic transformation of Goethe's "simplest object" within the frame of this card. With this card Goethe undertakes a methodological move, a metamorphosis of Newton's procedure for projecting a narrow slit of white light through a prism. Goethe's respecification can be summarized as follows. When the top rectangle in Card 4.5 is viewed through the two angles of the prism at "normal" viewing distance, the following bands of color are seen:

downward angle	upward angle
black	black
red	violet
yellow	blue
white	white
blue	yellow
violet	red
black	black

When the white space between opposing fringes narrows to the point of merging, green appears where yellow overlaps blue from opposing fringes. This methodological metamorphosis respecifies Newton's "homogeneal" green so that it becomes a mixture of blue overlapping yellow. Green is no longer a primary component of white light, since it now has been shown to emerge from a *particular* placement of contrasts in the figure. It can be made to appear or disappear by widening or narrowing the white slit against the black background. Newton's rainbow appears in either of two orientations when the narrow white slit is viewed through the prism (Goethe, 1840/1970, para. 214):

downward angle	_upward angle_
black	black
red	violet

yellow]	blue]
white } Green	white } Green
blue]	yellow]

violet	red
black	black

Goethe then undertakes a further metamorphosis of Newton's spectrum by generating an entirely different spectrum through an inversion of the contrasts in Card 4.5 (see Card 4.6).

Observations (either angle, distance 12-15 inches):

(1) First, examine the top of the three black rectangles, and compare what you see to Card 4.4A.

(2) Next, examine the middle rectangle. Notice the relation between the color fringe along the top edge of the rectangle and the fringe along the bottom.

(3) Examine the bottoms of the three rectangles. What has happened to the fringes? Have any colors emerged other than the blue/violet and red/yellow fringes described previously?

(4) Compare the distribution of colors emerging in the bottom rectangle to the "Newtonian spectrum" emerging in the narrowest of the three white rectangles in Card 4.5.

In the delimited case of the black slit against a white background an entirely different color spectrum than Newton's now emerges. By analogy to the reasoning in Newton's third experiment, the spectrum is produced by the prismatic separation of the components of _black_ light. But, of course, in Newton's system there can be no phenomenon of "black light," since black is the absence of light, while pure white light contains every color. Goethe has thus inverted the relation between dark and light in Newton's demonstration to produce a Newtonian _absurdity_. The absurdity disappears, however, if the spectrum is seen to be generated through a prismatic spreading of the white background over and against the dark figures. The violet and red fringes created at the opposing edges spread over the black figures and merge in the narrowest of the three figures. The opposing violet and red mingle to produce

Card 4.6. Goethe's Spectrum Generated Through Inversion

a bright magenta band.[9] Goethe thus produces a distinctive spectrum through this mixture of overlapping colors in the special case of the narrow slit. The above metamorphoses lead us to see the *special* dimension of the "narrow" slit. Arranged in an order of complementary oppositions, Goethe's spectrum can be represented as follows:

downward angle			*upward angle*		
white			white		
blue			yellow		
violet	]		red	]	
black	}	magenta	black	}	magenta
red	]		violet	]	
yellow			blue		
black			black		

Goethe respecifies Newton's spectrum by recasting it as a matter of mixing boundary colors. His demonstration shows how Newton's rainbow, and particularly the color green, is not the result of white light refracting into its components. Rather, this rainbow results from a unique mingling of light and darkness. When brought close enough together, these create the boundary colors of green or magenta. Goethe

DUSAN BJELIC and MICHAEL LYNCH   73

relativizes Newton's spectrum in at least the following respects: (a) by situating Newton's experimentally produced beam of white light as a "slit" of white against a black background, (b) by situating Newton's narrow slit within a series of slits of variable width, (c) by situating the continuous band of colors in Newton's spectrum as a special case within the series, and (d) by producing an inverted series in which the non-Newtonian color of magenta occupies a place analogous to green in Goethe's spectrum. Newton's spectrum is as though "contained" within the series of metamorphoses, and it becomes an *artifact* in the sense that it appears and disappears as a particularized product of an "artist's" rendering. Goethe's artful arrangement has thus recontextualized Newton's beam of light and its components, producing them as a special case contained within a textual series of metamorphoses. Newton's third experiment becomes a result of his having produced a narrow slit for his beam of light, a "demonic coincidence" wherein the slit's size happened to fit his preconceived theory about colors and light.[10] Although his procedure is not nearly as complicated as the equipment modifications used by contemporary experimentalists to dispute rival phenomenal claims (see Collins, 1985; Pickering, 1984, p. 103), Goethe's card games demonstrably manage to *remake* Newton's green by other means.[11]

Conclusions

As stated earlier, our aim has been to conduct a primitive "scientific" demonstration, one using a set of textual specimens and a simple item of optical equipment. Readers may, of course, wish to question whether this demonstration is relevant to actual scientific practices. We have not been concerned to satisfy historians' standards of inquiry regarding Newton's and Goethe's circumstances, and we make no claims about the relative validity of their respective accounts of color. Still, it may be asked whether the demonstration presented here has any relation to what "scientists" do. This demonstration has been, after all, extraordinarily simple, and for all we know it may do little more than exhibit what ultimately stands as an "unscientific" version of colors.

Although we certainly approve of efforts to investigate what currently stands as bona fide scientific and mathematical inquiry, our aim here has not been to *represent* actual practices so much as to exhibit perspicuously some prototypical moves in the production of a visible demonstration. Our sense that these are related to what laboratory researchers do is based on prior studies by Garfinkel and his colleagues. In this case, we imagine that there is no one-to-one correspondence between the moves we have demonstrated and any extant "scientific" practice. Nor are Goethe's color games and their constituent modes of demonstrability exclusively associated with a conventionally defined "scientific" inquiry. To an extent, our project has a negative, and even a "paranoid," consequence, deepening our initial suspicions about all attempts to posit science, scientific talk, scientific work, or scientific action as analytic objects for a general social science. Our *unscientific* alternative has been to produce a textual *installation* within which readers may use the instructions, equipment, and figures at hand in order to elucidate a phenomenon.

In closing, we will mention some themes arising from this demonstration. But rather than give a full-blown exposition on the philosophical background and continued relevance of these themes in social studies of science, we offer them for the reader's "inspection" with prism in hand. We would like our text to be treated primarily as a facility, and we have made deliberately "thin" descriptions of the practices to be exhibited through such a use.

Perhaps the most obvious theme coming out of this project is that of the serial ordering of cards, what we have called the *methodological metamorphoses*. Cards were deployed in temporal series so that readers would discover "logical" orderings from one card to another.[12] Subsequent cards drew out and explicated inchoate "experiences" evoked by earlier cards. Orders of conditional relevance, of partial repetition, of inversion, and of prospective-retrospective assembly were apparent as we worked through Goethe's respecification of Newton. The relations between cards do not readily fall in line with generic figural syllogisms; rather, their "logical" orderings are shown in and through their visible inspection. Nor does the less determinate language of hermeneutics entirely capture the way the color games developed. Clearly, as readers and writers we collaborated in the production of an instructed and disciplined gaze, a progressive orchestration of the strange looks of the things at hand. To say that we were engaged in "interpretation" of the cards is to say both too much and not nearly enough. To the extent that the demonstration worked, the metamorphoses "contained" their interpretations. As authors, we wrote with great confidence that our readers would see colors that we could not see on the page until arresting our writing to reach for a prism.

Goethe's phenomena were tied to the work of "handling" the prism. We relied on the reader's ability to use a prism competently after minimal instruction and practice. Our instructions were vague, and we said nothing of the micromovements, the hesitant search for a directed gaze, and the accommodations to prismed space that every reader who followed our instructions no doubt worked through. Goethe's demonstration places the prismatic gaze at the center of the phenomenon. Unlike Newton's elegantly closed field of objective prism, light beam, and projected image, Goethe's demonstration takes place in an open phenomenal field: The beam of light becomes a narrow slit against a black background, and the spectrum appears only and entirely within the field of the directed prismatic gaze.

Goethe's metamorphoses are generated through systematic workings of the textual surface. The gaze is localized in a figure; the figure is then systematically aligned in accordance with a rectilinear scheme; and colors are fixed to an order of edges, contrasts, and alignments as these elements are systematically varied and reduced in a progression toward geometric simplicity (see Husserl, 1970; Lynch, 1985b, in press). Where Newton's geometric optics works behind the field, organizing its details along colorless mathematical lines and convergence points, Goethe's mathematics *is* the field's irreducible surface configuration of purified shapes and embodied alignments. A lesson is taught in the progression from card to card, in a primitive language of contrast, alignment, inversion, and juxtaposition. The systematically instructed gaze emerges in and through the series, neither as an explication of an a priori knowledge nor as an internalization of textual information. As Goethe (1982) has remarked:

> A phenomenon, an experiment, can prove nothing; it is a link in a great chain, having validity only in the context. If somebody were to cover up a string of pearls and show only the most beautiful in isolation, requiring us to believe all the rest were the same, who would enter into a transaction? (quoted in Proskauer, 1986, p. 27)

Goethe's metamorphoses bring us to an end point: his primal phenomena. We have not said very much about Goethe's substantive philosophy, about his protopsychology of vision, or the romantic movement that initially supported his tilting at Newton. Perhaps for Goethe, and for his faithful followers, these would be essential to any understanding of "primal phenomena." In contrast to Newton's science,

Goethe's views may also have some vague affinities to ethnomethodology. Our aim, however, has not been to adopt his version of primal phenomena so much as to respecify it. Simply, the primal phenomena are inseparable from the demonstration; they arise where the demonstration comes to an end. To say this is not to credit them with an independent existence, but to situate them in the textual culs-de-sac produced by Goethe's card games.

Notes

1. The presentation was titled "Newton's and Goethe's Experiments on Color: An Ethnomethodological Workshop," by Michael Lynch and Dusan Bjelic, at the First International Conference on Understanding Language Use in Everyday Life, University of Calgary, Calgary, Alberta (August 23-26, 1989).

2. The parentheses mark the contingent historical status of Goethe's demonstration. In a strong sense, it is none of *our* business a priori to decide whether Goethe's work does or does not count as "scientific" (see Brannigan, 1981). While we shall not try to settle whether Goethe's writings about color constitute a *scientific theory*, we point out that his demonstrations are conditionally relevant to Newton's prior experiments (see note 6).

3. It can be argued in favor of conversation analysis that it has established a technical program with a cumulative literature. A key feature of this achievement is the fact that conversation analysts constitute their phenomena as "ordinary" analytic objects. "Ordinary" structures of talk are evidently and accountably recognizable for technical analysts, their readers, and the lay participants they study. Moreover, the *ordinariness* of these structures assures their generality—perhaps even their universality—so that they can be shown to underlie singular events of "merely topical" interest (Schegloff, 1988b). This cannot be said about many of the more "unique" activities and "esoteric" competencies that scientists and others perform. The local organization of such activities is less transparent to social scientists and to their readers. Consequently, conversation analysts may find it more sensible to investigate how doctors interview patients or inform them of diagnostic outcomes than to investigate how they organize *diagnosis*. What gets lost in the bargain are the uniquely identifying features of the work studied. "Interview" and "diagnosis" are intertwined, but when diagnosis is treated strictly as an etiolated form of talk, medical practices are transformed into hands-on occasions of talk's work. The medical gaze becomes subservient to the interests of initiating and sustaining a line of talk, while the patient's body primarily becomes a site for the selective activation of the turn-taking system of conversation. We would not want to say that such a transformation leads to incorrect findings, only that it produces an *absurd* account of situated competencies.

4. Matthaei (1971) translates Goethe's term *Farbenspiel* as "color display" (p. 25). Although *display* is certainly relevant, we believe that the term is best translated as "color games."

5. We were guided in this by Garfinkel's discussion of his and a group of colleagues' efforts to perform Galileo's inclined plane experiment in an effort to respecify that experiment as an ethnomethodological production (Garfinkel et al., 1989).

6. Although we use the term *theory* here, in many respects Goethe's *Farbenlehre* is not formulated as a conventional scientific theory (Wittgenstein, 1977, sec. 70-71), and

it might best be considered as a pedagogical display of a unique naturalistic philosophy. Its appeal is not entirely limited to the "aesthetic" features of color and it has never been entirely rejected by physicists (Boehme, 1987; Proskauer, 1986, p. xiii).

7. To avoid possible confusion here, a "virtual image" is not related to what we earlier called (after Shapin, 1984) "virtual witnessing." In contemporary optics, the term *real image* describes what is projected on a screen, in contrast to a *virtual image*, which appears through the interaction of the viewer's eye and the light focused by an optical device. *Virtual witnessing* is quite the opposite, since it describes a viewer's *disengaged* appreciation of an experiment. Accordingly, our "virtual specification" of Newton's spectrum is a device that engages the reader in a "direct" witnessing of the spectrum, albeit one that is not organized through the projection of a light beam onto a screen.

8. These are the seven prismatic colors Newton described, but they differ considerably from the colors many viewers see through the prism. Goethe described the sequence differently, and many viewers describe fewer and somewhat different colors. So, for instance, one may easily describe the sequence as purple, cyan, green, yellow, orange, red.

9. Goethe (1840/1970) called this bright color "purpur," and described it as "a splendid pure red" (sec. 210). Some viewers may see "hot pink." Goethe asserted that this color had a maximum of intensity, and he was particularly fascinated by its appearing through the merging of dark colors (the deep violet and dark red spreading over the black background). He explained this in accordance with his theory of complementaries, saying that it was brought about through a uniting of extremes.

10. Newton's use of a narrow beam derived from Grimaldi's prior experiments (Ronchi, 1970, p. 127). However, Newton (1704/1952) did describe experiments with beams of light "almost as broad as the prism" (p. 161). Newton accounted for the separation of prismatic red/yellow and violet/blue along the edges of the projected image in his broad-beam experiment (pp. 162-163), and he also described how these colors appear when one looks through the prism:

> And if one look though a Prism upon a white Object encompassed with blackness or darkness, the reason of the Colours arising on the edges is much the same, as will appear to one that shall little consider it. If a black Object be encompassed with a white one, the Colours which appear through the Prism are to be derived from the Light of the white one, spreading into the regions of the black, and therefore they appear in a contrary order to that, when a white Object is surrounded with black. (p. 165)

It is quite possible that Newton's system could account for all of Goethe's observations. We have not fully explored that possibility here, since our main interest has been to demonstrate Goethe's card games and the respecification they achieve. But it does not seem to be the case that Newton saw the green in his third experiment to be the "demonic coincidence" that Goethe's series of cards exposes.

11. Prism experiments are not as simple as they might seem at first glance. For a fascinating account of the practical difficulties and controversies associated with Newton's experiments, see Schaffer (1989).

12. Husserl (1970) mentions an intriguing relationship between mathematical reasoning and the organization of a game of cards in the course of his exposition on the mathematical natural sciences:

> One operates with letters and with signs for connections and relations (+, ×, =, etc.), according to *rules of the game* for arranging them together in a way essentially not different, in fact, from a game of cards or chess. Here the *original* thinking that

genuinely gives meaning to this technical process and truth to the correct results (even the "formal truth" peculiar to the formal *mathesis universalis*) is excluded. (p. 46)

By respecifying Goethe's *Farbenspiel* we have textually tried to "install" not only the rules and symbolic structures of the game, but a set of formal structures (the cards viewed through a prism) enabling a course of "play" that cannot be retrieved from even the most rigorous description of the game or its rules. In contrast to Husserl's genealogy of the "original thinking" in a Galilean science, an ethnomethodological genealogy exhibits "first time through" as the very "here and now" *performance* of the demonstration. (We would like to thank Harold Garfinkel for pointing this out to us in his comments on an earlier draft of this chapter.)

5

Mishearings

JACK BILMES

Conversationalists frequently engage in negotiations and controversies about meaning. To understand these occurrences, two basic features of utterances-in-conversation need to be taken into account. One is the dual nature of utterances as doings and as hearings. An utterance can thus be regarded as a locution and an illocution, a saying of something with a certain "force," as well as (if it is a response) a kind of claim as to what was meant by the previous utterance. (There are, however, exceptional cases, as we will see later.) This kind of utterance puts forward a hearing, an appreciation, an analysis, an interpretation of the utterance to which it is a response, at least in the sense that it presents itself as a relevant next utterance. (Of course, a hearing is also a kind of doing, but for convenience of expression I will use *doing* to refer to all those aspects of what an utterance does *other than* offering a hearing, unless that hearing is the explicit subject of the utterance.)

Even utterances that contain "misplacement markers," such as "At any rate, what I wanted to talk about was . . . ," offer hearings in that they themselves can be misplaced. Such utterances should not follow, for example, questions or other first pair parts. Moreover, the use of such an utterance reveals the speaker's awareness that what he is saying

AUTHOR'S NOTE: I would like to express my gratitude to Michael Moerman for his insightful comments on an early draft of this chapter. I should point out that some of the data presented here were collected under a grant from the National Science Foundation (No. BNS-8103585).

is discontinuous with the prior utterance.[1] Thus, in a number of ways, even a misplacement marked utterance reveals the speaker's analysis of the prior utterance.

The foregoing addresses a possible misconception about the problem of miscommunication in conversation. Hayes and Reddy (1983), for example, say that "unless the listener can determine that he has not received the message correctly, the error will go undetected; the conversation will continue uncorrected and may become quite confused" (p. 236). On the contrary, the conversational resources for both detecting and correcting mishearing are ubiquitous and sensitive. "Conversation requires its participants to demonstrate their understandings turn by turn, and makes available powerful devices for the repair of misunderstandings" (Moerman, 1988, p. 45). Hayes and Reddy add that "the listener normally has enough expectations about the sorts of things the speaker might want to say to make this [mishearing] a rare occurrence" (p. 236). Although I will not attempt to prove the point here, I think it is fair to say that it is not at all uncommon for a respondent to offer a hearing that the speaker finds in some respect unacceptable. This chapter contains examples of precisely this contingency.

The second feature of utterances-in-conversation is that what is heard, as implicitly or explicitly claimed in a subsequent utterance by the recipient, may be at variance with what the speaker claims to have meant. Utterances are taken (by participants) to have a single correct interpretation, even when what was said is open to more than one interpretation. In the case of ambiguous utterances, the correct interpretation is known to the speaker, and he, therefore, has the authority to say what he "meant." This way of handling matters is based on the assumption that expressions—when they are uttered—have a fixed meaning and that the interpretive problem, if any, is to determine what that meaning is, and that words merely express or encode meaning, which exists in people's heads in some perfect, unambiguous, nonverbal form, and is then, perhaps imperfectly, translated into words. The speaker, therefore, ordinarily "knows what he means." When he unambiguously says something other than what he subsequently claims to have meant, either he makes a mistake in encoding his thoughts into words or he is lying. Things, of course, are not really that simple. Participants often struggle over the meaning of utterances. This chapter investigates some of the many ways in which conversationalists manipulate one another's understanding of utterances.[2]

We begin with the observation that interactants employ various techniques to ensure understanding before there is any manifestation of misunderstanding. Speakers frequently reformulate their utterances, sometimes prefacing the reformulation with "I mean" (Garfinkel & Sacks, 1970; Heritage & Watson, 1979). Moreover, because the illocutionary force of utterances is usually not made explicit in the utterance, speakers sometimes instruct hearers as to the force of the utterance. As an illustration, I was present at an occasion where two persons got into an argument. A made a point; B strongly disputed it. B finally realized that she was wrong and conceded the point. She then turned to me and said: "I get impassioned." Then, turning to A, she said: "I get impassioned. That's an apology." [3] A particularly common instruction is: "Don't take what I just said seriously." This instruction appears in such expressions as: "I was just kidding."

I have suggested two important distinctions: one between the doing and the hearing aspects of an utterance, and the other between the speaker's and the hearer's claims regarding the meaning of an utterance. I want to draw to the reader's attention a third distinction that I have employed in the previous paragraphs. Most utterances can be said to have both a propositional content and an illocutionary force.[4] (There are utterances, such as "hello," that may have force but no content.) The significance of this observation for the matter at hand is that, as regards some utterance, speaker and hearer may disagree as to its content or its force or both.

The hearer has his own techniques to ensure that he has accurately understood what the speaker said. He may simply call for a restatement, minimally with "What?" or "Huh?" (Schegloff, Jefferson, & Sacks, 1977), or he may declare his lack of understanding. He may focus on a problematic element ("She said *what*?" "Who did you say you met?"). Or he may offer a candidate hearing for confirmation:

[1] [FTC: L 7/13][5]

```
01  C:   Okay wait you're asking do we know how many people we're
         talkin' about here we know how many loans 're outstanding
         (1)
02  P:   Right
         (3)
03  C:   That what y'r saying?
04  P:   That's one question.
05  C:   And you're saying th't s:ome o'these 're gonna be:(.) repeats=
```

06 *P:*   =I'm//not assuming anything but it (.) occurs t'me
07 *C:*   Yeah

Note that at turn 5, C is offering two hearings. One is an explicit candidate understanding of what P had said at some earlier point. It is the very business of this utterance as a doing to offer a hearing. But utterance 5 also offers an implicit hearing of 4. It appears to take 4 as an acceptance of the accuracy, if not the completeness, of utterance 1, since 5 is built on 1. Note also that P is accorded the authority to say what she meant. As we shall see, it is not always the case that the speaker has such uncontested authority.

Hearers have other ways to test and to repair their understanding. I will not try to enumerate them here. The topic of interest is: What happens when the hearer's response is such that the speaker takes it that he (the speaker) has been misunderstood? In a discussion that took place in the Federal Trade Commission (FTC), H asked a question; when it became apparent that the response was based on a mishearing of her question, H interrupted:

[2] [FTC: F 10.5]

01 *H:*   Wait wait wait wait (.) that's the regulation=I'm talking about
           (ths) the statute
02 *B:*   Oh (.) okay

The mishearing here relates to content rather than to force. H does not appear to be claiming that it was inappropriate to offer an answer, but rather that the particular answer offered was inappropriate. This mishearing is cited by H as grounds for cutting off and reorienting the discussion in progress, and these grounds are taken by B as new information, as evidenced by his "oh" (see Heritage, 1984a), and also accepted by him as adequate. H's cutoff of the discussion and invocation of "what she was talking about" constitute an exercise of her conversational rights.

Of course, it is possible (and not unusual) to claim that the force of one's utterance has been misconstrued.

[3] [FTC: 1977]

01 *R:*   . . . because you keep saying we need more and I'm not certain
           what more is.
03 *A:*   I-I didn't say that I you know I raised it as a question.

In this exchange, R, referring to an earlier utterance of A's, characterizes it as an assertion that "we need more." A rejects that interpretation, claiming that he was merely raising a question.

I close this section with a well-known example from Schegloff (1978). In this exchange—taken from a call-in radio show—A implicitly indicates that B has misconstrued the force of A's utterance. B then manages a rehearing of A's utterance.

[4] [Schegloff, 1978, p. 81]

01 *B:*   He says, governments, an'you know he keeps-he feels about governments, they sh-the thing they sh'd do is what's right or wrong.
02 *A:*   For whom
03 *B:*   Well he says-//he
04 *A:*   By what standard
05 *B:*   That's what-that's exactly what I mean.

Contested Hearings

In the examples offered so far, the speaker's authority to decide the meaning of his utterance has not been contested. The following exchange, quoted in a lecture by Harvey Sacks, is also from a call-in show; it contrasts with example 4 precisely on the question of who has the authority to decide the proper hearing of the speaker's utterance. In this excerpt, A is the host and B is a caller who is blind.

[5] [Sacks, 1965-1972: lecture, 22.2.68]

01 *B:*   I hev a gurripe. hhhnh!
02 *A:*   What's the gr//ipe dear.
03 *B:*   And oh boy hhhnhh heh hhh!
04 *B:*   Well, Eh-eh The trai::ns, Yuh know Theh-the-the people hh Uh-why:::, eh dizat-do not. They. hh respec'. The so called white ca:ne (bohk). In other words, if they see me wih the ca:ne, trav'ling the city essetra, hh why do they not give me, the so called right of way. Etcetera.
05 *A:*   Well they probably//do, once they see it.
06 *B:*   Wah dintenehh
07 *A:*   Uh, The//trouble is-
08 *B:*   No they don't Brad.

```
        09  A:  Ha'd'yih know.
        10  B:  Becuz I've been on th'trai:n before they don't care whether I
                live 're die hh
        11  A:  Well,
        12  B:  //Uh-
        13  A:  May-
        14  B:  //Yihknow
        15  A:  Maybe-
    →   16  A:  //Dear wait, wait?
    →   17  B:  (              )
    →   18  A:  //Wait.
    →   19  B:  Go'head
        20  A:  No:w. N:d-d-
        21  B:  //Okay.
    →   22  A:  Don'ask a question 'n then answer it.
    →   23  B:  Go'head.
        24  A:  Uh::, You see what happens, with-specially with New Yorkers,
                i:s? thet they get a::ll preocuppie::d with their own problum::s
        25  B:  //Yes
        26  A:  -with the::-fallout an'the pollution, en the//b-en the landlord,
        27  B:  Yeah mm hm,
        28  B:  Yeah.
        29  A:  //And they don't-
        30  B:  (          )-
    →   31  A:  Nuh waitaminnit, Lemme finish,
    →   32  B:  Guh head.
        33  A:  And they don't notice.
```

Excerpts 4 and 5 contrast in interesting ways. In 4, A produces what is apparently a question and then gets B to interpret it as not a question at all. In excerpt 5, B produces what is on its surface a question, and A insists on treating it as such, despite B's apparent desire to have it treated as a troubles telling. In excerpt 4, when B's answer is cut off, he understands that an answer is not what is called for and achieves a rehearing, but in 5, A refuses to do a similar reanalysis when he is interrupted, and it is B who bows to A's interpretation. In both cases, the host of the show is in control. It is in these delicate ways that hosts and callers play out their roles.

The point of primary interest for present purposes, however, is that it is not necessarily the speaker who has the final word on how his utterances are to be interpreted. In example 4, B could have pointed out—as A did in 5—that he had been asked a question and demanded space in which to answer. Whereas the speaker has the authority of "knowing his own intentions," the hearer is not without resources. Whereas the speaker's intentions are reserved for his own use, his words are available to whoever has heard them.

Given that both speaker and hearer may legitimately claim to know what an utterance means, there is a possibility that they will disagree and enter into a negotiation or quarrel over who is right. The following exchange, concerning a proposed passage in a memo being composed by Federal Trade Commission attorneys, is particularly interesting in that it deals not only with the meaning of the passage but also with the meaning of the underlying intention.

[6] [FTC: S9/13]

01 *P:*   Well (.5) then we s- I mean if we're gonna say why we should
         say: (2) we don't believe there is an appropriate remedy for an
         impermissible request for information (.5) it's no:t

02 *M:*   hm (.5) yeah

03 *P:*   because there wasn't any injury (.5) which is what you seem
         to be saying here or at least implying here (3.5) you're saying
         (.5) we're not asking for consumer redress for this violation
         because it did not lead (*) (.5) to an even greater violation (2)
         and I don't wanna

04 *M:*   Yeah=

05 *P:*   =I don't wanna rub their noses in that fact hhehheh

06 *?:*   huhhuh
         (1)

07 *P:*   U:m
         (1)

08 *M:*   That isn't really what we meant (1) I mean (.5) what we meant
         was (1) not that it's not an illegal practice but (.5) they didn't
         use it for the reasons Congress (.5) said you can't have that
         information (.5) in other words they didn't go ahead and dis-
         criminate once they had gotten that information (1.5)

09 *P:*   Why? Which is=

10 *M:*   =which is
         (1)

11 *P:*   which is saying:because you didn't (1) commit an even greater
         violation we're not going to ask

12 *M:*   W'll
13 *P:*   redress//for the
14 *M:*   you c<u>ou</u>ld s<u>ee</u> it that way=
15 *P:*   =hhuhhuh but that that's what I'm (.5) that's how I'm afr<u>ai</u>d it
            will//be=
16 *M:*   Yeah
17 *P:*   =seen
18 *M:*   Yeah

P begins by offering an interpretation of a passage in the memo
composed by J and M. P stands in a supervisory-consultative relationship to J and M. She is helping to refine the memo, which is aimed at
convincing higher authorities in the FTC of the desirability of certain
legal actions. P begins by characterizing the meaning of the passage,
what it *says.* M replies with a claim as to "what we *meant.*" This offers
a sort of compromise. We meant to say X, but (she seems to be
conceding) perhaps we said it in such a way that it could be interpreted
as Y. P does not accept this compromise. What you claim to have meant,
she says, is nothing more than a rephrasing of what I just claimed the
passage actually says. The passage is an accurate expression of your
intention; it is your intention itself that is faulty.

In this exchange, M uses the common ploy of distinguishing between
what the passage could be taken to mean and what she meant by it. Thus
she can find P's reading to be a misreading, without questioning P's
competence. This tactic frequently produces agreement, since the
speaker has admitted to a certain degree of fault (in having produced
an ambiguous utterance) while finding no fault with the hearer. P rejects
the ploy by insisting that there is no difference between her interpretation of what M wrote and what M said she meant by what she wrote. M,
that is, has failed to provide any grounds for contesting P's reading.

At this point, the talk becomes constructively fuzzy. M says: "you
could see it that way." The referent of "it" is not clear—is "it" the
passage or the intention or P's claim of identity of the two? At any rate,
this is a very clear offer of compromise, and P accepts it. In P's reply,
"but that's . . . how I'm afraid it will be seen," she seems to be allowing
both that the passage is somehow ambiguous and that the interpretation
that she is afraid it will be given is not necessarily the one that J and M
had in mind. The indeterminacy of M's "it" has facilitated this slide in
P's position from refutation to something less harsh. It is this final
position that elicits M's agreement.

It should also be noted that an utterance may refuse to give a hearing of a previous utterance, and that refusal, if it is recognized as such, may itself be meaningful. This is illustrated in the following exchange:

[7] [FTC: S 1 0/7]

((P wants to include in the case against XYZ Loan Company the charge that they illegally asked applicants about their marital status. However, she is not recommending that a penalty be assessed for this violation. She is explaining why she wants the charge included.))

01 P: Uh (3) for the deterrence value: of having this in an order (.5) If creditors don't ask (1) and don't have the information (1) then they can't intentionally discriminate on the basis of marital status .hh If they have the information (i) then we have to con- then- we are put to: a much greater burden as an enforcement agency in determining whether or not they've used it illegally.=

02 B: =(It will happen) if the deterrence: if you charged them ten thousand dollars for each time we were able to and no deterrence if it's issued in (**) (1) Nothing.
        (1)

→ 03 M: So why don't we charge 'em (1) I don't have any prob//lem with not charging

→ 04 B: ((to P)) You know that. I mean it's just another piece of paper (4.5)

05 P: I have to believe that my work is meaningful

M's utterance in line 3 is spoken clearly and is not overlapped until her suggestion has been completed. One cannot suppose that B did not hear it. On the other hand, B's utterance 4 does not deal with M or her utterance in any way. B ignores M's utterance, and precludes anyone else from responding to her, by readdressing himself to P with a remark that calls for a response from P. There is ample time after B's 4 for M to protest that she has been misheard, that her 3 called for some response, or alternatively for her to repeat her suggestion, but she says nothing. B has told her in effect that she spoke out of turn, that the exchange at this point is between him and P. B communicates this by readdressing P with an utterance that calls for a response from P and no one else. Thus M is doubly inhibited from speaking. Not only has an organizational superior indicated to her that she currently has no speaking rights, but he has done so in a way that selects someone else to speak.

I bring up this example as a way of pointing out that what might, under certain circumstances, be thought of as a mishearing ("Oh, sorry, I didn't realize that was a question") might also be a failure to hear or a refusal to grant a hearing. Sometimes, in fact, there may be some doubt as to whether the other has misheard, not heard, or refused to hear. The state of an individual's social relations with the other may hinge on such ambiguities.

Prefatory "No": A Mishearing Marker

When an interactant, A, begins an utterance with "no," it may not be clear whether A's "no" responds to B's utterance as a doing or as a hearing—whether A is saying "No, what you said is wrong" or "No, what you said is not a proper reply to what I said and suggests that you misunderstood me." As we shall see, this is more than an abstract possibility. This possibility sets the stage for further ambiguity. B's response to A's "no" may itself be open to different hearings according to whether A thinks that B has heard that "no" as referring to a hearing or a doing. Furthermore, the "no" is in itself a hearing. It may, for example, be taken to indicate that A heard B's previous utterance as serious, and B may go on to claim that he was only joking. In theory, the involutions have no end, and in fact such possible misunderstandings appear sometimes to remain undiscovered by either interactant. Later, both may claim to have meant something other than what the other claims to have understood.[6]

These considerations are sufficient to indicate that utterance-initial "no" is an analytically interesting object. Utterance-initial "no" has a number of functions; among them, answering questions, refusing offers and requests, and disagreeing.[7] We will be interested here in its function as a marker of disagreement or correction.

When initial "no" is used to correct a mishearing, it is often followed by "I mean." Such cases are perhaps the clearest examples of the use of initial "no" as a mishearing marker.

[8] [Schegloff, 1987b]

```
01  D:   Well, whaddya y'gonna do about it.
         (.2)
02  K:   Give it to my parents and have em sign it,
→ 03  D:   No, I mean about hh
04  K:   heh
05  D:   Not this,//I'm not talking about this
06  K:   heh
```

[9] [Schegloff, 1987b]

```
01  S:   Well, what are you going to do, Mr Greenberg.
02  G:   Well that's true. When you are a charity patient, when you are
         a beggar, you just can't do anything about it, you just have to
         take what's handed out to you, and-
→ 03  S:   No, I mean about yourself. What are you going to do for
         yourself.
```

In examples 8 (utterance 3) and 9 (utterance 3), the speaker says, "No, I mean" in a clear attempt to correct the previous speaker's apparent mishearing. In 8 the "mishearing" was apparently deliberate and nonserious. This means that D's correction could itself have been treated as a mishearing by K. He might have said, for example, "I was just kidding," and then proceeded to answer the question seriously. Instead, he chose to convey his nonserious intent by producing laugh tokens.

It is not necessary, however, to follow "no" with "I mean" in order for it to stand as a correction of a mishearing. The following exchange lacks "I mean" but is nevertheless rather close to the previous two:

[10] [FTC: S 10.7]

((P wants to include in the case against XYZ Loan Company the charge that they illegally asked applicants about their marital status. However, she is not recommending that a penalty be assessed for this violation. She is explaining why she wants the charge included.))

```
01  P:   Uh (3) for the deterrence value: of having this in an order (.5)
         If creditors don't ask (1) and don't have the information (1)
         then they can't intentionally discriminate on the basis of mari-
         tal status . hh If they have the information (1) then we have to
         con- then- we are put to: a much greater burden as an enforcement
         agency in determining whether or not they've used it illegally.=
```

02 *B:* =(It will happen) if the deterrence: if you charged them ten
thousand dollars for each time we were able to and no deterrence if it's issued in (**) (1) Nothing.
(1)

03 *M:* So why don't we charge 'em. (1) I don't have any prob//lem
with not charging

04 *B:* ((to P)) You know that. I mean it's just another piece of paper
(4.5)

05 *P:* I have to believe that my work is meaningful//because (*)

→ 06 *B:* No I- I- I- I just I just I just don't think (1) merely=

07 *P:* =(*)=

08 *B:* =having it in as a provision in a consent order has any impact
beyond the company.

B's "no" is clearly directed to the hearing that P has given his previous
argument. But note that his "no" is, upon its occurrence, ambiguous, at
least in theory, and is clarified by the rest of his utterance. It is
ambiguous because it could be referring to the previous utterance as an
assertion rather than as a hearing. That is, he might have said: "No, you
don't have to believe that your work is meaningful." This same observation applies equally to examples 7 and 8.

The next exchange is more subtle. In example 11, the sense of "no"
is once again clarified by what follows (although I argue that it remains
ambiguous), but what follows is not an account of what the speaker
meant or thought. Rather, it can be read as a continuation of what she
had begun to say earlier.

[11] [Jefferson, 1985]

01 *E:* Isn't this FUNNY YOU AND I: WOULD HAVE IT.h
(.4)

02 *E:* This is ri//diculous

03 *L:* E:VERYBODY'S GOT ih. hh=

04 *L:* =Isn't tha:t funny we were in a p-uh//::

05 *E:* Oh: God it's terrible Lottie m:y toenails .hehh they're just look
so sick those big t:oenails it just u-makes me: sick. You know
they're just (.) u-dea:d. (.) Everything's dead I d- I sat ou:t (.)
today and I said my Go:d am I just (.) DY:ING it's: (.) like I'm
ossified.

06 *L:* No I- We were in:some//pla:ce I don't know if it was=

07 *E:* ((sniff))

08 *L:*   =Abel's or somepla:ce (.4) I <u>guess</u> it was <u>A</u>bel's. a:nd <u>so</u>mebody
           was <u>ta</u>:lking about it a:nd <u>I</u>: bet there were .hhh <u>TE</u>:N <u>PEO</u>PLE
           arou:nd the:re, and they all started to <u>say</u> well <u>they had</u> the
           <u>sa</u>:me th<u>ing</u>? and I k<u>no</u>:w like D<u>o</u>ctor <u>Ba</u>rton s<u>ay</u>s it's from the
           <u>da</u>mn .p detergent.

E apparently thinks that L has provided her with a propitious place
to complain about her toenails and begins to do so in utterance 5. As
Jefferson points out, E may suppose that L's "we" in utterance 4 is a
reformulation of E's "you and I" in 1. In 6, instead of commiserating
with E, L apparently continues what she had begun to say in 4. Her
"we," as it turns out, did not refer to you-and-I but to I-and-them. She
prefaces utterance 6 with "no." In this example, the "no," I think, is
truly ambiguous. It could mean either "No, you're not ossified. It's just
the detergent" or "No, you heard me wrong. The line I was pursuing
was . . . ." Jefferson's analysis appears to favor the latter interpretation,
although she does not specifically address the occurrence of "no." The
way E hears that "no" may be consequential in determining the form of
her response, which, unfortunately, Jefferson does not supply.

As Schegloff (1987b, 1988b) has observed, "no" is also used to point
out that what preceded was not meant seriously, whereas what is to
follow is meant seriously. Sometimes this use of "no" can be seen as
correcting a possible mishearing by the recipient. The speaker says
something that is claimably nonserious, the recipient gives no indication that he has taken it as nonserious, and the speaker then says
something on the order of "No, I was just kidding" or just "no" followed
by some contrasting, serious utterance. The problem with this interpretation of the function of initial "no" in this context is that initial "no"
is also used for transition from nonserious to serious when the recipient
has clearly appreciated the nonseriousness of the preceding utterance.
Here are two examples:

[12] [Schegloff, 1988b]

01 *S:*   You didn't get an ice cream sanwich,
02 *C:*   I kno:w, hh I decided that my body didn't need it,
03 *S:*   Yes but ours di:d=
04 *S:*   =hh heh // heh // .hhih
05 *?:*   ehh heh
06 *?:*   (   )

```
07  C:    hh Awright gimme some money en you c'n treat me to one
          an I'll buy you a:ll some // too
08  S:    I'm kidding, I don't need it.
          (0.3)
09  C:    I WA:N' :ON//E, ((in "whine" voice))
10  S, R?:  ehh heh h//uh
11  C:    hhehhuh.=
→ 12  C:    =No they didn' even have any Ta:b
```

[13] [Schegloff, 1987b, pp. 215-216]

```
01  A:    . . . like Tuesdays I don't go in until two thirdy
          (0.5)
02  A:    E//n I'm home by fi:ve
03  B:    mm hmm
          (0.3)
04  A:    I have- th' class is two thirdy tuh fouh.
          (0.5)
05  B:    Mm
06  A:    En then, the same thing is (uh) jus' tihday is like a long day cuz
          I have a break,
          (0.7)
07  B:    Hm:.
          (0.6)
08  B:    .hh- NOt me:, hhuh uh-hhuh .hhh! I go in late everyday hh!
09  A:    Eyeh hh //!
→ 10  B:    No this'z- No I have my early class tihday et four thi:rdy.
```

We might begin by asking why "no" in these exchanges does not appear to mean "No, you need not have laughed. I was not joking." Although I do not have an actual example at hand, I think it is safe to say that "no" is frequently used in precisely this way. Just as we may say, "No, I was kidding" when our previous utterance does not elicit a laugh, we may also say "No, I'm serious" when it does. In examples 12 and 13, "no" is directed not at the response to the speaker's previous utterance but to the speaker's previous utterance itself. It instructs the recipient to put aside the previous utterance and replace it with whatever follows the "no." It is in fact what follows the "no" that tells us how to interpret "no" on this occasion. This provides a solution to a conversational problem; once we have been recognized as speaking nonseriously, we face the problem of "closure" (see Bilmes, 1985, for further discussion of closure as a conversational problem). Given that we have begun speaking nonseriously, how is the recipient to know whether further utterances are to be taken seriously or to be taken as a continuation of the nonserious talk? Initial "no" is a device for making clear the status of further talk. So, just as the talk that follows may clarify the meaning of the "no," the "no" may instruct us on how to interpret that very talk.

In discussing the previous cases, I have stressed possible ambiguities in the use of initial "no." My final example is a case where the ambiguity becomes palpable for the participants.

[14] [FTC: S 10/7]

((H, the head of the division, has entered a meeting where a discussion of a case has been under way for some time. Shortly after she enters, this exchange takes place.))

01	*H:*	Well let's see where our calculations would come out
02	*P:*	hhh huh
03	*B:*	That's what we//re just doing
04	*H?:*	Well
05	*?:*	Yeah
06	*?:*	(*)
07	*B:*	And <u>why</u> don't we just do the who:le summary here
08	*P:*	Well I have it written down here
09	*B:*	Okay why don't you just//tell her what
10	*P:*	S<u>e</u>venty gra:nd (1) fo//r the seven
→ 11	*B:*	No:
→ 12	*P:*	Y-//y
→ 13	*B:*	Tell her what we c<u>o</u>vered first and then tell her where we are in the calculations
14	*P:*	Okay we:ll anyone can tell her what we c<u>o</u>vered

In utterance 1, H says, "let's see where our calculations would come out." In 7, B calls for "the whole summary." At this point, there might be some ambiguity as to what B is calling for. Is he asking for a whole summary of the discussion thus far (or perhaps even more than that) or a whole summary of all suggested penalties, which is what H seemed to be asking for? The notion of a "whole summary" is inherently problematic (perhaps even verging on oxymoronic) in that it leaves unspecified how much detail must be included before wholeness is achieved. The problem here, however, is different. The problem is that the phenomenon to be summarized has not been sufficiently specified. The indefinite reference of P's "it" in utterance 8 does nothing to clarify the situation. In 7, B makes a suggestion-request (a directive, a call for action). P then makes what seems to be an offer, and B accepts the offer, which P, in 10, begins to carry out. As the nature of her report becomes clear, B interrupts her, saying "no."

As noted at the beginning of this chapter, a response has a dual nature in that it is both a doing and a hearing. What is at issue in example 14 is whether B (in 11) is taking exception to 10 as a doing or as a hearing. A second possible ambiguity that does not surface in this example is: If B is objecting to 10 as a hearing, is the problem that P has misheard the force of 7 and/or 9 or their content? In this case, the problem is clearly one of content. The problem is not that P has heard B as calling for a report and has begun to give one, but rather that she has not understood the kind of report he is calling for. But P herself apparently sees B's "no" as a comment on 10 as a doing. She sees him as claiming that her report is inaccurate. In 12, she apparently begins to say "yes," in contradiction to B's "no." B then clarifies the nature of his objection.

The ambiguity here can be given a structural representation as shown in Figure 5.1. B's call for action in 7 is followed by an offer by P. Since this offer commits P to carrying out the action, provided the offer is accepted, I view 8 and 9 as a subunit preliminary to 10, and 8, 9, and 10 as a unit paired to 7. The ambiguity derives from the way 11 is related to what precedes. P regards B's "no" as pertaining to the content of what she said in 10. B's claim, on the other hand, is that his "no" pertains not to 10 as such but to the understanding exhibited in 10 to the meaning of 7.[8]

We see in this example that particular utterances (7 and 9) can be claimed to have been misheard and, further, that the claim itself can be misheard. The possibilities for complication obviously go well beyond this. P might, for instance, claim that B had misheard her, that what she meant with 10 was not what he thought she meant, and so on. Infinite regress is a constant threat, and one that perhaps we sometimes escape only by abandoning attempts at correction or by terminating the line of talk or even the conversation itself.

P's analysis

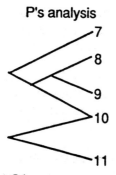

B's analysis

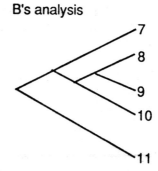

Figure 5.1.

Conclusion

The ability to ensure accurate hearing and address mishearing is what Hayes and Reddy (1983) refer to as "robust communication," which is a component of "graceful interaction." For them the significant characteristic of robust communication is that it facilitates the accurate transfer of messages. This essentially goal-oriented approach, one that is quite appropriate to their concerns with man-machine interaction, is not, I think, the one best suited to conversation analysis concerns. When one party claims to have been misheard, the analyst cannot assume that the hearing being called for now is the one that the speaker had "in mind" all along. We cannot assume that the meanings that get elaborated in conversation were there (in some mysterious mental form) all along, so that the only problem is accurate transmission. Nevertheless, for the sake of discussion, let us suppose that a speaker's utterance is an attempt to encode some meaning or intention that he has in mind. When the recipient gives this utterance a hearing, as reflected in his response, one possibility is that the original speaker will identify the hearing as an accurate reading of what he had in mind and accept it. Another possibility is that the response will evidence an inaccurate understanding of the utterance and will therefore be corrected. But there is a range of other possibilities. An accurate hearing may be rejected because the speaker has changed his mind about how he wants to be heard. An inaccurate hearing may be accepted because the speaker is satisfied to be understood in that way. Or a hearing may elaborate or specify a speaker's meaning in a way that the speaker never thought about, in a way such that the speaker cannot "simply know" whether or not that meaning was what he had in mind. That is, even if people do have their meanings "in mind," surely those meanings are not "complete" in the sense that every possible hearing is either unambiguously right or unambiguously wrong. When a recipient gives our utterance a hearing, we must make a judgment as to whether that hearing is an acceptable reflection of what we had in mind or want to be heard as having had in mind. This judgment is far more than a mechanical matter of matching meaning to hearing. Rather, we must ask, Is this particular hearing one that we can accept as a specification of our meaning? We may even experience our recipient's hearing as a revelation of what, after all, we had in mind in the first place.

Therefore, we should treat "mishearing" as primarily a topic of conversation analysis rather than as an analytical resource. That is, it is up to members to locate and correct or negotiate mishearings. The conversation analyst will not ordinarily want to say that a particular utterance evidences a mishearing unless a participant has treated it as such. Even when a participant produces a clearly irrelevant response, it may be treated by an interlocutor as a deliberate evasion, a snub, or an admonition (as in example 7) rather than as evidence of mishearing. From the analyst's standpoint, mishearing is best viewed as an interactional stance, something that can be claimed and disputed or agreed upon, rather than as an objective phenomenon existing independently of participants' claims and noticings.[9]

Three features of conversation are especially relevant to the study of mishearings. The first is what I will call *density*. Through conditions such as cultural and biographical knowledge and situational context and through mechanisms such as presupposition, implicature, and preference, conversation permits and demands inferences far beyond what is said in so many words. (I will not struggle here with the question of what it means to say something in so many words. Whatever it might mean, it is clear that our interpretations do not stop there.) These inferential processes are complex, subtle, and fluid. Conversation is built in such a way as to engender ambiguity and opportunities for claims of mishearing.

The second feature is *interpretive feedback*. We cannot think of conversation as built on a solid foundation of independent, preexisting meanings. Meanings are defined by and within the very conversation they support. While natural language is built to engender ambiguity, it is also built to reveal how utterances have been interpreted. In this way it provides for the third feature, *negotiability of meaning*, including corrections and retrospective claims. If conversation were not dense, if meaning were explicit and unambiguous, or if there were no interpretive feedback to reveal the other's hearing, there would be no need for negotiation. It is beyond the scope of this chapter to speculate on either the causes or the consequences of this state of affairs, although both are worthy subjects. I have merely tried to show—to some small extent—how the system works.

Notes

1. In using the masculine form as the unmarked pronoun, I am following the policy suggested by Dorothy Smith (1978): "The general pronoun follow(s) the sex of the speaker" (p. 53).

2. In a 1987 paper, Schegloff (1987b) discusses some sources of "misunderstandings," that is, some features of linguistic interaction that may produce a situation where a speaker may claim that he has been misheard by a recipient. In this chapter, I am concerned not so much with the conversational phenomena that may produce claims of mishearing as with the nature and sequential aspects of the claims themselves.

3. There are situations where the hearer may be considered to be a better judge of utterance force than the speaker. For instance, when the father in a family therapy session explains that he was going to take his son fishing but did not have the time and ended up taking him crabbing instead, the therapist comments, "You're apologizing."

4. There is yet another aspect of utterances—their style. The difference between "hello" and "hi" would seem to be a matter of style rather than of content or force.

5. I am using standard conversation-analytic transcription conventions (Button & Lee, 1987), with one modification. When I cannot make out the words on the tape, I put asterisks in parentheses. Each asterisk represents about .5 seconds of speech.

6. "No" produces, in certain contexts, another interesting ambiguity. The following exchange is from a collection made by John Heritage on troubled understanding:

P: Jees I've had a hell of a time
M: Ha- have you?
P: Since the eighth of October
M: Wh-what's that?
P: Well I've nothing to do.
M: Oh you mean you're not working?
P: No:::
M: Oh I did't know that

In this exchange, P's "no" is possibly ambiguous ("No, I'm not working" versus "No, I don't mean that"), although M's response does not reveal any recognition of that ambiguity. Sentences with two verb phrases, one subordinate to the other, tend to create this kind of ambiguity.

7. Utterance-initial "no" can also be used to express agreement, and this may give rise to ambiguity, as in the following exchange:

[FTC: S 10/7]

((B is expressing his understanding of a passage in a memo that he is reviewing with the memo's authors))

B: Okay and so then (1) an' the and so then but (1) it's hard for me to tell: I mean we're not alleging that our footnote says we- we don't care about that we don't care that they ask are you single or
(2)

M: No we care about did you ask marital status not whether you said are you single married or divorced.

M's "no" might indicate agreement ("No, you're right. We don't care that they asked are you single") or disagreement ("No, you're wrong, although we don't care about their using the words 'single,' 'married,' and 'divorced,' which technically is a violation in itself, we do care that they asked about marital status in whatever words"). M's proposition, given a knowledge of the memo and the legal context, is clear enough, but her stance in relation to B's understanding is ambiguous.

8. This sort of hierarchical, one-to-many structure has been recognized in C.A. since its inception. Schegloff (1968) writes that we can treat the summons-answer sequence "as a unit; it has the status of a first item in a sequence for which further talk becomes the second item, expectable upon the occurrence of the first" (p. 1084). See also Sacks on puns (1973) and on narratives (1974).

9. It is possible to overemphasize negotiability. While there is a certain amount of "play" or ambiguity in any utterance, any particular utterance is simply not open to certain interpretations. Also, an utterance may have a conventional "first hearing," an interpretation that any hearer would (on first hearing) give it, but one that a speaker can plausibly claim is incorrect. Perhaps exchange 5 is an example of this. The analyst, therefore, is not entirely without resources in his attempts to specify the meaning of utterances.

6

The Study of Extended Sequences

The Case of the Garden Lesson

GEORGE PSATHAS

Extended sequences in interaction need to be understandable and analyzable as whole units because they represent complex systems of action or activity systems. Explicating extended sequences entails paying attention to their overall structure rather than to any restricted set of contiguous utterances or turns. The structure of extended sequences is marked by a beginning and an ending and, possibly, by sections or subunits, each of which may be differentiated internally.

The extended sequence to be presented here, an "instructional examination formatted lesson," is understandable "as a lesson" only in terms of what it is about, what its purpose is as formulated by those who are collaboratively producing it, and in terms of what it comes to, what it achieves. The strategy for studying extended sequences or activity systems requires locating extended sequences in naturally occurring interaction and then explicating their structures.

The Extended Sequence

Three issues are fundamental to extended sequences. First, how do the parties in talk enter into the activity? This is the *entry* problem.

Second, how do they exit the extended sequence to move to other topical matters or to a closing of the interactional encounter? This is the exit or *closing* problem. Third is the *internal structure* of the extended sequence itself, whether it is a "simple" set of interrelated and interconnected microstructures, such as a series of adjacency-pair organizations or insertion sequences, or whether there are structures that are particular to the type of activity the extended sequence is about.

Some of the prior work on such extended sequences includes studies of stories (Sacks, 1970), troubles tellings (Douglas-Steele, 1988; Jefferson, 1980), teaching lessons (Mehan, 1979), and direction giving (Psathas, 1986a, 1986b, in press; Psathas & Kozloff, 1976). These types of sequences have generally been more than four turns long and may be of an indefinite length. The extended sequence relates to some type of activity that can be said to characterize the sequence, that is, it is about doing something, some type of social action.

In the case analyzed here, the entry into the lesson is marked by the two parties coming into an enclosed garden on what was once a large estate in a residential suburb of Boston (see Figure 6.1). I have named it the "Garden Lesson" in order to differentiate it from other lessons in which the same teacher and student were involved. The participants are an instructor of the blind and a blind student.[1] The lesson takes place (outdoors) in a garden. The student has never visited this place before. The student holds a long cane. He has been receiving instruction in long cane mobility and is reasonably proficient at it.

The end of the lesson, or exit from the extended sequence, is marked by the instructor's taking the student to another location, where he begins additional instructional activities. These entry and exit activities are not examined in detail here. Instead, the focus is the internal structure of the extended sequence. This particular type of instructional sequence is one in which there is a determinate correct answer, as decided by the instructor; the student is examined on his knowledge or achievement of the correct answer; and the student's answer is evaluated by the instructor as to the correctness of the solution. It can therefore be referred to as an "instructional examination formatted lesson."

Further, this type of lesson has additional internal features, namely, the use of particular recommended or previously taught methods for achieving the correct solution. In this respect the evaluation of the student's performance includes the evaluation of the correct use of the appropriate methods for solving the problem.

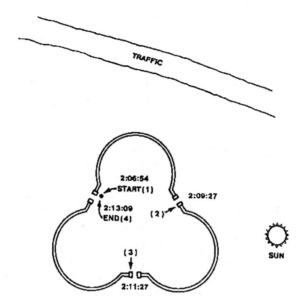

Figure 6.1. Garden Lesson

The Lesson

The lesson is built, stepwise and sequentially, as a series of sequenced actions. These can be subdivided analytically into sections and their internal organization studied. Each of the sections can also be examined in terms of what it accomplishes in relation to the overall lesson, how it relates to the prior section, and how it relates to the next in a series of interconnected sections.

The prestart section. The first part of the lesson, referred to as the prestart, is marked by the entry into the garden through what the instructor later calls a "gate" or "opening." The prestart is divided into approximately three parts with some subdivisions: Lines 1-12 involve "sitting squarely," lines 13-16 involve "locating the sun," and lines 17-20 involve "locating the traffic." The first of these can be called *achieving proper body orientation*; the second and third, *locating external orientational reference points*. A prototypical sequence for achieving a correct response to an instructor's directive would be as follows:

14 *T:*   point to the sun   directive
15 *S:*   ((points to the sun)) response: achievement/nonachievement
16 *T:*   awright   assessment: positive/negative

Some variations on such a sequence might occur. For example, the student might fail to respond in the second turn, due to refusal, nonhearing, or nonunderstanding, thus leading the instructor to repeat, elaborate, reformulate, or even abandon his directive. The student's response might be incorrect due to mishearing or misunderstanding rather than to inability to perform correctly. The student's response might go unobserved or be incorrectly observed by the instructor and either no assessment or an incorrect assessment made.

Underlying all this is the question of whether the student has achieved the correct response by using the correct means. In this case, pointing to the sun may be done with one's face, one's nose, one's hand without using one's face, and so on. The instructor might have a criterion for which of these is the correct means for achieving the solution. In this respect, if the student uses the correct means and achieves the correct solution, the instructor evaluates both the means and the solution.

If the instructor corrects the means before accepting the solution, the third turn may be further differentiated. This is what happens in the first sequence (lines 1-12), where many more turns are taken before the teacher accepts the student's response as correct. Let's look at this sequence in detail.

01 *T:*   face me squarely
02   just as you came in t'du-
03   just//as you came in the gate
04   ((motions with his two hands and arms forward and parallel to each other))
05   facing me face me (.5) squarely
06   feel=the=block behind you (1.0)
07   ((takes S's left hand and places it on the block))
08   awright now
09   now sit square on it
10   ((motions with his two hands and arms directly in front of his body and parallel to each other))
11 *S:*   ((moves his body twice, hitches over to his left while seated on the block))

12 *T:*   that's it
13   so you're facing me (.2) awright (.2)

It is clear that, whatever the student is doing from line 1 until line 11, it is not the correct response to the directive that is given in line 1, "face me squarely," because it is not until line 12 that a positive assessment is given by the teacher and line 13 when the teacher finally concludes this segment with a pause of (.2) and an "awright," a disjunct marker, after which he goes on to another directive on a different topic.

The failure of the student to provide the correct response elicits several further elaborations from the teacher, which can be heard as his providing means by which the correct response could be achieved. In lines 2-4, for example, the means indicated suggest that the student remember the orientation he had when he came through the "gate" with his shoulders parallel to the plane of the gate. "Squarely" is now elaborated to include not only the student's face but also his upper body as represented by the alignment of his shoulders.

The absence of a response by the student then elicits (in line 5) a reiteration of the earlier formulation, "face me" (line 1), the (.5) pause representing the turn transition space in which the student's response would be expected. Since there is no response, the instructor adds again, "squarely."

Now he proceeds to elaborate with an additional means by which the student can solve the problem, namely, to "feel the block" on which he is sitting and to "sit square on it." It is possible (as the student shows in lines 1-10) to align one's face in the sought-for direction without aligning one's upper torso. The student does feel the block with his hand as the teacher takes the student's hand and places it on the block. This action is assessed as correct by the teacher (line 8: "awright"), but this assessment does not refer back to the prior directive. Thus this sequence is a directive-response-assessment sequence and is itself embedded within another directive sequence. (We could also refer to it as an "insertion sequence.")

Finally, in line 11 the student moves his body, hitches over to his left, and realigns his upper body and shoulders, keeping his face also in the proper alignment. This obtains the teacher's positive assessment, "that's it" (line 12).

Following this first directive sequence, there are two additional sequences of similar types. These deal with two different topical matters, "point to the sun" (line 14) and "where's the traffic?" (lines 17-18), reformulated to "where do you hear the traffic?" Each of these is concluded in a sequence of three turns.

D	14	*T:*	point to the sun
R: ach	15	*S:*	((lifts face, places left hand up to face, etc.))
A: pos	16	*T:*	awright
D	17	*T:*	where's the traffic?
	18		where do you hear the traffic?
R: ach	19	*S:*	((gestures with left hand and arm raised . . .))
A: pos	20	*T:*	perfect
	21	*T:*	okay?

After this, the instructor begins a different sequence that represents the entry into what I shall call the "lesson proper" beginning with an instruction section. This entry thus marks the prior sequences as preliminary. Although the three directives are assessed as to their correctness, they do not appear to be "the lesson." At this point, their relevance for the lesson can only be guessed, but that they are relevant cannot be denied. Their relevance stems from (a) their sequential positioning, (b) the fact that they occur after the garden is entered and before any information is provided as to the purpose for their being in the garden, and (c) the fact that a correct response is sought. If just any response would do, there would not have been elaborations, repeats, reformulations, and so on, until a correct response was achieved. Thus, for the student as well as for us, *that* being able to "sit squarely," "point to the sun," and "locate the traffic" are relevant for what is to follow seems apparent. Just *how* they are relevant, however, is not.

In order to indicate the significance of these directives for the overall lesson, I would like to refer to them by terms that are oriented to their lesson relevance. The first, "sit squarely," involves achieving a consistent bodily orientation in relation to an external orientational reference point. That is, the post of the gate is the one on the left of the gate as it is entered. Sitting on it squarely involves aligning one's upper body, shoulders and upper torso, in a plane parallel to the line formed by the inner edge of the post. This can be achieved by sitting with one's legs at a perpendicular (or 90 degree) angle to the inner edge of the post and aligning one's upper body accordingly. The use or significance of achieving such an alignment is yet to be discovered by the student, but its importance is emphasized by the amount of attention given to its achievement by the teacher. I shall refer to it as *achieving proper bodily orientation*. The next two directives are similar in that each requires locating an external orientational reference point and describing its location with bodily actions. In the case of the sun, a point with one's nose, hand, and/or face represents an acceptable response, and in the case of the traffic, which flows linearly, a movement of a hand and arm that traces the line of flow is an acceptable response. I shall refer to these as *locating external orientational reference points*.

The end of the prestart section of the lesson is marked by a "solicit" (line 21: "okay?"), a disjunct marker (line 22: "now:"), and a pause (.4). The solicit refers backward to the prior series of directives and their consequences, and, since it does not obtain any response or request or further talk on the prior topics, serves to close that prior section. The disjunct marker, particularly in the form of the expression used here ("now"), serves to announce that a new section of the lesson is upcoming. Together with the pause of four-tenths of a second it is clear that the prior section is ended and a new section is forthcoming.

Instruction section. This next section (lines 23-54), until the camera clicks on, can be considered the *instructions for the lesson proper.*

```
22 T:   now, (.4)
23      we have come into uh a garden this (.4)
24      closed in by this little wall
25      you feel the little wall beside you there?=
26 S:   ((feels wall with left hand, head turns toward left))
27 T:   =awright.
28      I want you to follow that wall all the way arou:nd (.2)
29      and then when you get throu:gh
30      I want you to draw me a picture (.)
31      of the shape of this garden. (.8)
32 S:   (you wan I gonna go blip blip)
33 T:   you're gonna follow it all the way around (.2)
34      ⌜with your cane
35 S:   ⌞(I'm gonna walk)
36      ((moves left hand and arm in tracing motion from right to left,
         describing an arc in space))
37 T:   you're gonna walk yeah.
38      now an a in your mind (.2)
```

39   (wer's) you g<u>o</u>
40   I want you to notice all the changes in direction (.2)
41   that the wall makes. (2.)
42   all the changes in <u>c</u>haracter
43   sometimes it might be straight
44   sometimes its curved (.)
45   whatever it is
46   you keep=it=in=mind
47 *S:* okay
48 *T:* and if there's an (.) uh uh uh
49   an architectural feature like a <u>ga</u>teway
50   like <u>this</u> one (.5)
51 *S:* ((nods head from up to down))
52 *T:* keep that in mind, okay?
53 *S:* (this way it goes there too?)
54 *T:* ((nods head up and down))
        ((camera clicks off)) ((Time 2:08:06))

We can note that these instructions do not involve obtaining answers or responses that are evaluated as to their correctness in terms of solving a problem. The questions that are embedded here are questions and answers that deal with assuring an understanding of the instructions and their related parts. For example, prior to the instructions we hear the teacher describe the location and one of its features (lines 23-24: "we have come into uh a garden this (.4) closed in by this little <u>w</u>all"). This description locates the lesson as being carried out within the enclosure of the garden. The wall is now mentioned for the first time. Up to this point the student has no way of knowing that the garden is enclosed by a wall. All he knows is that he has entered the garden through an opening, called a gate, and that the gate has a post on its left side, which is square and low, about 18 inches high and 16 inches wide. Now he is told that the garden is enclosed by a wall. Unresolved is how the post is connected to the wall.

The resolution of this matter is provided in the next utterance (line 25: "you feel the little wall beside you there?"). That is, as the student is sitting on the post he is asked to feel the wall that begins at the post on his left. This interchange (lines 25-27) is in the form of a directive, stated in question format, a response that achieves the correct answer, followed by a positive assessment by the teacher.

D	25	T:	you feel the little wall beside you there=
R: ach	26	S:	((feels wall with left hand, head turns toward left))
A: pos	27	T:	=awright.

In the next turn, the teacher begins instructions about what the student is to do, what he will be examined on at a later point, and what will constitute a satisfactory answer to the examination questions (lines 28-31).

I1	28	T:	I want you to follow that wall all the way arou:nd (.2)
	29		and then when you get throu:gh
I2	30		I want you to draw me a picture (.)
	31		of the shape of this garden. (.8)

The lesson thus requires bodily movement around the garden, assuming the student's ability to use the long cane during his walk to maintain contact with the wall that encloses the garden, to arrive at a completion point, which is a return to the starting point, to know that he has so arrived, and to be able, at that time, to describe the shape of the garden (i.e., the shape of the path he has traced bodily in his walk) in a pictorial format. (Although the student is blind, picture tracing is something that we shall see can be done by using one's cane on the ground, one's hand in the air, one's finger on the palm of the hand, either one's own or the instructor's, and so on.) At the completion of the utterance (in line 31) there is a pause that provides an opportunity for the student to ask questions, obtain clarification, or whatever. In this case, he asks a question and obtains an answer, and then asks a second question and obtains an answer to that question.

Q1	32	S:	(you wan I gonna go blip blip)
A1	33	T:	you're gonna follow it all the way around (.2)
	34	T:	⌈with your cane
Q2	35	S:	⌊(I'm gonna walk)
	36		((moves left hand and arm in tracing motion from right to left describing an arc in space))
A2	37	T:	you're gonna walk yeah.

These Q-A sequences are embedded within the instructions and represent insertion sequences. The questions request clarification and obtain clarification with elaboration. The elaboration in the Q1-A1 sequence adds information with regard to movement: "you're gonna follow it all the way around." The second question requests clarification with regard to how the wall can be "followed," that is, by walking with cane in contact with the wall, and obtains confirmation. The student's question overlaps with the teacher's "with your cane."

Thus we can see that both questions tie back to the instructions in lines 28-31, where it is not specified as to how the instructor wants the student to "follow that wall." We see that the means to be used to solve the problems being posed are inextricably linked with the solution and can also be considered to be an intrinsic part of the problem itself. That is, the solution that is to be tested at a later point requires the use of particular methods for its achievement. What we shall see is that not any methods will do. Rather, the methods to be used are those that the student has been tested on in the prestart section of the lesson, and that he has demonstrated an ability to use and to use correctly.

The instructions section continues with further elaborations by the teacher, who now states that there is more to be done and remembered in the course of the walk around the garden. Presumably, the information he now directs the student to acquire during his walk will also be tested at the conclusion of the lesson. These instructions presume the satisfactory understanding of the prior instructions. That understanding seems to meet the instructor's approval as evidenced by his utterance in line 37, "you're gonna walk yeah," followed by "now," which serves as another disjunct marker and announces the next part of the set of instructions, lines 38-52.

```
38  T:   now an a in your mind (.2)
39       (wer's) you go
40       I want you to notice all the changes in direction (.2)
41       that the wall makes. (2.)
42       all the changes in character
43       sometimes it might be straight
44       sometimes its curved (.)
45       whatever it is
46       you keep=it=in=mind
47  S:   okay
48  T:   and if there's an (.) uh uh uh
49       an architectural feature like a gateway
50       like this one (.5)
51  S:   ((nods head from up to down))
```

52 *T:*   keep that in mind, okay?
53 *S:*   (this way it goes there too?)
54 *T:*   ((nods head up and down))

The instructions are that the student is to "notice," that is, attend to as he walks around the garden, "changes in direction" of the wall and "changes in character." Changes in direction would refer to the wall's going around or going straight and could be in the form of such shapes as an S or a T or U or an O, whereas changes in character could be changes in height of the wall, protrusions in the wall, openings in the wall, such as the presence of a gate, all of which have shapes themselves. Thus the gate might have an opening of a certain width, that opening marked by a post on either side, and the posts might be square or curved or whatever. However, by specifying changes in character in lines 43-45 as "straight," "curved," "whatever," he seems to be elaborating on the earlier utterance's term "changes in direction." Whether these are identical or not is not clear, and the elaboration following the prior "changes in direction that the wall makes" would at first seem to mean that "changes in direction" and "changes in character" are not the same. However, since "changes in direction" is not elaborated, but "changes in character" is, we are left with an ambiguity. One interpretation is that they are equivalent.

The further instruction, to "keep in mind"—that is, to attend to and remember—"an architectural feature like a gateway" now adds the notion of architectural features to "changes in direction" and "character."

The directives in this part of the set of instructions then are multifold. The student is expected to notice and to keep in mind (for later recall, presumably), as he goes, all changes in direction, character, and architectural features. If this is connected to the prior instruction of following the wall all the way around and then drawing a picture of the shape of the garden, we now see what is required for the successful achievement of the solution and the answers to the test to come.

Lines 38-54 consist of two additional instructions, the first with an elaboration of four parts and the second with one elaboration. Each instruction receives an indication of understanding by the student (line 47 and line 53).

I3 elab 38 *T:*   now an a in your mind (.2)
         39   (wer's) you <u>go</u>
         40   I want you to notice all the changes in direction (.2)

		41		that the wall makes. (2.)
I3	elab	42		all the changes in <u>char</u>acter
I3	elab	43		sometimes it might be straight
I3	elab	44		sometimes its curved (.)
I3	elab	45		whatever it is
I3		46		you keep=it=in=mind
R3		47	S:	okay
I4		48	T:	and if there's an (.) uh uh uh
		49		an architectural feature like a <u>gate</u>way
I4	elab	50		like <u>this</u> one (.5)
R		51	S:	((nods head from up to down))
I4		52	T:	keep that in mind, okay?
R4	Q	53	S:	(this way it goes there too?)
	A	54	T:	((nods head up and down))

It is only at this point that the student begins to move with his cane to walk around the garden. The next series of actions constitutes the carrying out of the instructions.

These actions are now further subdivided into three parts. Within each of these parts or sections the instructor asks the student to stop and to answer one or more questions. These several sections are thereby linked with the overall lesson in that they are connected to the prestart topically and to the instructions and the anticipated ending or test section functionally. That is, the solution and correct answer to each of the questions asked in each of these next sections can be understood as having a bearing on the student's ability to solve the overall problem, namely, at the end of the lesson being able to describe or draw a picture of the shape of the garden.

In this sense each section stands as a subsection leading up to the final or test section. The correct response to questions posed in each of the subsections is possibly prerequisite for the achievement of the correct solution to the questions to be posed in the test section. Considering that there is only a restricted set of questions asked on a restricted set of topics within each of the subsections, their character as prefatory and prerequisite to the achievement of the correct overall solution is graspable both by the student and by us.

Note that the overall problem is one of movement through an enclosed space, tracing a shape, remembering the changes in direction one has made while in the process of this movement, and noticing changes in the character or architectural features of the wall that is traced. The overall problem can be characterized as kinesthetic shape tracing using tactile contact with shaped outlined architectural features and remembering the traced shape and features. The ability to provide a correct answer to one or a series of verbally formed interrogative utterances at the conclusion of the traced movement through the enclosed space requires more than a verbally shaped answer. The answer instead is to be provided through a representational tracing using hand, finger, and/or cane, an answer that is noticeable/readable by a sighted other.

However, the continuing presence of the instructor during the student's actual movement through the space provides the instructor with additional information concerning the "correctness" of the means used for the solution. No shortcuts are taken or allowed; each subsection is begun when the student arrives at and can locate an opening or gate in the wall, and each set of questions within a subsection is begun only after the proper post of the gate is not only located but sat down upon.

Internally Differentiated
Problem Divisions: Subsections

Basically, three questions are asked at each of these subsection stopping points. These repeat the specific directives presented in the prestart section, namely, body orientation (sit on the same block in the same way) and external reference point location (Where is the sun? Where is the traffic?). The correct solution to each of these problems enables the student to answer correctly the question based on these, namely, "Are you back where you started from?"

A second question concerning the "picture of the shape of the garden" thus far requires attending to the kinesthetic shape-tracing activity of walking around inside the wall of the garden while maintaining contact with it with the cane. Posed as a statement or as a question, the basic issue is: "What is the shape of the garden up to this point, as you know it?"

Related to this and to the prior three questions is: "Are you back where you started from?" That is, "have you followed the wall all the way around?"

These questions are not really separate questions, because the answer to "Are you back where you started from?" can be provided only by locating the two external orientational reference points, the sun and the traffic, and doing the locating while in the same bodily facing orientation in relation to the interior/exterior of the garden post/gate. Drawing or describing the shape of the garden "thus far" is preliminary to the final test question and can be considered as anticipating it. It enables the student to obtain assessments as to his descriptions of shape tracing and to "keep in mind" the shape of the wall. Rather than ask this question only at the end of the lesson, in the test section, the instructor produces (in each subsection) a replica of the final test section.

Subsection 1

75		okay. now there's your block.
76		sit down on that block
77	S:	((follows wall with cane, passes the block))
78	T:	back this way a little bit
79	S:	((starts to sit down))
80	T:	no not on the wall
81		on the block ( )
82	S:	((continues past the block))
83	T:	at the opening here
84		Inky Inkyala
85		come back here
86	S:	((starts back toward T))
87	T:	right there
88	S:	( )
89	T:	feel that block
90		feel the block
91	S:	((feels with right hand the block))
92	T:	that's the gate
93		awright
94		an here's the opening right around here ((T moves through the gate))
95		right
96		awright now sit that on that (1.0)
97		((student sits))
98		now tell me the character of the wall that you have followed
99		Was it straight or was it curved?
100	S:	( )
101	T:	huh?
102	S:	( ) ((draws a shape in air with right hand))
103		square then go ( ) ((traces a shape))

104 *T:*   awright
105   now we've been walking around a curve a long time.
106   right?
107   we have made a complete circle?
108   are we right back when we started?
          ((camera clicks off)) ((Time 2:10:32))
109 *T:* now uh and also where's the traffic now?
110 *S:* ((looks toward his right)) behind me
111 *T:* oh listen carefully
112 *S:* oh oh du ((motions with right hand and arm, an arc in space at
          right side, from front to back along his side))
113 *T:* that's right
114   okay
115   so this is not the same one? right
116   okay well then let's explore still further tha-
117   this wasn't just a circle with an opening in it
118 *S:* ((shakes head right to his left))
119 *T:* this is a second opening you s-
120   two openings at least okay
121 *S:* ((nods head up and down))
122 *T:* lets go on an see wha-
123   what we have now
124 *S:* you wan me to continue?
125 *T:* you continue
126   ((they walk: S with cane in left hand maintaining contact with
          wall)) . . . ((camera clicks off)

Subsection 2

128   ((S walks, cane in left hand, in contact with wall))
129 *T:* (awright   ) come to another post.
130   awright. go by the post
131   ((S walks another step, cane in contact with the wall lifts head
          up and faces sky))
132 *T:* see if there's an opening beyond it
133   like there was before
134   ((S walks cane in contact with low step in the opening))
135 *T:* raise your cane an see if there's an opening there
136 *S:* (what is   )
137 *T:* an opening awright

138   go to the (gate) an sit down
139   okay sit down
140 S: ((sits down))
141 T: are we back home?
142 S: if you mean back (   ) back home
143 T: are we back where we started from?
144 S: no:o:o:o
145 T: why not?
146 S: because. the sun is here
147   ((points with right hand to right side of face))
148   uh hah hah hah
149 T: an where's the traffic
150 S: ((S points with right hand and arm—traces a line from left to right))
151   (is there)
152 T: awright
153   okay
154   so we keep going,
155   we gotta get ⌐back home
156 S: ⌊uh hah hah hah (its   )
157   ((S stands up and begins to move again, cane in left hand in contact with wall)) ((camera clicks off and on again)) ((Time 12:12:10))

We now see, in Subsection 2, that the question "Are you back where we started from?" can be answered by using these reference points while seated on the post next to the gate opening, which is on the same side of the opening (i.e., the left side) as the first gate. When the external orientational reference points are in the same configuration as they were at the start of the lesson, the answer has to be affirmative.

However, we also see that a correct verbal answer to whether we are back where we started from is not necessarily acceptable, because it could be a "guess." The only means whereby the instructor can determine whether the student achieved the correct answer through the correct means is to ask also for a bodily display, in contrast to a verbal reply, of his awareness of the location of the two major external reference points, the sun and the traffic.

In Subsection 2 we see that the student produces a correct verbal answer (line 144) to the question "Are we back where we started from?" but is also asked "why not?"—that is, how do you know, or show me the means you used to produce the correct answer. The student shows with his hand and face the location of the sun and with his hand and arm the location of the traffic. Both of these answers are accepted as correct and the answer to the first question is also therefore accepted as correct. In this case, the assessment comes only after the answer to the third question (line 152). Since the three questions are internally related in the manner I have described above, the one assessment can serve to indicate that the instructor accepts the answers to all three. That is, by the following:

Q1	143	*T:*	are we back where we started from?
A1	144	*S:*	No:o:o:o
Q2	145	*T:*	why not?
A2	146	*S:*	because. the sun is here
	147		((points with right hand to right side of face))
	148		uh, hah, hah, hah
Q3	149	*T:*	an where's the traffic
A3	150	*S:*	((points with right hand and arm—traces a line from left to right))
	151		(is there)
asmt	152	*T:*	awright
	153		okay
	154		so we keep going,
	155		we gotta get back home . . . .

This is to be contrasted with Subsection 1, in which (although the recording had been switched off during the sequence) we see the same questions: "are we right back where we started?" (line 108); (answer not recorded); ". . . where's the traffic now?" (line 109); The last question is answered incorrectly and the teacher prompts with "listen carefully," whereupon the student points to the traffic correctly and gets a positive assessment, "that's right" (line 113).

Subsection 3

Here we find the instructor and student at the same gate at which they had started. The same questions occur: "is this where we started from?" (line 181); "where's the sun?" (line 178); "where's the traffic?" (line 183).

Q1	174	*T:*	now, is this where we started from?
A1	175	*S:*	oh, no:o (.5)
	176		((listens, moves his head toward his left))
	177	*S:*	⌐oh
Q2	178	*T:*	└ where's the sun?
A2	179	*S:*	ye:es
	180	*T:*	okay!
Q1R	181		((stands up)) this is where we started?
A1	182	*S:*	yes
A3	183	*T:*	where's the traffic?
A3	184	*S:*	((points with left hand. moves it from forward to back, along the left side of his body))
asmt	185	*T:*	awright. now.

Test Section

Only when these have been successfully and correctly answered does the test section begin: "now. what's the shape that you walked?" (lines 185-186). The next sequences deal with obtaining a drawing of the shape, and the instructor confuses things by first asking the student to "draw it for me on the ground with your cane or draw it in the air." The student looks downward but then starts to draw in the air. He names shapes as he draws: "we do like a circle" (line 198) and changes in the character of the garden wall "sometimes it change like so we cross one so like . . . circle go one again open here (go one again) rrr (one open again) rrr come one back" (lines 199-205).

The instructor then asks for a short verbal descriptor: "if you tried to tell me what that was in something that its like what would you say?" (lines 208-210) and the response is, "uh (1.5) circle" (line 211). This is not accepted and it is not until line 226 that the instructor traces the shape in the student's hand (see the Appendix to this chapter).

The test section is concluded when (in lines 206 and 207) the instructor accepts the student's first response as correct. When the name of the shape is requested in line 208-209 the answer is not accepted until lines 267 and 269. Before the name is accepted, however, the instructor draws the shape of the garden in the student's hand and provides a hint (line 251: "do you play cards?") before he names the club shape and follows this with "a three leaf clover" (line 263).

The student has shown that he knows he has arrived at the starting point and displays that he solved this problem by the use of the correct means, that is, sun, traffic, and bodily facing orientation. It is only then that questions with regard to the shape he has traced in his movements are asked. The inadequate shapes actually traced by the student are not accepted, although he does have the basic elements of the shape correct, namely, "like circle" and "open"(ings) with each one like a "half moon." The correct shape is drawn on the student's palm by the instructor (lines 226-243), whereupon he asks for the name of the shape traced in the hand (lines 245-248) and finally obtains what he accepts as a correct answer (lines 258, 263, and 268). The instructor supplies the latter answers, and the student the recognition. Because they come sequentially after the student's own effort to trace the shape on the ground and to describe the shape he walked, his recognition of what the instructor is providing can be seen as tying back to his own less-than-adequate description. That is, the instructor has indicated that the student's answer is not accepted without an upgrade to a description that fits with the instructor's own criterion of correctness. The "answer" to the lesson's problem is thus seen to be a multiple-part rather than a single-part answer. The answers are interrelated, as noted, and the conceptual naming of the shape is clearly provided last, after the solutions to the prior questions regarding the means of knowing that the starting point has been reached and the provision (by the student) of some line drawings roughly corresponding to the shape traced.

Conclusion

The lesson can be broken up into several parts:

prestart section
  subsection 1: bodily facing orientation
  subsection 2: locating sun
  subsection 3: locating traffic
instruction section
  subsection 1: preface
  subsection 2: instruction 1
  subsection 2: instruction 2
  subsection 4: instruction 3
  subsection 5: instruction 4

```
performance section
  subsection 1: next gate
  subtest: interrogatives
    answers
    assessments
  subsection 2: next gate
    subtest: interrogatives
    answers
    assessments
  subsection 3: next gate
    subtest: interrogatives
    answers
    assessments
test section
  test question 1
    answer
    assessment
  test question 2
    answer
    assessment
  test question 3
    answer
    assessment
exit
```

Extended sequences like this one have been shown to be complex systems of action (or activity systems). Their explication requires attention to their overall structure rather than to any restricted set of contiguous utterances or turns. Further, any restricted examination of two or four or six or eight turns with alternating speakers would not yield the same understanding of the overall structure of the activity system.

An activity as complex as a lesson can obviously extend over a lengthy period of time (e.g., an entire classroom period). The lesson examined here is organized not by time but by the problem solution's own requirements. It cannot be solved in the prestart section or the problem introduction section, but only after a series of actions have been directly engaged in, that is, walking all the way around the garden. This division into discrete stages, based on the garden's own character-istics (i.e., three openings), represents a natural division and can be referred to as the lesson's "internally differentiated problem division."

We have been able to discern four major divisions: prestart, instruction, internally differentiated problem division, and test section. These are interlinked and interdependent, with the prior section leading to the next and with the beginning section providing materials that allow for the interpretation of what the possible end (problem solution) will be. This extended sequence has its parts interconnected by virtue of the *problem* to be solved, by the instructor's *instructions*, and by the *interconnected activities*, such as maintaining bodily orientation, locating external orientational reference points, and kinesthetic shape tracing, that constitute the problem *and* its solution.

At the level of presupposition, at the level of problem formulation and solution, and at the level of task itself, linkages and interconnections constitute the sequential organization of the interaction. Dividing up the interaction into adjacency pairs or insertion sequences or directive-response-assessment sequences would not have told us what the activity is about, what the purposes of the collaborating parties are, and what the lesson will come to. We must, instead, use our own member competencies to delineate the overall organizing feature of the activity-as-a-lesson, as what is being collaboratively produced in and through the interconnected and interrelated discriminable "parts." The whole is not the sum of its parts; rather, the whole is constituted in and through all relevant elements as a "gestalt-contextured configuration." The analysis of such "elements" as "sections" and "paired utterances" was undertaken to reveal the "machinery" of the lesson's organization. The study of extended sequences should not be thought of as an expansion of two- or three-part sequences into longer and longer strings. Rather, complex social actions need to be examined in their own right. Their division into subunits is designed to enable us to see more clearly how the whole is organized. We must not lose sight of the social action, "teaching and performing a lesson," that is being collaboratively produced by the parties.

Appendix: Test Section

185 *T:* awright. now.
186   what's the shape that you walked?
187 *S:* umm
188 *T:* draw it for me (.) on the ground with your cane.
189   or draw it in the air.

190   or uh
191 *S:*   ((looks up then looks down at cane and ground))
192 *T:*   on the ground (.) that's okay
193   whatever you like
194   yeah ⌐yeah
195 *S:*   └(do)
196 *T:*   to it like that
197 *S:*   ((draws with right hand in the air but camera is focused on
              cane on ground))
198 *S:*   we do like a circle
199   sometimes it change like so we cross one so
200   like (go like two like) circle
201   go one again
202   open here. ⌐(go one again
203 *T:*   └right
204 *S:*   rrr one open again
205   ⌐rrr come one back
206 *T:*   └good
207 *T:*   awright. (1.0)
208   uh, (.5) if you tried to tell me what that was
209   in something that its like
210   what would you say?
211 *S:*   uh (1.5) circle
212 *T:*   yeah but
213 *S:*   (half-) half a-
214 *S:*   half half moon (.5)
215 *T:*   no:pe
216 *S:*   ye::s
217   ((starts to draw on the ground with cane))
218 *T:*   each one is like a (.) ⌐half moon maybe
219 *S:*   └half
220 *T:*   ⌐but not (.) the three of them=
221 *S:*   └yes
222 *T:*   =together don't make a half moon
223 *S:*   no=no they do like
224   ((draws on the ground with cane; traces out three semicircles
              with cane; each is connected with the other but the last is not
              connected with the first.))
225 *T:*   yeah (.2) let me have your hand

226 *S:*   ((offers his left hand, palm up. T holds S's left hand in his left
          hand. S draws on his own palm with his right index finger.))
227 *S:*   one, (two)
228 *T:*   that's right
229   ((T draws on S's left palm with T's right index finger))
230   but you- this one better come back
231   and start again. okay?
232   ((S withdraws his own right index finger))
233   so yo- you start here straight,
234   then when you loop
235   then a straight ⌜with an opening
236 *S:*   ⌞straight
237 *T:*   ⌜then another loop
238 *S:*   ⌞straight
239 *T:*   ⌜then
240 *S:*   ⌞(   )
241 *T:*   then another loop
242   an then you're back home
243 *S:*   yes
244 *T:*   awright?
245   now what's that shape,
246   if I draw a shape like this (.5)
247   with a little s- straight in between
248   wha- what's that shape look like
249 *S:*   I dunno whachucall (1.5)
250 *T:*   well, would you say somethin like-
251   (.) uh do you play cards?
252 *S:*   yes OH YES
253   I don't know wha-
254   whachu call it in a cards
255   is a a (slep)?
256   (tref)?
257 *T:*   do you know uh (.5)
258   clubs ⌜clubs
259 *S:*   ⌞I know wha's clubs
260 *T:*   clubs
261   okay ⌜or:
262 *S:*   ⌞yes (.5)
263 *T:*   a three leaf clover (.5)

```
264         ⌈or a flower
265  S:     ⌊yes (.)
266  T:     ⌈you know
267  S:     ⌊(flowers)
268  T:     with three ⌈leaves right?
269  S:                ⌊(nods)
270  T:     ⌈okay
271  S:     ⌊sure
272  T:     that's exactly (whu-) it is,
273         okay, now
274         we're gonna leave this,
276         take my arm
277         we got a lot more (way to go)
```

Note

1. I am grateful to Robert Amendola of the Carroll Center for the Blind and Visually Impaired in Newton, Massachusetts, for allowing me to videotape this lesson and for the many discussions we had concerning the problem of teaching spatial orientation to adventitiously blind persons. His brilliant insights, incorporated into his lessons, and his willingness to share these with me make him truly a collaborator in this research. The student is adventitiously blind (i.e., he once had sight but lost it). He is about 16 years old, African, from Zaire. He speaks French and English and has been in the United States only a short time. Eventually, he went on to high school in this country. The instructor has worked for many years as an instructor of the blind and as a practicing artist.

7

Normative Order in
Collaborative Computer Editing

JAMES L. HEAP

When sociologists address the problem of social order they often assume that members of society internalize a normative order and that
observed regularities of behavior can be accounted for in terms of a
shared knowledge of the prevailing rules and a cognitive consensus
regarding when and where the rules should be applied. Solutions of this
sort—which are based on the notion that rules inform social action—
have been the focus of much criticism. Ethnomethodologists contend
that, from the observer's perspective, the relation between behavior and
normative order is indeterminate (Garfinkel, 1967/1984); we can never
be certain that people follow rules or comply with particular normative
orders.

In this chapter I examine the problem of social order as it is mani-
fested in a specific, naturally bounded task that is undertaken in the
classroom. At issue is how the normative order informs the action of
two people in a combined grade one/two class who are engaged in collaborative computer editing. From the perspective of participants, compelling grounds exist for believing that one's collaborator is oriented

AUTHOR'S NOTE: I wish to thank Christine Bennett, a research officer on the SSHRC
research project, No. 410-85-0607, for her transcription and bibliographic efforts. Her
support was most appreciated. David Ross applied his editorial skills to reduce a much
longer version of this chapter to something approximating its current form. Finally, I am
grateful to Alec McHoul for trying to improve my understanding of Wittgenstein.

123

to a specific normative order. I argue that beliefs are based on what Other appears to do, when he or she takes a turn at talk or action, and that these beliefs provide grounds for Self's actions.[1] These actions, in turn, provide grounds for Other's beliefs about the normative elements to which Self is oriented. Thus a sense of normative order and social structure can be built up sequentially by means of sequences of well-defined and/or loosely defined turns at talk or action.

I focus on the normative features of editing during collaborative computer writing. Central to the study is the organization of options. The primary (or default) option invites a writer to execute "arranging" moves (keyboard moves that are performed with a view to arranging characters on the computer monitor). The secondary option invites a helper to execute arranging moves. The ordering of these options (to which the collaborators orient themselves) can best be understood in terms of the prevailing rights and responsibilities for editing. A system of ordered options for inputting and arranging is generated by means of "discourse-action machinery." The grounds for each party's beliefs regarding the relevant normative order for accomplishing the task at hand are made available by this instantiation. I cite data strips from my research to illustrate the discourse-action machinery at work and the instantiation of the system of weighted options for action.

Normative and Factual Order

A factual order consists of typical, uniform, repetitive, cohort-independent actions that can be recognized and measured independently of any reference to the point of view of the members-actors who perform those actions. A factual order can be accounted for in terms of a normative order, which involves

> essential reference to the point of view of the actor and includes his categories for classifying the social and physical environment, value elements that order such categories in terms of preference, duty, affect, etc., and the rules or norms that specify the particular kinds of actions appropriate to situations thus categorized and evaluated. (Zimmerman & Wieder, 1970, p. 286)

Following (and affirming) the ground-breaking work of Garfinkel (1967/1984), ethnomethodologists have produced perceptive commentaries on the problems involved in explaining action in terms of the factual-order/normative-order theoretical apparatus. It is not possible, experientially and thus epistemologically, to separate factual order and normative order. Normative order is used to *see* the regularities of factual order (Wieder, 1974b). Thus rules have a constitutive function (Heritage, 1984a, p. 110). With respect to the distinction Weber makes between behavior and action,[2] I argue that rules are used to see behaviors as instances of certain types of actions and that, when they are recognized, normative orders imply so-called factual orders.

Garfinkel (1967/1984) has claimed that an appropriate model for the member-actor is one in which the member-actor realizes that her or his actions will be interpreted by Other under some normative framework. Whatever Self does will be normatively interpreted in order to see what action Self is performing. Self will be held answerable for the action he or she appears to Other to have performed. Heritage calls this "normative accountability," and sees it as essential to what can be called ethnomethodology's theory of how social order is produced.

Two approaches to the problem of social action are usually taken. The first considers rules as directives for action and argues that action is underdetermined by rules. Ethnomethodologists have documented the type and the amount of interpretive work that goes into using rules (see Garfinkel, 1963; Zimmerman, 1970). That work is central to solving the problems of which rule should be applied, when, to what extent, and in what way. It consists of situated practices, including the practices of "ad hocing," "et cetera," "let it pass," "*factum valet*," and so on (see Garfinkel, 1967/1984). It would seem that, for some actions, there are no rules at all that direct or govern a member-actor's behavior (Dreyfus, 1979, chap. 8; Heritage, 1984a, pp. 126-127).

The second considers rules as explanatory devices. It seems to follow that, if action is underdetermined by rules, the analyst's formulation of rules will not be adequate to account for the behavioral regularities of interest. The interpretive work of members-actors in applying rules would have to be captured, described, and linked to the rules that the analyst has formulated.

Recovering the Normative

Environments that feature people completing tasks jointly serve as suitable sites for examining the place occupied by normative elements in the production of social action. These environments are normative in the sense that the actions performed there are oriented to task completion (see Parsons, 1937, p. 75). The study outlined here concentrates on schoolchildren who engage in collaborative computer writing.

Research. My study was conducted in a school located in a working-class neighborhood of a major Canadian city. The neighborhood has a mix of Southern European ethnic groups, largely Italian and Portuguese. Altogether, 32 students were enrolled in this class, a combined first and second grade; many of the students were repeating a grade. The teacher (who has pioneered the use of word processing at the early primary level) coauthored the word-processing program used in the class.

Two video cameras were used: One was mounted to give an overhead view of student keyboard use; the other was placed to give a side-angle view of the students at the computer. The signals from both cameras were fed into a special-effects generator to create a split-screen image. A second video recorder allowed us to capture all the screen states during student computer use.

Collaboration. Collaboration at our classroom research site consisted of the interaction between a designated writer and a designated helper. The teacher allowed each student to select a helper when it was her or his turn to write, but retained a veto over the writer's choice.

Editing. We defined editing as the preparatory work done by teacher and student(s) to reform one draft of a story into a final draft. (In any particular case, the latter may turn out to be just the next draft.) Editing thus conceived has two phases: hard-copy correction, and correction interpretation and screen document reformation. These phases are present for both solo and collaborative computer writing. The teacher carries out the first. Students have the responsibility to respond to the teacher's queries. The material focus of this phase is the hard copy of a story that was written on the computer by one of the students. The students carry out the second phase at the computer, generally without the teacher's direction or supervision.

Editing and keyboarding. Acts of inputting (which are effected by means of display keys) involve the production of signs and symbols on some type of display screen. Acts of arranging (which are effected by means of executive keys) involve the arrangement of the signs and symbols on the screen. Transcribing acts are here defined as inputting or arranging on the display screen.

Task accomplishment concerns. Editing, conceived in terms of correction interpretation and screen document reformation, consists of a variety of jobs, the accomplishment of which is oriented to a set of concerns. These concerns lie at the heart of the notion of joint task accomplishment. As competent speakers/actors, we have trouble understanding how persons who engage in a joint task such as editing at a computer could not share the three concerns contained in the questions, Where are we? What should be done next? and Who should do it? I call these location, direction, and normative concerns, respectively.

Rights and responsibilities. We noticed that, when it was the writer's turn to write, the story that was written was the writer's story, not the helper's story. The ownership of the story thus flowed from the allocation of a turn to write at the computer. This feature of the enterprise was carried over into the phase of correction interpretation and screen document reformation. The person who was selected to assist during the composing phase (i.e., the helper) generally continued in that supportive position in the editing phase, unless there was a long hiatus between story composition and editing or the earlier helper was not available when editing commenced.

The organization of the editing phase is best understood in terms of the prevailing rights and responsibilities. Rights and responsibilities may not qualify as rules (see Shimanoff, 1980), but they nevertheless act as normative elements. They inform persons as to what ought to be done and what is expected to be done, as well as under what circumstances it should be done. They provide the linkage between the situation and the action that Wilson (1970) has identified as the generic property of a rule.

I offer an account of the organization of student rights and responsibilities. In doing so I fully accept Coulter's (1983, pp. 51-72) stated limit on rule explanation. However, I maintain that my account *accords with* the way students behave. I will go one step further and claim that my formulations capture the way students interpret and understand their collaborators' orientation to normative elements over the course of their joint task accomplishment.

The formulation here is based (primarily) on the interactions of two students I studied. After the teacher corrects the hard copy of the writer's story, the writer sits in front of the computer. The helper sits in front of the printer, which is to the left of the computer. The rights and

Table 7.1. Rights and Responsibilities During Editing

| | Collaborators | |
Activities	Writer	Helper
Correcting	assertable right	delegated right and
Interpreting	ultimate responsibility	responsibility
Inputting	right, delegated	no right, ultimate
	responsibility	responsibility
Arranging	right, delegated	sufferance, ultimate
	responsibility	responsibility

the responsibilities (see Table 7.1) accord with student actions, given that the hard copy belongs to the helper. Because the corrected hard copy of the story belongs to the helper, he or she has the right as well as the responsibility to interpret the teacher's corrections. I argue that the writer delegates these privileges to the helper, who has watched the teacher correct the writer's story during the correction phase. At any time, the helper can assert the right to examine the corrected hard copy.

Throughout this enterprise the writer assumes the responsibility to input characters into the screen document. Owning the hard copy does not entitle the helper to claim the right to input. The directions of delegated and ultimate responsibility are thus reversed here. The helper (in control of the hard copy) assumes ultimate responsibility for what appears on the screen. This action follows from one of the organizational features of the enterprise (see Table 7.1). The helper tells the writer what to input while they are engaged in story correction. The writer's responsibility for inputting is thus "delegated."

These rights are the most interesting. During the story correction and story repair phases of editing, the writer assumes the right to arrange. This right is not simply delegated. The helper, too, has the right to arrange. This (lesser) right I here call a "sufferance." A sufferance is the tacit permission to execute a move, one that is suggested by the absence of objection. Under conditions where the writer does not object, the helper can assert the right to arrange. Of course, the possibility that the writer may object is a source of tension, but the collaborators must manage this tension if they are to complete the task and remain on good terms with each other. If we are to understand how collaborative computer editing can be socially organized, we have to see how they manage this tension.

Ordered Options for Arranging

The rights and the responsibilities formulated above tell us (and the collaborators) what can or must be done when an opportunity to make an arranging move presents itself. However, the rights and the responsibilities tell neither us nor the collaborators what should be done to satisfy the relevant normative elements. I suggest that the relation between the rights and the responsibilities for arranging can be seen as an organization of ordered options. I believe that the organization of these options provides a way of publicly satisfying the "normative concern" of joint task accomplishment.

It will be useful, before formulating the organization of these options, to introduce the features necessary for the operation of a normative system. The distribution of rights and responsibilities must be mutually established if a normative system is to be created. Each person must know her or his own rights and responsibilities, as well as those of her or his collaborator. Each person must be able to anticipate the consequences of breaching these rights and/or of not fulfilling these responsibilities. Such anticipation has to be mutual (see Heritage, 1984a, p. 117). These conditions are necessary for the smooth functioning of any normatively based interactional system of joint task accomplishment.

The helper has first rights in interpreting corrections, a "visual" activity requiring proximity to the corrected hard copy. The writer may assert the right to read/interpret the hard copy. Again, the writer has sole rights for inputting. Usually, however, the writer is not in a position to know what ought to be input; the helper learns this by reading and interpreting the hard copy. The writer exercises the right to hit the executive keys during the arranging phase of the exercise. If the writer does not exercise this right, if the writer exhausts it, or if the writer appears to relinquish it, the helper can exercise a sufferance to arrange.

The question for us is how this last "ordered option" is organized. How can a right be seen to be relinquished? How can sufferance be decided and acted upon? How is the normative concern for arranging satisfied?

Discourse-Action Machinery

The ordered options for arranging (during collaborative editing) are instantiated by means of (soft) machinery for the production of discourse and action.[3] This machinery bears a close relation to that formulated by Sacks, Schegloff, and Jefferson (1974) for understanding naturally occurring conversation. Discourse-action machinery is task oriented, whereas conversation machinery is task independent. Discourse machinery can be used for a wide variety of tasks, which, however, must be accomplished through, in, and as talk. The actions accomplished in conversation are primarily speech acts (see Searle, 1969). The actions accomplished by means of the discourse-action machinery of collaborative computer editing include speech acts. These acts are primarily devices for fostering the accomplishment of nonverbal acts, such as inputting, arranging, and getting help from peers or the teacher.

Not surprisingly, we observed variations on the turn construction design. Sacks et al. (1974) have noted that turns at talk regularly have a three-part structure: "one which addresses the relation of a turn to a prior, one involved with what is occupying the turn, and one which addresses the relation of the turn to a succeeding one" (p. 722). Turns at talk during student editing exhibit some of these "orientational" features. The turns conducive to the accomplishment of screen document reformation, however, need not be oriented to a prior turn at talk, nor to a next turn at talk. Instead, they need to be oriented to the consequences (which are displayed on the screen) of a prior *action* turn, of inputting, or arranging, and they need to be oriented to a succeeding action turn.

Discourse-action sequences relevant to arranging display most of the properties of sequences found in conversation. Conversation analysts call these sequences "adjacency pairs" (Sacks et al., 1974). The proffering of a "first pair part," such as a question, makes relevant and requires a "second pair part," such as an answer, which is produced by a second speaker (see Schegloff & Sacks, 1973). Such sequences of questions and answers are to be found in our transcripts of editing sessions, but they are ancillary to the primary sequence that is used in student editing, namely, the "directive-compliance" sequence. One student issues a directive, for example, "Put a period." The second student (as required) engages in an inputting action, such as hitting the period key. Whereas conversational adjacency sequences make relevant and required a turn at talk, primary editing adjacency sequences make relevant and required a turn at action. Conversational adjacency sequences can be expanded by means of "side sequences" (Jefferson, 1972) and used to expand directive-compliance sequences. Such expansion devices are utilized as turns at talk, but in the case of directive-compliance sequences, the goal (the required end) is an action rather than a turn at talk.

During directive-compliance sequences, the helper and the writer utilize the discourse-action machinery for connecting the correction-interpreting phase of editing with the screen document reformation phase. The helper interprets a correction and issues a directive, and the writer complies. What results is a reformation of the screen document.

The Machinery in Action

The rights for inputting and arranging are observed whenever the writer participates in directive-compliance sequences, that is, whenever he or she engages in inputting and arranging. The responsibility of the helper and the delegated responsibility of the writer are thus affirmed through their respective speech acts (directive) and keyboard acts (compliance). The discourse-action machinery instantiates the default option of writer arranging, whenever the helper believes that arranging is "what should be done next."

The same machinery that generates the writer's option to arrange generates the helper's option to engage in arranging moves. Logically, if the writer is unable to comply with an arranging directive or fails to achieve the directed end, the person who issued the directive (the helper) may take the opportunity to strike an executive key. Moreover, if the writer's effort to comply with either an inputting or arranging directive somehow misfires, an opportunity for arranging acts presents itself. In the case of inputting mistakes, the delete key (an executive key) can be struck to repair the screen state. However, given that, in making an inputting mistake, the writer has not shown her- or himself incompetent at *arranging*, the default preference for writer arranging moves would still hold. In this case, the writer would have to hit the delete key. We would expect that, when the writer makes a mistake (miskeys) in arranging, the helper would see an opportunity to engage in arranging moves.

After producing keyboard compliance moves and screen state repair moves, writers sometime utter expletives that are "singletons." The following are examples of writer singletons.

Whew!
Oh:: I'll kill myself!

> Yeah, fine.
> Now I know what I'm doing.
> Thank you God. I love you.
> Okay, I'm doing fine. Ah, um.
> I hate this.
> And, I'm brilliant!

What makes these utterances interesting is that they occur after key-board acts and they can be heard as reactions to the effects of those acts. Writer singletons do not make relevant, nor do they require, a next turn at talk or action. This does not mean, however, that the helper cannot topicalize the singleton and produce a turn at talk in the space adjacent to the production of the singleton. For example, after the writer says: "And, I'm brilliant," the helper says, "No you're not," and the writer comes back with, "I know."

If singletons are hearable as reactions to screen state changes, they usually occur after the writer's attempt to comply with a helper's directive. Expletives are usually issued in these slots when the state of the screen document changes from what it was when the helper issued her or his first directive.

Expletive singletons may also occur after a writer keyboard act that is not done in compliance with a helper directive. Such keyboard acts can be initiated by the writer in an effort to repair an unacceptable screen state that a prior compliance move had produced.

Most expletive singletons enable the hearer to make a judgment about whether the speaker is pleased with or dismayed by the change to the screen state to which the expletive is hearably a reaction. Many are hearably positive, such as "Okay, I'm doing fine," but others are hearably negative, such as "Oh:: I'll kill myself." The negative reactions are particularly salient to helpers as grounds for assuming sufferance to arrange.

One of the hypotheses worth pursuing is the proposition that the negative singletons produced by writers, as reactions to their own arranging moves, can be treated by helpers as lifting the default preference for writer over helper arranging moves. When the state of the screen is altered by a failed compliance move, the "direction" concern is altered. The effort to accomplish the task is shifted to a new "location." In such circumstances, the normative concern for "who should do" whatever should be done may be shaped by "who tried but failed." That is, "first rights" for the *next* arranging move may be relinquished if "first rights" for the prior move did not produce an acceptable screen state.

If the person who has the stronger right to do something fails at it *and* makes visible that failure (e.g., via a negative expletive singleton or negative gesture), the person with the weaker right can treat the admission of failure as grounds for believing that her or his turn at arranging will be unopposed. If this occurs, the weaker right can be called a sufferance.[4]

Thus it can be argued that the directive-compliance sequence instantiates the ordered system of options: The first right goes to (is given to) the writer to engage in arranging acts. The discourse-action machinery also provides for the second option, namely, helper arranging moves. This option takes effect when the writer fails to comply with the helper directive and marks that failure by uttering words (or making gestures).

Normative Order Once More

The toughest claim to substantiate is the claim that normative elements are indeed the elements to which actors are oriented in the course of their activities as collaborative computer users. All attempts to characterize actors' mental states (including their orientation to normative order) are interpretations based on behavioral displays or their artifacts. The relation of such displays and artifacts to mental states is, at best, one of "necessary evidence" (Heap, 1980; Wittgenstein, 1958). Under proper circumstances, we can use what persons do, and the results of such doings, as evidence that supports the claim that persons were in particular mental states. But in this case the rub is the realization that the evidence does not entail the presence or existence of that for which it is evidence.

So it is with the behavioral displays of the students I have videotaped. Those displays allow anyone who is competent in the ways of North American Anglo-Saxon/Celtic culture to make claims about the mental states of students, and to say, for example, what rules they are following. But these claims cannot meet the canons of rigor of literal description for deductive explanation.

While one task appears impossible to master, at least another looks as if it can be handled. I want to turn the hurdle of access to other minds into a resource for success. While behavioral displays do not guarantee access to the mental states of actors, they are all that actors themselves have to go on. While we do not know for certain that the writer was oriented to a right to arrange during an editing session, we can be certain that *the helper could take the writer's arranging move as grounds for believing that the writer believed that she had a right to arrange.* In what follows I illustrate my claims about the existence, nature, and operation of a normative organization of ordered options for arranging.

An Illustration of Ordered Options

The case examined here comes from a 37-minute collaborative computer editing session that occurred just after recess on the afternoon of May 27, 1986. The writer is Joan, who is repeating second grade. Her helper is Mary, who repeated first grade. Joan's 17-line story, titled "Miami Vice," has been corrected by the teacher, and the students are in the second phase of editing.

At first, correcting the document on the screen gave Joan and Mary a great deal of trouble. They deleted and/or erased[5] portions of the document that they had intended to "cursor through" to get to the end of the line, where a period should have been placed.[6] At the beginning of the editing session, the first line of the story, as it appeared on the computer monitor's screen, read:

Last week 1 went to the C.N Tower

When the editing session started, the time displayed on our videotape read 6:30.0: (6 minutes, 30). (The *1* was an uncorrected error.)

As a result of various "miskeys," the *s* and the *t* of *Last* had been deleted, and by 33 seconds into minute 8 they were being replaced. In the course of these adventures the writer had deleted a space. The first line then looked like the second line below. (The first line represents the numbering of the columnar spaces on the screen; the asterisk represents the placement of the cursor.)

1234*67890
Lastweek 1 went to the C.N Tower

We see that the moment this screen state is displayed, Joan turns to her left, looking at Mary but pointing to the screen with her index finger.

She crinkles up her nose, smiles a crooked smile, and says (with a self-conscious question intonation): "Oh:: wha:at?"

In response (at minute 8:36.7), Mary reaches out (just as Joan pulls her hand back from the screen), saying, "You have to put a space," and touches the space bar at minute 8:37.3. Joan removes her hand from the screen, looks downward, slaps her hand to her forehead, looks toward the screen, and moves her hand to the space bar at minute 8:38.2, depressing the bar a full second later, at 8:39.2. The space bar overtypes the w with a space and moves the cursor one column to the right. The resulting screen state appears below:

```
12345*7890
Last eek 1 went to the C.N Tower
```

Joan reacts to this screen state with "I hate your guts," which (while appearing harsh in print) is not said harshly. A second later (at minute 8:42), she depresses the right arrow key, inserting a space at the cursor.

On early viewings of this section of the tape, it appeared to us that Mary actually hit the space bar. Not until the tape was played in slow motion did we see clearly that Mary merely touched the space bar, while it was Joan who hit it. The overhead camera shows Mary's hand on the keyboard, but the side-angle camera reveals that her hand touched the key without depressing it (minute 8:37.3).

This vignette illustrates the use of the directive-compliance sequence. Mary (the helper) directs Joan (the writer) as to "what should be done next," thereby satisfying both the direction and normative concerns of task accomplishment. The directive is coupled with a "showing" of exactly "what should be done next." Mary gained access to the keyboard; at other times she was not able to do this. The issuing of the directive may have operated as an "umbrella" under which it was safe for Mary to invade the writer's terrain (the keyboard). The invasion of terrain was not treated by the writer as a violation of rights.

An important point is that Mary merely touched the space bar. She could have struck it. We cannot get inside Mary's mind to learn whether she was oriented to Joan's "first right" to arrange. However, *touching the space bar while uttering "You have to put a space"* could count as evidence that Mary was oriented to the system of ordered options, which gives the writer first right to do arranging moves. This action (for us as observers) could count as such a display. Joan could read this maneuver the way we do. Given Mary's behavior, Joan would have "necessary evidence" for believing that Mary was oriented to the normative system of ordered options for arranging.

Concluding Remarks

In this chapter I claim that sufficient evidence existed for each student to believe that her or his collaborator was oriented to a normative order of rights and responsibilities. If a member-actor desires or believes that he or she should work jointly with another person on a task, then he or she will have to orient to joint task accomplishment concerns, including the normative concern of "who should do" what next. Member-actors can use discourse-action machineries, such as directive-compliance sequences, for the local (public) management of their normative concerns. The talk and/or action each party provides for the other party (or parties) constitutes necessary evidence as to what normative orders are being oriented to. Hearer/witnesses may not be right in their beliefs, but they can have compelling grounds for holding those beliefs.

In that members-actors have what they need, we, as members-analysts, have something we can use. We can make warranted judgments as to what actions interactants can hold one another normatively accountable for. We can use such judgments to understand how normative order is implicated in the joint accomplishment of tasks. We can see the place occupied by normative order in the production of social order in real-life circumstances such as collaborative computer editing.

Notes

1. I follow the gender-fair convention of listing pronouns in alphabetical order (e.g., her or his, he or she).

2. Behavior is the directly observable movement of an organism through time and space. Action is "meaningful" behavior—that is, behavior that is motivated, goal oriented, purposeful, intentional, or the like. If one stumbles, that is behavior. If one stumbles "on purpose," that is action. See Weber (1968).

3. Of course, discourse is action, but for purposes of economy and exposition I shall contrast discourse action with nonverbal action. The former will be called *discourse* and the latter will be called *action*.

4. Since instances of helper arranging moves rarely occur in circumstances matching the simple state of affairs presupposed by my hypothesis, we shall have to treat it as a "working hypothesis"—that is, one that I like but cannot prove.

5. Deletion keystrokes remove characters as well as spaces in a document. Erasure keystrokes replace or overtype one character with another character or space.

6. The students' word-processing program is in permanent overtype mode, so hitting the space bar erases the character to the right of the cursor.

8

Psychiatric Records as Transformations of Other Texts

TONY HAK

The Sociological Use
of Psychiatric Records

Three approaches to the study of records can be distinguished in the sociology of psychiatry. The first, which is related to psychiatric epidemiology, treats the psychiatric record as a source of information about a patient's condition (e.g., Faris & Dunham, 1939; Williams et al., 1989). The record itself is not the object of study; in the rare exceptions in which it is, it is treated as a source of information about the expertise of the writer. In such studies, descriptions of mental problems and their psychiatric treatment as presented in psychiatric textbooks are used as the basis of sociological analysis. This approach, which I call "regular (medical) sociology," implies the acceptance of psychiatry's own claim that mental illness is an object that is disclosed by means of the appropriate psychiatric diagnosis. Because the sociologist uses the records in fundamentally the same way that the psychiatrist is assumed to use them, psychiatric practice itself remains uninvestigated.

The second approach, which I call "critical (medical) sociology," distinguishes between a patient's "real" problem and the description offered by psychiatry (e.g., Goffman, 1961; Scheff, 1966). According to the critical approach, the original trouble is quite different from the interpretation offered by psychiatry. In its most extreme version, the contention is that in reality there is no trouble at all; psychiatry itself creates the object of study (mental illness) out of nowhere. For instance, Rosenhan (1973) organized an experiment in which pseudopatients sought admission to a variety of mental hospitals, complaining that they had been hearing voices. When asked what the voices said, the pseudo-patients said that the voices were not very clear, that as far as they could tell the voices said, "empty," "hollow," and "thud" (Rosenhan, 1973, p. 251). Without exception, the pseudopatients were hospitalized; all but one were diagnosed as schizophrenics. A critical sociologist studies psychiatric records neither to obtain information about a patient's condition nor to understand psychiatric practice. In pointing to the differences between the psychiatric record and the "reality" for which the record stands, the sociologist merely criticizes psychiatric labeling.

Ethnomethodology represents the third sociological approach to the study of psychiatric records. It is critical of both the "regular" and the "critical" views. It might even be said that ethnomethodology grew out of attempts to solve the problems inherent in the "regular" sociology of psychiatry (see Garfinkel & Bittner, 1967a, 1967b). According to eth-nomethodologists as well as "critical" sociologists, the psychiatric re-cord is a description of neither "real" mental conditions nor a patient's career; however, from the ethnomethodological point of view, this "distortion" is not produced by psychiatry, but is a phenomenon intrin-sic to social practice itself. In other words, there is no "reality" against which psychiatric records can be compared. They can be studied only as part of psychiatric practice (which is partly constituted by them). My analysis of psychiatric records is based on this approach. Before pre-senting samples of my data and outlining my analyses, however, I shall discuss some fundamental aspects of this approach.

Sociological Description

According to Garfinkel, there are no positivistic sociological "facts"; there are only "findings" (achievements). Any sociological description is a "documentary interpretation." Sacks (1963, p. 5) considered this problem in terms of a "representative metaphor," namely, a "machine" consisting of two parts. While one part engages in some activity, the other provides (by means of a narration) a description of that activity. From the commonsense perspective, the machine might be called a "commentator," its parts being "the doing" and "the saying."

This commonsense perspective presupposes that the observer knows what the machine is doing and that he speaks the language of the accompanying narration. If the observer does not know what the machine is doing, he can look to the narration for an explanation. Conversely, if the observer believes he knows what the machine is doing, he can evaluate the narration. The observer may decide that the narration is not precise enough or that the machine is not functioning properly. The observer may even regard the narration as a metaphoric or ironic sketch.

> In his considering possible solutions for the problematic relation of the parts we shall say he is engaged in "theorizing." In posing as his problem "the problematic relation of the parts" for which a solution constitutes some "reconciliation" we shall say he is engaged in "practical theory." (Sacks, 1963, p. 6)

The commonsense observer and the sociologist are engaged in "practical theory" when they try to make sense of the behavior and the talk of actors. Both try to reconcile "the doing" with "the saying." Both formulate the reconciliation routinely in the language they share with the actors. According to Sacks, the sole difference between the writings of sociologists and the talk of lay people about society is that sociologists focus on the "etcetera problem." They recognize that the researcher must add an etcetera clause to any description of a concrete event, however long, so that the description can be brought to a close. According to Sacks, the difference between various sociologies is the difference in their solution to the etcetera problem.

In the eyes of a complete outsider who neither comprehends the actions of the machine nor understands its language (Sacks's "naive" scientist), it would not seem strange that the (regular) sociologist should attempt to formulate a reconciliation. However, it would seem strange that the sociologist should suppose that this activity, in which the machine's narration is taken as a description of what it is doing, should produce "scientific" descriptions. Sacks (1963) uses the machine metaphor to get across the point that it is strange that (regular) sociology should use members' descriptions instead of independent descriptions: "Sociology, to emerge, must free itself . . . from the common-sense perspective. . . . The 'discovery' of the common-sense world is important as the discovery of a problem only, and not as the discovery of a sociological resource" (pp. 10-11).

But avoiding "practical theory" is impossible. An unequivocal description of "doings" presupposes a language or theory that is independent of social interpretation, but inevitably such a language or theory is part of the social practices of (documentary) interpretation.

The Ethnomethodological Study of Psychiatry

The implication of all this for the sociological study of psychiatry is that psychiatrists' descriptions, be they in psychiatric records or in textbooks, must be taken as problems and not as resources. This means that psychiatric records cannot be read as information about patients' (or psychiatrists') behavior. This also means that we must dismiss the "critical" sociological evaluation of psychiatric accounts as distortions of reality, because in the end this evaluation turns out to be nothing but the comparison of the psychiatric account with another account, the sociologist's. What can an ethnomethodological study—taking the psychiatric account as the problem—offer us?

In their study of the records kept by a psychiatric outpatient clinic, Garfinkel and Bittner (1967a) show that, when treating the descriptions in the records as a problem, it is necessary to analyze the ways the records are used. The records they studied were not meant to be—and so they were not read as—descriptions of patients' behaviors. Instead, records should be regarded as "procedures and consequences of clinical activities as a medico-legal enterprise" (p. 198). This does not mean that a "contractual reading" of a record is the only possible—or even the most frequent—reading, but Garfinkel and Bittner (1967a) contend that "all alternatives are subordinated to the contract use as a matter of enforced structural priority." The contents of folders, according to these authors, do not "describe" events so much as "hint" at what might have happened or what might happen:

> As expressions, the remarks that make up these documents have overwhelmingly the characteristic that their sense cannot be decided by a reader without his necessarily knowing or assuming something about a typical biography and typical purposes of the user of the expressions, about typical circumstances under which such remarks are written, about a typical previous course of

transactions between the writers and the patient, or between the writers and the reader. Thus the folder contents much less than revealing an order of inter-action, presuppose an understanding of that order for a correct reading. . . .

The documents in the case folder had the further feature that what they could be read to be really talking about did not remain and was not required to remain identical in meaning over the various occasions of their use. Both actually and by intent, their meanings are variable with respect to circum-stances. To appreciate what the documents were talking about, specific reference to the circumstances of their use was required: emphatically not the circumstances that accompanied the original writing, but the present circum-stances of the reader in deciding their appropriate present use. (pp. 201-202)

What these characteristics suggest—according to Garfinkel and Bitt-ner—is that sociologists cannot read folder contents correctly, because they do not have the necessary knowledge of the people to whom the records refer, the people who constructed the records in the first place, the principles that shape the clinic's organization and operation, and the actual procedures the staff follow in going about their day-to-day business, including reading a record. Sociologists can only describe the ways competent staff members produce and use records as part of the practicalities of their bureaucratic work.

This view—in which records are regarded as locally organized re-flexive accounts of the sanctionable performances of the therapeutic relationship—is convincing. But one can, in stressing this point of view (as Garfinkel and Bittner do), underestimate two other matters. First, even though psychiatric records cannot be considered complete and independent descriptions, they contain some descriptions of a patient's condition, for the simple reason that the sanctionable performances clinical staff engage in must be justified by some kind of diagnostic procedure. Potentially at least, this means that these records can be studied as a product of a psychiatrist's "practical theorizing" about a given patient's behavior. Second, a competent reading of—and by implication a competent writing of—psychiatric records cannot com-pletely be defined locally, and the record must bear at least some relation to "ideal" psychiatric competence, for the simple reason that eventually sanctionable performances by clinic members must be eval-uated by outside experts. This means that even a local meaning for present use can be uncovered—at least partially—by using "ideal" procedures and theories as interpretive tools.

Psychiatric Theory

In his reading of psychiatric theory, Schegloff (1963) tries

> to discover not how psychiatry is done, but rather how it is written about and what proper accounts of it look like. We assume we will find described in the literature ideal psychiatric procedure and theory, i.e., procedure and theory as it is publicly avowed it ought to be. . . . The concern of this paper, then, will be to examine the kind of accounts that are given of dynamic psychiatric work, and which psychiatrists take it supply the warrant for believing their knowledge to be adequate. (p. 62)

For professionals as well as members of the public, then, these "proper accounts" form the "pattern" of which observed procedures are the "documents."

According to Schegloff (1963),

> The theory, as employed in reports of case materials in the literature, provides ways of seeing anxiety, hearing resistance, and knowing that the patient's stream of associations "followed" from the therapist's last interpretation. Thus, we find in the literature references to "withdrawn and inarticulate patients," "showing inhibition," "manifestations of increased resistance," and, following an interpretation, "The patient's response was to burst into tears and say with great feeling. . . ." (p. 71)

Psychotherapeutic theory provides the therapist with an interpretation not only of what the patient says and does but also with an interpretation of his own intervention. A distinction is thus made between "proper" interventions and interventions that are considered to be symptoms of countertransference:

> Explicit prohibitions on the introduction of the therapist's values and judgments, and the continuing search for counter-transference seek to guarantee that behavior will be understood and related to other behavior in strictly psychiatric ways. . . . It is the currently available theory that determines when behaviors have been understood and related to others in psychiatrically proper ways. (Schegloff, 1963, p. 74)

Schegloff also discusses how, according to the literature, the therapist can (given the features that characterize a proper psychotherapeutic conversation) organize a conversation in such a way that the client behaves as expected. The literature mentions the procedures employed by psychiatrists to "educate" the patient, for example, representing the patient's problems by means of transference; making impossible the reasonable accounting for in-session behavior by reference to features of the situation and, by extension, making impossible reasonable accounting for problematic behavior on the outside, by pointing out patterns connecting intrasession with extrasession behavior; interpreting reactions, including "negative" reactions, in terms of the theory from which these reactions are "derived," that is, understanding them as "resistance" (p. 90).

Schegloff emphasizes that his reading of psychiatric theory has not uncovered a description of the way therapists actually proceed. What he has found are therapists' descriptions of the prescriptions and the presentations they employ or have employed to manage a course of therapy.

> [A description of this kind] cannot say whether psychiatrists, in fact, employ the theory over the course of a session, whether they employ the procedures outlined above, or whether they succeed in cultivating a proper audience in their patients. It does seem, however, that in providing this account of their procedures, they have at least in part succeeded in gaining a more or less appreciative audience in their readers. (Schegloff, 1963, p. 90)

I contend in what follows that, in order to understand psychiatric practice, it is necessary to assume that it is done by more or less appreciative readers of "ideal" psychiatric theory.

Problem (Re)Formulation

In his study of the social organization of juvenile justice, Cicourel (1968) says that

> the police, like all members of a society, operate with background expectancies and norms or a "sense of social structure" that enables them to transform an environment of objects into recognizable and intelligent displays making up everyday social organization. The special skills, which the police acquire to enable them to decide "normal" and "unusual" circumstances, become

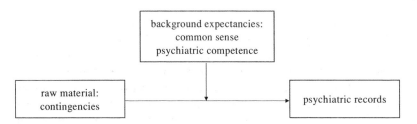

Figure 8.1.

crucial elements of their sense of social structure. . . . The contingencies of
the unfolding scene provide the officers with the raw material for generating
practical solutions. (p. 328)

I maintain that exactly the same holds for psychiatrists. However, it is
expected that psychiatrists interpret circumstances in ways that differ
markedly from the ways police officers (or people in other professions)
interpret the circumstances they face. This difference is due to the
specific psychiatric competence of which the "ideal," not the practice,
has been described by the experts themselves in their theory books.

The approach I propose for studying psychiatric records combines
Cicourel's description of an institutional interpretive process and
Schegloff's notion of an "ideal" procedure. The latter can be regarded
as a specific form of "background expectancies." My approach is
illustrated by Figure 8.1. This model suggests that psychiatric interpretation, as presented in a psychiatric record, can be understood as a
specific transformation of "raw material" into a description, under both
commonsense and "psychiatric" auspices.

We should be able to understand the dynamics of this transformation
if we compare the record itself with the raw material used to produce
the record. However, this comparison is not possible, because we do not
possess (as pointed out in the above discussion of sociological description) an independent description of the "raw material."

Solving this problem of the nonavailability of an independent description of raw material means distancing ourselves once more from
everyday understandings of psychiatric interpretation. The everyday
conception of psychiatry supposes that psychiatrists interpret behaviors, experiences, and feelings. But actually, psychiatrists seldom observe the appearances that count as documents of problematic behaviors

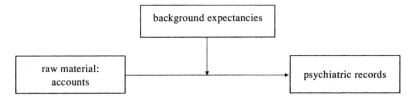

Figure 8.2.

and experiences, because the great majority of the "symptoms" under scrutiny are not presented but merely reported in psychiatric interviews. This point was made by Rosenhan's (1973) experiment, in which pseudopatients who said they had been hearing voices sought admission to a variety of mental hospitals. A psychiatrist cannot observe a patient's "voices." He or she simply takes the report as raw material for diagnosis. So far, the approach I propose squares with the conclusions reached by psychiatry itself to the effect that "many aspects of the patient's mental status cannot be observed directly, as in a physical examination, and [so] the interviewer is dependent on subjective data provided by the patient" (MacKinnon, 1980, p. 906). This means that the figure can be read as representing a relation between two kinds of texts, accounts to be read psychiatrically and its psychiatric readings (see Figure 8.2).

I should add that, in institutional settings, like those of psychiatry, experts rarely deal with what might be described as the "original" accounts, that is, those provided by initial observers, including patients themselves; instead, they deal with materials already professionally interpreted, materials that can be in oral as well as written form. The written form of this kind of already-available interpretation is the folder, which is read and reread and added to during the course of institutional work. The folder documents the institutional career of the patient, in the form of a historical or genealogical chain of successive interpretations of the patient's problem. As Cicourel (1968) puts it with reference to juvenile justice: "The 'delinquent' is an emergent product, transformed over time according to a sequence of encounters, oral and written reports, prospective readings, retrospective readings of 'what happened,' and the practical circumstances of 'settling' matters in everyday agency business" (p. 333).

The chain of possible reformulations of the "problem" goes on without end. In fact, there is no such thing as the "original" problem. Many studies of the lay interpretations of medical and psychological

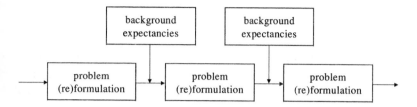

Figure 8.3.

problems have made it clear that problems undergo many transformation (reformulations) before they are offered to an expert such as a
doctor or a psychiatrist. This observation leads us to the final version
of the model sketched in Figures 8.1 and 8.2, in which any interpretation
of a problem can be represented as a transformational link in a genealogical chain, without a beginning and without an end (see Figure 8.3).

A Psychiatric Case

I propose to illustrate the use of the model in Figure 8.3 by means of
a partial analysis of a case report made by a Dutch service for emergency psychiatry. This institution takes action when a person is reported
to be in need of assistance, usually by a general practitioner. An
assistant—a psychiatrist, physician, or social psychiatric nurse—visits
the person immediately in order to size up the situation and to decide
what action to take. The possible courses of action range from arranging
psychiatric admission to concluding that no treatment is required.
Sometimes, as in the case considered here, a decision on psychiatric
admission cannot be reached immediately; this means that an appoint-
ment for another contact (a "repeat visit") has to be made. Some kind
of referral is always required; this means that decision making is almost
always explicitly recorded. Observations made during the patient's
contact with the staff member are written down as well.

Anna-Lize, a woman of about 20, had been reported in order to
establish whether or not she should be admitted to a hospital (a psychiatric hospital or a psychiatric department of a general hospital). It was
decided to pay her a repeat visit. The document to be analyzed here is
the result of that repeat visit. (The full report is provided in the Appendix to this chapter.) Actually, the repeat visit consisted of two separate
visits, the first at her home address (in her parents' presence) and the

second at the crisis intervention center to which Anna-Lize had reported at the assistant's advice. What was said during these visits was tape-recorded so that the exchange could be transcribed. In addition, two other conversations were taped and transcribed: a telephone conversation in which an assistant discussed—with staff at the psychiatry department of a general hospital—the possibility of admitting Anna-Lize, and a consultation with a colleague from the crisis intervention center.[1] Altogether, then, the corpus of texts is composed of the following:

Text 1: the first report (not discussed here)
Text 2: the transcript of the staff member's home visit and interview with Anna-Lize and her parents
Text 3: the transcript of the assistant's consultation over the telephone with staff at the hospital
Text 4: the transcript of the interview conducted at the crisis intervention center
Text 5: the transcript of the staff member's discussion with colleague at the crisis intervention center
Text 6: the second report (see the Appendix to this chapter)

I do not have the space at my disposal to discuss in detail how the assistant organized the process of reformulating the problem; however, I can illustrate the process in part by reference to the following part of the report (Text 6). I analyze this report as the product of a complex reformulating process.

It is obvious that the client has delusions. She fancies that her sexual past is being disclosed on the radio. And that her father can hear her all the time as well. On the other hand, she frequently hears voices. She seems to hear the voice of her father, even when he is not present. It is not clear to me to what extent these are hallucinations.

In the presence of her parents she tries to provoke her father. She spews out rather vulgar descriptions of her sex life. Her father reacts with much agitation. Threatens to throw her out of the house, to beat her, etc., and still he cannot cope with her.

I present my analysis in two parts. In the first I describe the transformation process that has produced the above fragments. In the second I discuss the background expectancies. I argue that these expectancies have shaped the transformations.

Psychiatric Interpretation
as Transformational Practice

The fragment reproduced above can be read as an expansion of both parts of the "diagnosis" as it is mentioned at the beginning of the report: "Borderline state of paranoid coloring and severe protracted disturbance in relationship with father." Although this fragment presents the father—at least partially—as a source of trouble (e.g., by mentioning his "agitation"), it is in the first place a description of the client. Anna-Lize is the one who hears her father's voice ("even when he is not present"), who "fancies that her sexual past is being disclosed on the radio," and who "tries to provoke her father" by spewing out "rather vulgar descriptions of her sex life." Four conversational fragments extracted from Text 2, which consists of the transcripts of the visit and the interview, are arguably the "sources" of the "findings." [2] (Note: In the material that follows, IR is the assistant, IE is Anna-Lize, and F is her father.)

Text 2: Interview   *Text 6: Report*

[Fragment 1]

IE: I've just been used all my life.

IR: By whom?

IE: By boys.

IR: And how does the whole country know about this?

IE: Yes, it is broadcast.

IR: Broadcast where? On the radio or something?

IE: And on TV.

IR: That you're being used?   She fancies that her sexual past

IE: No uh who I went to bed with.   is being broadcast on the radio.

[Fragment 2]

IE: My dad also hears every move   [She fancies] that her father can
     I make upstairs.   hear her all the time as well.
                                      She seems to hear the voice of
                                      her father, even when he is not
                                      present.

[Fragment 3]

IE: When I suddenly heard voices, I went completely crazy.

On the other hand, she frequently hears voices.

[Fragment 4]

IE: He is bothering me all his life, and he has told me that already.

F: I will beat you up. Please get dressed and get the hell out of here. . . . When I can't hold out with sexual life any longer, I go to the whores. I'm not gonna use my kids for that. What she reels off now!

She spews out rather vulgar descriptions of her sex life. Her father reacts with much agitation. Threatens to throw her out of the house, to beat her, etc., and still he cannot cope with her.

In the reformulation that takes place in Fragment 1, the assistant succeeds in securing the patient's confirmation of his reformulation of her words as "who I went to bed with is broadcast on the radio and TV." This statement is reformulated in the report as "She fancies that her sexual past is being disclosed on the radio." The most important transformation effected in this reformulation is the conversion of "who I went to bed with" into "her sexual past." The reformulation that occurs in Fragment 2 effects much less change.

The reformulation that takes place in Fragment 3 brings about, among other things, the transformation of "suddenly" into "frequently." In the report, the reformulation is followed by the statement: "She seems to hear the voice of her father, even when he is not present." I cannot find the corresponding fragment in the interview. By transforming "suddenly" into "frequently" and by identifying one of the voices, the assistant constructs the symptom as "hearing [her father's] voice."

Two major transformations occur in the complex reformulations that make up Fragment 4: (a) the transformation of "my [i.e., father's] sexual life" into "her [i.e., Anna-Lize's] sex life," and (b) the transformation of the proposition "He uses his kids" into a mere opinion ("vulgar descriptions") about the quality of the proposition.

Three features warrant comment. The first feature (seen on two occasions) is the transposition of a description of behavior into an abstract classification: "who I went to bed with" becomes "her sexual past," and "He is bothering me all his life" becomes "vulgar descriptions of her sex life." The last transformation displaces the father from the center of the situation. The second feature, then, is the arbitrary inclusion or exclusion of mention of the father from the transposition. An example of addition is the following formulation: "She seems to hear the voice of her father, even when he is not present." The third feature is the interpolation of such words as "frequently," which suggests that a more or less stable symptom already exists.

Background Expectancies

This account of the process of psychiatric reformulation demonstrates that very specific background expectancies are operative. In the first place, these are the background expectancies of the father. He reads his daughter's utterance "He is bothering me all his life" as an allegation that he uses his kids to satisfy his sexual needs. This is understandable, given the "protracted disturbance" in the relationship between father and daughter. What is remarkable here is that the report has been structured to convey the father's view. This is clear when we reconstruct the process of reformulation:

Anna-Lize:	He is bothering me all his life.
Father:	What she reels off now! She has been used to satisfy [my] sexual life.
Report:	She spews out rather vulgar descriptions of her sex life.

What is not made explicit in the assistant's report and what serves as the source of his description of Anna-Lize's talk as "vulgar" is his acceptance of the father's reading of the statement "He is bothering me" as the assertion "that I [Anna-Lize] am being used by my father [to satisfy his sexual life]." In not making explicit the reasons for calling her statements "vulgar descriptions," the assistant conceals the fact that he actually quotes the father and that he identifies with him.

The sense of the formulation "She spews out rather vulgar descriptions of her sex life" cannot be decided by the reader, as Garfinkel and Bittner (1967a) say,

> without his necessarily knowing or assuming something about a typical biography and typical purposes of the user of the expressions, about typical circumstances under which such remarks are written, about a typical previous

course of transactions between the writers and the patient, or between the writers and the reader. Thus the folder contents much less than revealing an order of interaction, presuppose an understanding of that order for a correct reading. (p. 201)

It should be clear by now that the assistant and the father share a certain understanding about "a typical biography" and about "typical purposes of the users [daughter and father] of expressions," and "typical circumstances" under which such remarks are made. While writing his report, however, the assistant cannot be sure that it will be read in the light of these understandings. He must, therefore, rely on another kind of understanding, namely, the one he is assumed to share with his professional readers. The assistant's report is not just a story about Anna-Lize; more than anything else, it is a psychiatric case history. The "psychiatric" nature of this story is based on the relations among its elements as understood by a competent reader. It can be assumed, following Schegloff's (1963) reasoning, that these relations in their "ideal" form are formulated in "psychiatric theory."

The fragment of the report studied here consists of two parts, each of which bears a distinct relation to "ideal" psychiatry. The first part describes "delusions" and "hallucinations." The second part describes the patient's "provocative" behavior. These two parts correspond to the two parts of the "diagnosis": "Borderline state of paranoid coloring and severe protracted disturbance in relationship with father." Strictly speaking, the second part of this diagnosis is not a psychiatric interpretation. Rather, it is an everyday description, one that could have been produced by anyone. This also holds for the assistant's emphasis on the patient's "provocative" behavior. Consequently, the "psychiatric" sense of this description cannot be decided without finding a relation between it and the other parts of the report. The descriptions of a "mental illness" in other parts of the report convey a "psychiatric" sense to the everyday descriptions of the patient's behavior. The first part of the report offers a clear example of "ideal" psychiatric writing, in contrast to the second part, which is a description of the patient's provocative behavior.

In the first part, correct terms for the designation of well-known symptoms, such as "delusions" and "hallucinations," are employed. Moreover, symptoms are referred to throughout. Fancying that details of one's sexual past are being disclosed on the radio, for example, is an "ideal" instance of the general class of hallucinations. The same holds for hearing voices. It is, therefore, somewhat surprising for the competent reader to read "It is not clear to me to what extent these are hallucinations." As I have already shown, the text—"She fancies that her sexual past is being disclosed on the radio. And that her father can hear her all the time as well. On the other hand, she frequently hears voices"—consists of reformulations of fragments of the interview. Suggesting that these observations can be interpreted as hallucinations provides justification for including them in the report and for selecting them from an extensive interview.

I cannot expand here upon the details of "ideal" psychiatric knowledge, such as the differences between such terms as *delusions* and *hallucinations* and the relevance these differences have for the diagnosis of "borderline state of paranoid coloring." It should be quite clear by now that the psychiatric report can be read competently only with recourse to both "everyday" and "ideal psychiatric" background expectancies.

Conclusions

This chapter has shown how psychiatric practice can be described as an ongoing process of reformulating earlier formulations, be they more or less "original" accounts recorded by initial observers (including those of the patient herself) or preceding professional interpretations. The process of reformulation takes place under the auspices of "everyday" as well as "ideal professional" background expectancies. These expectancies can be analyzed by means of a detailed comparison of formulations and their reformulations.

Psychiatric practice can be described as the transformation of both "original" and "secondhand" accounts into a competent interpretation. The result of this process—a psychiatric report—provides evidence of an "ideal" competence and produces a professional (oral or written) dossier sketching a patient's particularities. The latter in particular is important. If a report had to meet only the requirement that it could be read as evidence of ideal competence, it would consist of a mere collage of statements lifted from psychiatric textbooks. Only a very small proportion of the many "observations" made by the assistant in the interview are turned into "findings," but these are necessary if the report is to refer to one particular, not just any individual, case.

In other words, the report serves as the locus of two simultaneous "reading processes." A situation is read for the purpose of discovering "findings"; at the same time, psychiatric "knowledge" is consulted for diagnoses. Psychiatric practice apparently consists of the ability to ensure that both processes result in a common product, that is, a "case," in which the representation of a particular person and the evocation of specific "knowledge" are intertwined.

Appendix: Text 6 (Report)

Reason for referral:
  Paranoid state of borderline of drug addict. Repeat visit.
Preliminary diagnosis:
  Borderline state of paranoid coloring and severe protracted disturbance in relationship with father.
Home visit information parents (pat. is still asleep).
  Pat. is alleged "to be difficult." She wants to play the boss according to her father. Pat. is said to have always been changeable. Was at school for retail trade.
Interview with pat.
  Little by little pat. joins the conversation. She seems a little inhibited in conversation; she is rather reserved/evasive. After some hesitation she gives clear questions an adequate answer. At present her problems are cardiac.

  During our conversation she frequently reaches for the heart region. On the other hand, she sometimes laughs when she formulates her "cardiac problems."

  It is obvious that the client has delusions. She fancies that her sexual past is being disclosed on the radio. And that her father can hear her all the time as well. On the other hand, she frequently hears voices. She seems to hear the voice of her father, even when he is not present. It is not clear to me to what extent these are hallucinations.

  In the presence of her parents she tries to provoke her father. She spews out rather vulgar descriptions of her sex life. Her father reacts with much agitation. Threatens to throw her out of the house, to beat her, etc., and still he cannot cope with her.

  Agreed to let pat. go to crisis intervention centre and see there if admission to psychiatric hospital is necessary. In the crisis intervention centre in the afternoon everything is much calmer. State of condition not changed. Pat. is to stay there a few days. Admission to Essenland Psychiatry was not possible for lack of room.

It is difficult to diagnose this pat. There are delusions. She does not give the impression of being manifestly psychotic, even though she is often evasive. Feels quickly injured.

Drugs don't play a role at the moment. (Last use of speed + hallucinogens in Dec.) There are also theatrical/stubborn components in her behavior.

Address:

Already in crisis intervention centre.

Repeat visit:

New contact by ass.

Medication:

Advise on neuroleptica for the time being.

If necessary, seresta forte.

Notes

1. These texts were collected during research on a project called "Sex-Specific Criteria Used in Decisions on Psychiatric Admission," which was carried out by Fijgje de Boer. The project, which was made possible by a grant from the Dutch National Foundation for Mental Health, investigated whether sex differences are constituted in the discourse of assistance and, if so, how. See de Boer and Hak (1986).

2. Actually, I used a more or less "formal" method in order to find these four fragments. Because it is not the object of this chapter to discuss that method (described in Hak, 1989a, 1989b; for a critical discussion, see Hodge, 1989), I do not give details here. I am convinced that, at least with reference to the fragments discussed here, a "careful" reading would have produced the same results.

9

Recognizing References to Deviance in Referral Talk

STEPHEN HESTER

Within the interpretivist tradition in the sociology of deviance there is an extensive literature providing answers to the question: What is deviance? Assuming that deviance is a matter of interpretation, numerous studies have documented how deviance, in a variety of settings, is socially constructed (e.g., Bittner, 1967; Cicourel, 1968; Emerson, 1969; Emerson & Pollner, 1978; Hargreaves, Hester, & Mellor, 1975; Jeffery, 1979; Mercer, 1973; Sacks, 1972a; Sudnow, 1965). Interpretive resources such as "commonsense" and "practical knowledge," "interpretive procedures," "mundane reason," and "definitions of the situation" have been the major foci of attention in this research tradition.

It is therefore somewhat ironic that these studies should have neglected a fundamental interpretive issue, namely, how "interpretations" or "definitions" of deviance are identified in the first place. This chapter describes some methods for producing and recognizing references to deviance.[1] The intelligibility of references to deviance, and therefore the intelligibility of the sociology of deviance as a subdiscipline of sociology, depends upon these methods. Unless speakers are able to produce recognizable references to deviance and, in turn, unless hearers can recognize them as references to deviance, intelligible talk about such a subject is impossible (see Jayyusi, 1984, p. 3).

156

The data upon which this study is based consist of the transcriptions of 28 tape recordings (which were made over a two-year period) of "referral meetings" involving teachers and educational psychologists. In these meetings teachers were invited to describe (and answer questions about) children they had referred to the School Psychological Service, an agency that formed part of the Child and Family Guidance Service, one of a range of special education services provided by the local education authority or school board in a large northern city in England. These meetings comprised occasions when the teacher described for the psychologist "the problem" in detail for the first time. They contain numerous references to deviance in school.

The conceptual framework in terms of which the analysis proceeds is derived from the work of Sacks (1967, 1972a, 1972b), R. Watson (1976, 1978, 1983), and others on "membership categorization" (e.g., M. Atkinson, 1980; Cuff & Francis, 1978; Drew, 1978; Jayyusi, 1984; Lee, 1987; Payne, 1976). "Membership categories" are classifications or social types that may be used to describe persons and nonpersonal objects (see Jayyusi, 1984, p. 212). These categories are linked together to form "membership categorization devices" (Sacks, 1972b, p. 332). "Rules of application" provide for the pairing of a category from a device and a population member. The "economy rule" provides for the adequacy of using a single membership category to describe a member of some population (although in some settings, e.g., referral meetings, there may be a preference for "multiple referencing"; see Hester, in press). The "consistency rule" holds: "If some population of persons is being categorized, and if a category from some device's collection has been used to categorize a first member of the population, then that category or other categories of the same collection may be used to categorize further members of the population" (Sacks, 1972b, p. 333). Sacks also identifies a corollary or "hearer's maxim" of the consistency rule. The hearer's maxim holds the following: "If two or more categories are used to categorize two or more members of some population, and those categories can be heard as categories from the same collection, then: hear them that way" (p. 333). Finally, when Sacks speaks of "category-bound activities," he means those activities that are expectably done by persons who are the incumbents of particular categories. Subsequent researchers (e.g., Jayyusi, 1984; Payne, 1976; Sharrock,

1974; R. Watson, 1978, 1983) have observed that category-bound activities make up one class of predicates that "can conventionally be imputed on the basis of a given membership category" (R. Watson, 1978, p. 106). Other predicates include rights, expectations, obligations, knowledge, attributes, and competencies.

References to Deviance in Referral Talk

An initial distinction may be made between two aspects of references to deviance, namely, what the references are "to" and what the reference consists "of." Previous researchers have explored the first of these aspects, but have not paid much attention to the means or methods whereby this deviance is described or referenced (e.g., Barton & Tomlinson, 1981; Ford, Mongon, & Whelan, 1982; Tomlinson, 1981). Two aspects of the issue of "how" deviance is referenced will be considered in this chapter. The first (a "preliminary" issue) concerns the range or variety of references that are used. For this purpose, references are classified into six main varieties. The second (to which the main part of this chapter is devoted) concerns how *intelligible* references are produced and recognized. Six main ways of referring to deviance are listed below.[2]

Deviant Membership Categories

This type of reference makes use of culturally available names, types, or "category concepts" of persons, such as "bully," "slow learner," "nuisance," "menace," and "thief."

[1] [WJS/5578]

```
01 EP:   So: the: what is the nub of the problem?
02       Truancy doesn'ₜt sound like it₁'s
03 FT:               [well that's not ¹ no it'ₛ nₗot=
04 EP:                                 [no]
05 FT:   =that no it's really it's thieving for a start
06       that brought things to light but she's a very
07       good bully
08 EP:   Mm hmm
```

Deviant Type Categorizations

Type categorizations often make use of membership categories such as "criminal type," "Hell's Angel type," or "hippie type" (see Jayyusi, 1984, chap. 1). For example:

[2] [MP/69]

```
01  SW:   Mm⌈hmm⌉
02          ⌊Er⌋ rm (.) perhaps that last year (.) errm in the
03          lower school was something of a wasted opportunity I
04          don't wan-to (.) sort of (.) chuck responsibilities
05          around (0.6) but (0.5) the boy's getting older (0.7)
06          an:d umm (.) at a time like that one might 'ave
07          said (.⌈) here's a maladjusted type of=
08  SW:         ⌊mmhm         (0.5)             get the=
09  EP:   =boy (⌈(s.v.)) is this the school for him
10  SW:   =child⌋ served yeah
```

Another form of these categorizations makes reference to activities. This form is used in the following extract.

[3] [WJS/11]

```
01  HT:   You see he's the sort of boy who you will meet on the
02          corridor (.) at break time chasing around in an
03          immature sort of way
04  MT:   Mmhmm
05          (0.4)
06  EP:   Mhmm
```

Descriptive Statement of Deviant Attributes

This type of reference consists of a description of the deviant qualities or attributes of the individual pupil. They may be expressed in terms of qualities, properties, or features, in short, "attributes" that the individual pupil *is* or *has*.

[4] [MP/49]

```
01  EP:   ((.s.v.)) Mmhmmm mmhmm
02  MT:   Errm (0.5) at the moment I've taken him from his
03          classroom down in the gym waiting for Joseph to come
```

04   down .hhh but it's reached such a stage with me:
05   that-errm you know I find that the boy's completely
06   uncooperative

[5] [WJS/20]

```
01 FT:   He's a bit of an anomaly, isn't he, Peter because I
02           ┌think he's (.) he's got maturity=
03           └oh he is┘
04 FT:   =problems (.) he's got ┌ a ┐ very (0.5) errm acute=
05                               └mm┘
06 FT:   =brain really=
07 MT:   =mmhmm, ┌oh yes┐
08 FT:           └but he┘'s got a very poor attention span
```

One particular class of attribute references is that of *pupil incompe-tence*. This class of references is evident in the following extract:

[6] [AN/1]

```
01 HT:   Now, when she brought him in she said er e-e wasn't a
02           good talker
03 EP:   Mm hm
04 HT:   And er I think I said was there anything else wrong
05           with him and er she said no
06 EP:   Mm hm
07 HT:   And (.) I asked her as usual you know her first name,
08           her husband's first name
09 EP:   Yeah
10 HT:   So she gave her husband as Paul and she's Pauline
11 EP:   Mm
12 HT:   And (.) I accepted this er
13 EP:   Mm hm
14 HT:   Quite happily (. . .) and er we saw his birth
15           certificate (.) but it wasn't very long before we
16           realised that it was more than just a poor speaker,
17           he-he can't speak very much at all, he-he doesn't
18           know the=
19 EP:                              ┌Mm hm┐
20 HT:   =language, he doesn't know the names of common
21           objects, no response to various simple instructions
```

22   such as "stand up," "sit down," he's really
23   functioning like an=
24 *EP:* =Mm hm=
25 *HT:* =eighteen month or two year old baby
26 *EP:* Mm hm

Descriptive Statement of Deviant Behavior

This class of references consists of references to *how the pupil behaves*. One subclass of these can be heard as references to behavior that is a general, persistent, and present feature of the pupil. Such *generalized* references are contained in the following extracts:

[7] [AN/1]

01 *HT:* And he talks to his mum in this sort of gibberish
02   which she understands but nobody else does at all and
03   she replies which means he isn't being stimulated at
04   all ⌜ to t⌐ry to talk
05 *EP:*   ⌊Yeah⌋
06   Mm.

[8] [AN/1]

01 *EP:* mm hm
02 *HT:* (and) he keeps running away, apparently he's been
03   running away this morning
04 *EP:* mm hm
05 *HT:* down the corridor

A second subclass of these behavioral references (illustrated below) consists of references to *particular incidents*.

[9] [MP/55]

01 *MT:* Yeah well look I-I-I'll say what happened today then
02   before you got 'im Derek because he must have been
03   high as a kite by the time you got 'im today (.) it's
04   wet weather (0.7) so the school's in difficult
05   turmoil CSE examinations are goin' on so they can't
06   go to their normal ports of call in wet weather .hhh
07   an:d (0.5) in the dining hall today (.) he was

```
08          messing around (0.6) doing ridiculous things (0.7)
09          throwing some potato at somebody
10  T2:     Yeah that's him
```

One distinctive class of "behavioral" references uses membership categories and their predicates that belong to the membership categorization device "crime." In the data presented here, such references pertain to "theft." They make use of the category "thief" and the activity "thieving" (extract 1), as in the following extract:

[10] [RMSJ/311]

```
01  EP:    yeah
02  HT:    so I won't give you the whole story, ahmm, but in a
03         nutshell his behavior has deteriorated, they can't
04         trust him in the house at all on his own, even if
05         they pop up to the shops the house is in a mess when
06         they come back and he's stealing, he's been caught
07         three times stealing from supermarkets on the local
08         terrace
09  EP:    mm
```

Negative Comparisons with Other Pupils

This class of references makes use of comparison, either with other pupils specifically or with the "average" or the "norm" for other pupils.

[11] [AH/1/LM]

```
01  EP:    Mm hmm yeah I see err does he have any friends in the
02         classroom?
03  FT:    (. . .) January when I came into the class Alfred
04         was very sort of quiet shy he was always weighing up
05         the situation but I think all children do with a new
06         teacher .hhh initially (.) then he started running
07         round the room screaming "I'm taking no notice" "I'm
08         not bothered by you" "I don't care what you say" and
09         if you didn't (.) take notice of him (.) he wanted
10         your attention fair enough all young children do
11         want attention sometimes some more than others but if
12         you didn't notice him he would go and punch there's
13         two children in the class that seem to be picked on
```

14   more than anyone else and he'd go and punch them or
15   kick them or swear at them

References to Problems and Troubles

This class of references consists of those in which the words *trouble* or *problem* are actually employed by the speaker. On some occasions, the "trouble" is located *within the individual child*. On others, the "problem" posed by the child *for the school* is emphasized.

[12] [WJS/20/2]

01 *EP:* ┌Mmhmm┐
02 *FT:* └ .hhh ┘ and then he has err (.) coordination problems
03   in a sense that he can't sit still for two minutes
04   and he can't .hhh err physically root himself (.) for
05   more than te┌n (.) I-h mean=┐
06 *MT:*   └no, that's true ┘
07 *FT:* =(.) that's too long, isn't it?

Recognizing References to Deviance

The sense of references to deviance, especially to deviance in school, appears obvious. However, these references can be used in various ways; hence they can have different meanings. Thus such designators of deviance as "murder," "kill," "stab," "bully," and "rob" can be used to accomplish a variety of interactional tasks besides designating deviance. So, for example, with respect to categories of "theft," persons may be described as having "stolen the show" when they have outperformed an established celebrity in a theatrical performance, of having "robbed Peter to pay Paul" when borrowing to repay debts, and of having been "robbed" when narrowly missing a shot or target in some sport. Similarly, when the English language is said to have been "murdered" or when a person is said to have "taken a stab" at something, it is possible for us (and appropriately so) to hear these descriptions as (respectively) descriptions of improper language use and of an attempt at an activity or project.

Just as references with "criminal" or "legal" connotations may be used in various ways, so also may the school-based references. References to pupils "running away" (extract 8), "talking gibberish" (extract 7), "not paying attention" (extract 9), being "uncooperative" (extract 4), "throwing potato" (extract 9), "acting like a two year old" (extract 6), "running round the room screaming" (extract 11), and so on may be interpreted in ways other than as references to deviance. Persons might "run away" from danger and other sets of circumstances, they might be "taken to the toilet" for a variety of reasons, and occasionally they might quite acceptably talk gibberish, act like 2-year-olds, not pay attention, run around the room screaming, and act uncooperatively. None of these activities is inherently deviant. Each can be heard as a reference to deviance in school. At issue, then, is how these references are heard sometimes as designating deviance, while on other occasions they are heard to designate something very different, something "normal" and "acceptable."

One way to approach this matter is to recognize that references can belong to different collections or membership categorization devices. Membership categories and the properties conventionally tied to them can belong to a range of collections. For example, "stealing" may belong to the collection "criminal acts" or to the device "theatrical performances," depending on the context of use; "running away" may belong to the collection "methods of avoiding danger" or it may signify a form of deviance in school. It is possible to find an alternative contextually "acceptable" collection for each reference to "deviance." To find a sense for a reference, then, one needs to find the collection of which it is a member. One of the methods members use to do this is *coselection*. Payne (1976) describes this method:

> One general method or procedure available to members is to hear words as collections or co-selections. That is to say, members hear any one word as a co-selection with the words which precede and follow it. The parts of an utterance can be heard as mutually constitutive in that how any part is heard can depend upon, among other things, how other parts are heard. It is the speaking and hearing of words as co-selections which helps to constitute situations to be observably what they are. (p. 35)

In other words, speakers and hearers rely upon the assumption of consistent coselection of words. It is assumed that words are not chosen randomly or incoherently but, rather, that they are selected because there is a discernible coherence and consistency between them. They are designed to "go together" as mutually elaborative selections for describing or constructing meaning. In terms of the consistency rule, the coselected items composing the reference are heard to go together, if they can be heard that way.

Consider extract 10 and, in particular, the reference to the pupil's "stealing" and of having "been caught three times stealing from supermarkets on the local terrace." If "stealing" does not have a "literal" meaning but rather is an "indexical" expression, which is to say it "points to" different things on different occasions, then a method of isolating the particular sense of the word on this occasion must be employed. It has to be shown to be and figured that it is a reference to theft and not, say, to stealth. What has to be provided for as well as figured out is whether or not this category/activity is a member of the collection "criminal acts" or some other collection, for example, "ways of walking" or "types of theatrical performances."

In "helping" to achieve a sense of the reference to "stealing" as a reference to "deviance" the method of coselection "works" in conjunction with two other methods. The first of these is the orientation to "standardized relational pairs" (Sacks, 1972a, p. 37). Payne (1976) describes this method as follows: "In our culture, certain categories are routinely recognized as paired categories, and the pairing is recognized to incorporate standardized relationships of rights, obligations and expectations" (p. 36). These standardized relational pairs include not only the "intimate" pairings of husband-wife, aunt-uncle, girlfriend-boyfriend, and the like, which Sacks and others (e.g., Eglin, 1990) have found to be relevant, for example, in the case of suicide discourse, but also those relevant in particular "institutional" contexts. Examples of such institutional standardized relational pairings include doctor-patient, lawyer-client, teacher-pupil, teacher-psychologist, and offender-law enforcer.

The second method is the orientation to category predicates. This method provides a link between membership categories, such as those in the preceding paragraph, and certain predicates, such as activities, attributes, obligations, and entitlements, in that such features are "bound" or conventionally tied to those categories.

In combination, these methods permit the inference that the reference to "stealing" is a reference to "theft" and not, say, to "stealth" or to a type of theatrical performance, because an inferential relationship conventionally exists between membership categories and their predicates. Several features of this relationship may be noted. First, it is possible to infer a category from a predicate. For example, to describe someone as having "obeyed" may permit the inference that he or she is a "servant" or a "worker." Second, just as membership categories are relationally paired, so are their predicates. Examples of this include buying and selling in the customer-shopkeeper relationship and teaching and learning in the teacher-pupil relationship. Third, predicates may "stand for" their relationally paired membership categories such that through a substitution procedure a category may be implied by or inferred from mention of the predicate of a category with which it is paired. Thus saying that a person has been "arrested" permits the inference that this activity has been performed by a "law enforcer" and that the arrested individual belongs to the category "offender."

On the basis of these inferential procedures, "stealing," when coselected with the item "caught three times," can be heard to mean "theft." First, "being caught" can be heard as a predicate relationally paired with the activity "catching." Second, "catching" can be heard as an activity bound to the membership category "catcher" (e.g., store detective and police officer). Third, "catcher" can be heard as relationally paired with one whose category-bound activity is "stealing," that is, a "thief." In this way, "stealing" can be heard as belonging to the device "theft" rather than to some other possible collection of categories.

Although the use of the orientation to consistent coselection may "help" in finding a collection for a reference and hence in making sense of it as a reference to deviance, this method will not, either by itself or in combination with the orientations to standardized relational pairs and category predicates, be sufficient to *situate* the references. Thus, while a hearer could reasonably achieve a sense for a reference, from the words alone he or she could not tell whether it was a description of a film, a play, or some other event. To situate or to contextualize a reference other methods are used in conjunction with those already considered. In particular, orientations to the category membership of the speaker, hearer, and person of whom they speak, and to the type of occasion in which their talk occurs, are also involved in the recognition of references to deviance.

Referrers, Referees, and Referral Talk

The relations among context, category membership, and the character of talk as talk about deviance are reflexive. Each of these components constitutes and is constituted by the others. The sense of the occasion as a "referral consultation" is constituted through the identification of the category membership of the participants and the character of their talk as referral talk. The category membership of the participants is constituted by the character of their talk and the context in which it occurs. The character of the talk as talk about deviance in school is, in turn, constituted by the category membership of the participants and the sense of the occasion as a referral consultation.

Like any identifiable social event, referral consultations require a "complement of specific category members to be observably present" (see Payne, 1976, p. 34). A person recognizable as a teacher is required, as is another person identifiable as an educational psychologist. The participants' category-relevant talk constitutes the situation for what it is, namely, an occasion in which talk about deviance in school occurs. By identifying the membership categories of the participants as those of teacher and psychologist, and the character of their talk as referral talk, the occasion can be recognized as a referral consultation.

While the sense of the occasion as a referral consultation is achieved by reference to the talk that occurs within it and to the participants' category incumbency, membership of the categories "teacher" and "psychologist" is achieved by reference to the talk and the sense of occasion constituted by it. Thus category membership is a reflexive and contextually elaborated interactional achievement.[3] "Referral talk" is the stock-in-trade of the talk of "teachers" and "psychologists" about pupils in the referral consultation.

Constituted by the sense of occasion and its talk, the category membership of the participants may be used, then, as a resource in making sense of their talk as talk about deviance in school. It has already been suggested that the teacher and psychologist can be considered to be an institutionally standardized relational pair of membership categories. In the context of the referral consultation, the categories "teacher" and "psychologist" imply each other. Together they "involve a collection of rights, obligations and expectations for each other" (Payne, 1976, p. 35). This collection of predicates can be seen to be used in recognizing references as references to deviance in school, because in the context of a referral consultation an activity bound to membership categories of both participants is the production of referral talk. For the incumbent of the category "teacher" this involves making reference to referral problems, including pupil deviance. Making reference to deviance in school, describing pupil problems, complaining about pupils—these are simultaneously rights, expectations, and obligations bound to the category "teacher." The teacher is able, as a "right," to tell the psychologist the kind of problem being experienced with the referred pupil. The teacher is also obligated to produce such talk. The reason for the consultation in the first place (from the teacher's point of view) is the production of talk of this kind. Talking about deviance, then, is an activity that is bound to this membership category in this context. Knowing the membership category of the speaker, then, permits the inference that this task is about deviance in school because such talk is a predicate of this membership category in this setting.

With respect to the category called "educational psychologist," it may be observed first that an activity bound to it is the "reception" of referral talk. Such recipiency is typically associated with this membership category in this type of setting. The psychologist is obliged organizationally to receive and to listen to teachers' descriptions of "pupils" as deviant. The psychologist expects that schools will refer bona fide cases to him or her. The reason for the meeting in the first place (from the psychologist's point of view) is the reception of referral talk. Knowing, then, that the recipient of the teacher's talk is a psychologist, and hence one for whom in this situation a category-bound activity entitlement and obligation is the reception of referral talk, permits the inference that the teacher's references are references to deviance.

Referrals, Pupils, and Deviance

Just as the membership categories of the speaker and the hearer are implicated in recognizing references to deviance in school, so also is the membership category of the referred pupil. It may be observed that one of the coselections in these references is the pupil (the "he" or the "she") who is the subject of discussion. In fact, these references invoke not one, but two membership categories. The first is the category "referral" and the second is the category "pupil." The subject's membership in these categories is achieved in and as the speakers' talk about him or her, and both categories, through the orientation to their category-bound features, provide a resource for the recognition of references to deviance in school.

The use of these membership categories yields a sense of a reference as a reference to deviance in two different ways. The first—the orientation to the predicates of the category "referrals"—yields such a sense through a course of practical reasoning, which finds the reference as *consistent* with these predicates. The second—the orientation to the predicates of the category "pupils"—yields a sense of a reference as a reference to deviance through a course of *contrastive* practical reasoning. In this case, the reference is found to *contrast with* the features bound to the category "pupil."

Incumbents of the category "referral" are expected to display "a cluster of expectable features" (Jayyusi, 1984, p. 26). These may be attributes, activities, *in*competencies, appearances, habits, and so on. When the child is recognized as being spoken about as an incumbent of the category "referral," the predicates of this category can be brought into play. Referrals are expected by the Child and Family Guidance Service to display some "cause for concern" or problem; they are expected to exhibit the referral attributes, activities, and other predicates that fall within the domain of legitimate organizational intervention by the school psychologist.

One way to hear a reference as a reference to deviance in school is to use as a resource the membership category "deviant pupil" or "referral." If the pupil were described as "cooperative," "well coordinated," "attentive in class," and "no trouble at all," then it would be difficult for hearers to make sense of these references as references to deviance. These attributes, activities, and traits are not hearable as references to deviance, they are hearable as references to "conformity."

However, "running away," "stealing," "bullying," "throwing potato," and "running round the room screaming" are readily hearable as the kinds of activities, attributes, and problems that referred pupils (i.e., expectably "deviant" pupils) do and have. As a resource, the category-bound features of the membership category "referral" are used to make sense of the references to the pupil as references to deviance. Such pupils are expected to display a cluster of category-bound features. The selection and the use of items from this cluster confirm their category membership just as their presumed category membership permits the inference that the references are references to deviance.

So far, this discussion has centered on how a sense of a reference as a reference to deviance might be achieved through a procedure whereby the reference is aligned—that is, found to be consistent with—the predicates of the category "referral." If attention is focused on the membership category "pupil," it is possible to recognize a reference as a reference to deviance in school via a contrastive procedure. The reference in this case can be heard to identify *departures* from norms, obligations, and expectations that are bound to the membership category "pupil." As with the membership category "referrals," the category "pupil" "orientably and expectably" carries with it "a cluster of expect-able features" (Jayyusi, 1984, p. 26). When the child is recognized as being spoken about as an incumbent of the category "pupil," the predicates of this category can be brought into play to arrive at a sense of the pupil's conduct as deviant. The references listed above can all be heard as infractions of category-bound norms.[4] These norms may pertain to classroom conduct, competencies, attainment, social relations, and a variety of other aspects of the category "pupil." By invoking these norms it is possible to recognize that what is contained in the reference contrasts with the normatively acceptable and is therefore hearably deviant.

The recognition that "running away" (extract 8) is a reference to deviance is achieved through a course of contrastive practical reasoning, in which the reported conduct is analyzed in terms of the norms bound to the category "pupil." In terms of these category-bound norms, "running away" can be heard as deviant because all schoolchildren are expected to remain within class or some other teacher-supervised location in school, leaving at the end of the school day and not before.

A background of normality, consisting of membership categories, attributes, activities and competencies, and so on of "normal" pupils, is invoked. An underlying "normal school conduct and competence" is being drawn on to throw into relief the problematic behavior of the pupil in question. Against that background, the pupil's "running away" stands out as deviant, as a departure from the norm.[5]

The pupil in extract 12 is described as having "coordination problems," a description that is hearable as a description of deviance. That it is heard this way rests upon the use of the category-bound norm that the pupil can and should sit still for more than the amount of time mentioned in this reference, namely, two minutes. Likewise, the sense of "cannot physically root himself" (extract 12) as a reference to deviance derives from the expectation that the "normal" pupil can remain so "rooted" for considerably longer periods than is the case with this particular pupil.

Finally, the identification of deviance in extract 11 can be heard to work in the following way. First, in describing Alan's behavior in January, the teacher invokes the "normal" behavior of young children with a new teacher. She says that "all children" are "shy" and that they spend time "weighing up the situation." Recipients of this reference to Alan's behavior can hear the reference as a description of the behavior of a typical child. Second, the teacher then contrasts this behavior with the behavior Alan exhibited later. This description (i.e., "running round the room screaming") is plainly heard as a contrast not only with Alan's own preceding behavior but also with what is "normal behavior" in the classroom.

It is against the background of an assumed category-bound response to the problem of obtaining the teacher's attention that this particular reaction stands out as deviant. All children seek attention sometimes, according to the teacher, but if they do not obtain it, it is incumbent upon them to refrain from running around the room, screaming, and swearing at the teacher.

An underlying pattern of normality runs through all these references, one that is organized as membership categories and their predicates. It is this pattern that is used as grounds for recognizing references to deviance. Only against such a background are recipients able to achieve a sense of, say, "running away," "running round the room screaming," "stealing," and "bullying" as references to deviance.

Using the Stage-of-Life Device
in Reference to Deviance

One special class of references to deviance makes use of the "stage-of-life" device. This is a device onto which the category or the device "pupil" may be easily "mapped" (Watson & Weinberg, 1982). It is a positioned-category device that can be arranged in terms of "age" (e.g., 1-year-old, 2-year-old, 3-year-old) or in terms of such categories as "baby," "child," "adolescent," or "adult."

The recognition of references to deviance that use the stage-of-life device is also achieved contrastively. Certain attributes, activities, and competencies are predicated of different age categories. When a pupil is described as having attributes bound to an age category lower in the arrangement of categories than the one to which he or she belongs, such a description can be heard to identify deviance. The use of this device is evident in extracts 6 and 7. In extract 6, a 4-year-old pupil is described as "functioning like an eighteen month or two year old baby." In extract 7, the same child is described as "talking to his mum [in] gibberish." By themselves, these references may not be heard as a references to deviance at all. After all, what is "wrong" with these activities? In certain settings, it is not difficult to imagine, such activity might be regarded as praiseworthy. However, in the context of referral talk, these references can be heard quite plainly as references to deviance.

With respect to "positioned categories," such as those arranged in the stage-of-life device, it has been observed by Sacks (1972b) that describing a person in terms of a category positioned lower in a collection of categories than that to which they belong constitutes a degradation. The force of the degradation derives from a contrast between the predicates of the two membership categories. In extract 6, in particular, it depends upon a contrast between what is expected in terms of the predicates of the stage-of-life category to which the child belongs, namely, "4-year-old," and what is received, namely, a level of "functioning" that is typical instead of the category "2-year-old." As a member of the category "4-year-old" the child is expected to have certain attributes and to be able to function in ways that are bound to such a category. "Normal" children display and are expected to display predicates of the categories to which they ostensibly belong. Hence the child's being a 4-year-old but behaving like a 2-year-old may be heard as deviant.

Similarly, in extract 7, the pupil's "gibberish" is heard as deviant because of what is commonsensically predicated of the category "4-year-old." It is expected that 4-year-olds speak in a way that is understandable. Against such a background, the pupil in question can be heard as behaving in a deviant manner. By filling in what is normal in terms of membership category organization, the recipients of the description are able to hear it as a description of deviance.

The hearing, as in the previous example, relies upon a course of contrastive work; it depends upon contrasts among the behavior in question, what is being described, and the predicates of the stage-of-life category to which this pupil belongs. For a "4-year-old," certain linguistic competencies are expected. Against the background of, and in contrast with, these expected predicates the pupil can be heard as deviant.

Concluding Remarks

In this chapter I have considered some methods of membership categorization whereby the sense of a reference as a reference to "deviance" (in school) may be achieved.[6] Before concluding this chapter, I should comment on several features of the use of these methods. First, category membership and the recognition of references to deviance are mutually constituted. These references can be heard as references to deviance because of the assumed membership categories of the referent, speaker, and hearer. The membership categories of the referent, speaker, and hearer are constituted by and through these references (to deviance).

Second, these methods reveal the mutual constitution of normality and deviance (see Douglas, 1970; Lynch, 1983). In particular, the discussion of the contrastive procedure for achieving referential recognition indicates that deviance and normality are mutually constituted in the course of the work of membership categorization. Just as a sense of "deviance" is constituted by reference to a presumed normality, so it is that normality is constituted through the recognition of deviance.

Finally, the methods and procedures explicated in this chapter not only provide for the intelligibility of particular references to deviance, but also establish the ground for the subject matter of the sociology of deviance. Without these methods of practical reasoning—according to which references to deviance may be recognized—such subject matter would be unintelligible.

Notes

1. That *description* or *referencing* rather than *interpretation* is the preferred term here reflects the critique of the mentalistic model of interpretation. See Hester (1985).

2. This list is an analyst's device; it does not address what distinctions members themselves may make among "types" of references.

3. Payne (1976) has observed this reflexivity in the context of classroom lessons: "The double aspects of the hearing of the utterance as performing some activity and as membershipping the speaker and the hearers are mutually constitutive productions; each analysis informs on the other analyzed elements and together they provide for the constitution of the situation for what it is" (p. 36). This applies to referral consultations in the same way: The membership categories are used to make sense of the utterances as "referral talk" and the "referral talk" confirms the sense of occasion as a referral consultation between teacher and psychologist.

4. The analysis presented here suggests that "normative sociology" is not so much a form of sociological explanation (largely discredited) as it is a members' method of practical reasoning. It is by reference to category-related norms, for example, that a sense of references to deviance may be understood. The intelligibility of these notions—deviance and conformity—rests upon these methods.

5. The invocation of the category-bound norms in terms of which the pupil's features appear contrastive presumes that the membership category to which these norms are bound is already known. This, as has been shown in the case of "stealing," involves the method of coselection. "Running away," like "stealing," may be used in a variety of senses. For example, it may refer to running away "from home," "from danger," "from

the teacher," or "from school." A first task then is to achieve the sense in which the "running away" is intended. This achievement is possible through inspection of the words coselected with "running away." These include "this morning" and "down the corridor." There is no mention of danger, fire, bullies, or other causes that might make running away sensible. Given the membership category of the speaker—a teacher—and the reference to "down the corridor," it is possible to hear this as a reference to running away from a teacher or from school rather than as some other category of "running away."

6. This discussion does not exhaust the analysis of such methods. Indeed, space does not permit an examination of their full range. Other methods, not discussed here, include the use of the consistency rule and the use of location descriptors.

10

Two Incommensurable, Asymmetrically Alternate Technologies of Social Analysis

HAROLD GARFINKEL
D. LAWRENCE WIEDER

In 1987 Harold Garfinkel was invited by Richard Heyman and Robert M. Seiler to write an article for the *Discourse Analysis Research Group Newsletter* to mark the twentieth anniversary of the publication of *Studies in Ethnomethodology.* He collected the work of a company of ethnomethodologists with the theme of their work's achievement as the claim that a corpus of ethnomethodological studies offered evidence for locally produced, naturally accountable phenomena of order*,[1] logic, reason, meaning, method, and so on, in and as of the unavoidable and irremediable haecceity[2] of immortal, ordinary society.[3] That claim was explicated in three articles that precede this one: Part I was called "An Announcement of Studies," part II was "The Curious Seriousness of Professional Sociology," and part III was called "Instructed Action." [4] This chapter is an abbreviated version of the fourth in that series.

In this chapter two cases in which a *topic* of order* is respecified as a locally produced, naturally accountable *phenomenon* of order* are examined.[5] With two cases the argument is sketched that whenever this is done, but just in any actual case in vivo, the respecified phenomenon of order* demonstrably possesses two incommensurable, asymmetrically alternate technologies in and as of the particular phenomenon's production, observability, recognition, accountability, demonstrability, and so on. The paired technologies and their relationships are unavoidable, irremediable[6] details of the particular phenomenon of order*.

In this chapter we shall briefly describe two pairs and their relationships. We will mention several other pairs. Each pair, described or mentioned, is a case of a phenomenon of order* in its own right. The two described pairs and their relationships are collected and summarized as the first rendering theorem.

Necessarily undemonstrated, because the argument's materials are abbreviated, the argument's principal claim is this: A comparison of EM policies and methods with those of classic studies in the studies by each of order* in and as immortal, ordinary society reveals EM's distinctive policies and methods. On the grounds of the distinctions between classic and EM studies of achieved phenomena of order* a general result is proposed, as follows: Just and only in any actual case in vivo, every phenomenon of order* exists as, in that it is composed of, two incommensurable, asymmetrically alternate technologies for the production, analysis, understanding, description, disclosure of, and observability of order* in and as of practical action's and practical reasoning's chiasmically embodied details. These pairs are collected as cases of a phenomenon of order* in its own right. This phenomenon is specified with a schedule of rendering theorems.

After "An Announcement of Studies" appeared in their newsletter, Heyman and Seiler asked Arthur Frank to explain it for newsletter readers. Frank (1988) offered this synopsis: "It is Garfinkel's central contention that order is already complete in the concrete." His synopsis gives to the parts of this series their direction as steps of an argument.

Why Be Concerned?

An expanding academic industry is committed to exhibit the pairs with careful, technical scholarly specifics. We want to offer an alternative to its programs. We want to recommend about these pairs, as phenomena, that there is more to these pairs than taking note of their separate components provides or can provide no matter with what scholarly care the two are distinguished; no matter with what skill the members of the pair are unified in devices of generic representation and formal analytic theorizing; and most particularly no matter with what technical dedication the members of the pair are specified in formal analytic descriptions of fact. The more there is to these pairs makes up a domain of phenomena that this industry depends upon the existence of, requires and uses as indispensable details of its own enterprises, and ignores.

That domain of phenomena can be addressed with the question: Just what in the world *can* a pair *look like* in and as the actual in vivo achieved relevances as of which the phenomena of order* consist? What *can* a pair look like in the real-world occasions where *a* pair is to be found composing an object in detail? What in the world can a pair look like composing the haecceities of a phenomenon of order*? What in the world can a pair, by what it consists of, look like composing the instructably reproducible haecceities of phenomena of order*?

Issues that specify this phenomenon are collected and come to a head in EM studies of discovering work in the natural sciences. Many of these issues are luminously the teachable achievement of Dusan Bjelic and Michael Lynch in their brilliantly original and seminal chapter in this volume.

A Comparison of Classic and Ethnomethodological Studies of the Workings of Immortal, Ordinary Society

Professional sociology and ethnomethodology agree that the animal they are hunting is the production and the accountability of order* in and as immortal, ordinary society. Not *any* old immortal, ordinary society, but immortal, ordinary society really and not imaginably; actually and not supposedly; and these evidently, distinctively, and in detail. For both, every topic of order, reason, logic, meaning, and method is to be discovered as the workings of immortal, ordinary society.

To carry out this program both disciplines reconstrue the endless *topics* of order* as *phenomena* of order*. Both do so by adding to a topic of order* the suffix, in-about-and-as-immortal-ordinary-society. For example, the topic rational action becomes the candidate phenomenon rational-action-in-about-and-as-immortal-ordinary-society. The same is done for rules, signs, production, causes, inquiry, evidence, proof, knowledge, consciousness, reason, practical action, comparability, uniformity, reliability, validity, objectivity, observability, detail, and structure. For both disciplines no terms of order* are excepted or need to be excepted.

Further, both insist that a certain emphasis be incorporated into the technical work of respecification. The emphasis is that in actual inquiries and not otherwise the production and accountability of order*, in and as the workings of ordinary society, be worked out to accord with the commitments of professional sociology and the social sciences to the problem of social order. We understand by these commitments that professional social analysts are required, as the day's work, seriously to specify the production and the accountability of the phenomena of order* in and as immortal, ordinary society while requiring that the practical objectivity and the practical observability of immortal, ordinary society, which are vexed issues, be consulted *just because* these are vexed issues, to settle all issues of adequacy. Among these issues is the omniprevalent and controlling issue of descriptive precision.[7]

Both understand by descriptive precision that their overriding concerns for adequacy contain the probativeness of social analysis. Both disciplines insist on that. By *probativeness* is meant that an issue can get settled. Straightforward cases of probativeness are found in the natural sciences—in physics, for example (Holton, 1978).

There is unanimous agreement in both disciplines, classic studies of ordinary activities and EM studies, and in the social sciences, that wherever issues of adequacy are of concern, the issue of descriptive precision is primordial, and unavoidably so.

It would look like classic studies and EM studies agree, and entirely. It is true that they have very much to do with each other, and this is the case wherever the work of one or the other is done, as we hope to show. Nevertheless, they do not agree.

Distinctive emphases on the production and accountability of order* in and as ordinary activities identify ethnomethodological studies of order* and set them in contrast to classic studies as an incommensurably alternate technology of social analysis. We use the expression *classic studies of order* to speak of essentially incarnate inquiries, that is, inquiries that in the work of being carried out are locally produced and locally managed and accountable details of the setting's phenomena they have under examination, and that *therein* make up the technical goods of the indefinitely many arts and sciences of practical action: budget analysis, arbitration law, operations research, management science, sociology and the social sciences, artificial intelligence, histories of this and that, industrial engineering, clinical psychiatry, laboratory methodologies in the natural sciences, and the "occult" aids to decision making in everyday life, such as astrology. Their inquiries address the *lived* work of order* production; they make use of the orderlinesses that are found in the lived work of order* production. They know of its existence. They depend upon its existence as grounds for their own demonstrable adequacy. And in all these respects, and in just these respects, their inquiries, being unavoidably and without remedy incarnate, are nonetheless conducted (a) as naturally theoretic inquiries, (b) with the policies and methods of constructive analysis, and (c) for all questions of adequate accountability of the phenomena of practical action use established theories of logic to make them decidable as issues of truth and correctness.[8] So, for example, an inquirer's privileged use of a transcendental analyst can provide for the real worldness of the phenomena under examination as being prior to, indifferent to, and independent of the methods that are used to obtain access to them. Another privileged use provides for what talking, speaking, recording, reading, writing, diagramming, counting, representing could *possibly* be doing that makes up the achievement of instructable production and adequate accountability of real-world phenomena of practical action and practical reasoning. These are two of many privileges that can be exercised by an inquirer's use of one or another transcendental analyst as a device.

In order to compare classic studies of order* with ethnomethodological studies, consider the distinguishing emphases of each on demonstrable structures as a topic of order*. Each in its distinctive ways is preoccupied with studies of structure in order to claim just what real-worldly ordinary society is, just what adequate analysis of it could be, and just what real ordinary society and its adequate analysis have to do with each other. But it is their point, too, that in the material particulars of that preoccupation, in the craft of that preoccupation, they differ profoundly and without the possibility of reconciliation. On every topic in sociology's many visions of the problem of social order they are irreconcilably claimants to what ordinary society and its analysis could be. Thus they differ on the nature of "immortal" society; on the work of its production and reproduction; on its objectivity and observability; on its "account-ability"; that "it sits in judgment on every account of itself" on its status as source and grounds of effective practices, objective knowledge, reasoned discourse, or rational action; on its intelligibility; on its exhibitable analyzability in and as distinctive and technical detail, and on what detail, let alone on what *such* detail could possibly be.

Furthermore, for the endless topics of order, reason, logic, meaning, and method they "agree" only in a Pickwickian sense of "agree" that what these topics consist of as phenomena is posed by ordinary society as the origins and grounds for their production, observability, objectivity, and accountability. Similarly, only in their distinctive and different ways of speaking tendentiously[9] of these topics of order*, and only by conflating each other's lingoes, do they "agree" on the availability "in, about, and as" ordinary society of its awesomely massive and consequential, local achievements of these phenomena.

They do *not* agree. Of course they do not agree. Not only do they not agree, but in their differing treatments of these phenomena each exhibits itself as a distinct technical preoccupation with these phenomena, and incommensurable with the other. The preoccupation of each with the phenomena of order* in, about, and as ordinary society identifies classic versus ethnomethodological studies of order* as an incommensurable, asymmetrically alternate technology of social analysis.

But merely to call attention to their differences distracts us from attending to their differences as positive phenomena of ordinary society and thereby misses the point of the distinctions: that the identifying task of ethnomethodological studies of order* is to furnish to the phenomena of order* production their genetic origins in and as immortal ordinary society; that every received topic of order* without exception is a candidate for these interests; that these topics include classic accounts of the phenomena of order* production and classic accounting technologies; that because of this inclusion, classic studies of order* and ethnomethodological studies are asymmetrically related alternate technologies for the analysis and demonstration of the production of order*; that their incommensurable asymmetric alternativity is an order* phenomenon in its own right; and because this is so their reconciliation is pointless.

Ethnomethodological Policies and Methods

Ethnomethodologically, every *topic* of order*—every topic of order, logic, meaning, reason, and method—is eligible to be found as a *phenomenon* of order*. Every *topic* of order* offers to ethnomethodological study its candidacy to a search for a *phenomenon* of order* as an achievement in and as of practical action. Every topic of order* will

offer itself to the craft of ethnomethodology as an achieved phenomenon of order*, to finding the topic as a phenomenon of order*, finding
it with the use of EM policies and methods, finding the phenomenon as
an only discoverable achieved phenomenon of order*, or to collecting,
examining, describing, indicating, respecifying, or teaching a topic of
order* as a phenomenon of order*. Any of the indefinitely many topics
of order* are eligible for discovery.

The technical, distinctive jobs of EM, the *craft* of EM, consist of in
vivo tasks of discovering phenomena of order* as instructable achievements in and as of their coherent details. EM's results are identical with
radical phenomena of order*.

Its maxims, policies, instructions, and methods are singular to and
distinctive of EM studies. They are incommensurable, asymmetrically
alternate to the corpus of policies and methods of classic studies. They
furnish the sole grounds for explicating EM findings. With their use
EM findings are to be treated as corrigible claims written as sketch
accounts. They are to be read praxeologically as first segments of
lebenswelt pairs. And they had to be found out.

About Ethnomethodological Methods and Policies

What are these methods? Since EM's methods are discoverable phenomena of order* in their own right, they are not methods as methods
are "straightforwardly" understood. The fact that EM's methods are
discoverable phenomena of order* in their own right is not, however, a
mere nicety or convenience, or simply an automatic EM response to any
topic, problem, or issue (a sort of standard EM turn or twist). The fact
that EM's methods are discoverable phenomena of order* in their own
right is central to EM's treatment of methodogenesis, the relation of EM
methods to EM knowledge, its position on phenomena of order* as prior
to and independent of their EM study, the place of competence as a
reflexive constituent of the "work" to which that competence is addressed, and more. These features are partially expressed in the unique
adequacy requirement of EM methods and in EM's use of perspicuous
settings. Space permits only brief discussion of other EM methods and
policies.

The Unique Adequacy Requirements
of Methods

This policy accompanies the policy that a phenomenon of order* is available in the *lived* in-courseness of its local production and natural accountability.

In its weak use the unique adequacy requirement of methods is identical with the requirement that for the analyst to recognize, or identify, or follow the development of, or describe phenomena of order* in local production of coherent detail the analyst must be *vulgarly* competent in the local production and reflexively natural accountability of the phenomenon of order* he is "studying." We will replace the abbreviation "studying" with the specific requirement that the analyst be, with others, in a concerted competence of methods with which to recognize, identify, follow, display, and describe phenomena of order* in local productions of coherent detail. These methods are uniquely possessed in, and as of, the *object's* endogenous local production and natural accountability.

In its strong use the unique adequacy requirement of methods is identical with the following corpus-specific finding of EM studies. Available to EM research, the finding is used and administered locally as an instruction: *Just in any actual case* a phenomenon of order* already possesses whatever as methods methods could be of [finding it] if [methods for finding it] are at issue. Comparably, a phenomenon of order* already possesses whatever as methods methods could be of [observing], of [recognizing], of [counting], of [collecting], of [topicalizing], of [describing] it, and so on, if, and as of the in vivo lived local production and natural accountability of the phenomenon, [observing], [recognizing], [counting], [collecting], [topicalizing], or [describing] it is at issue.

For example, say the analyst is concerned to find *a* single conversation at a cocktail party and say *any* single conversation will do, then *a* single conversation—*just that* single conversation—will already be possessed of whatever [finding just it] could consist of that someone as an adequate finder of just that single conversation, with others, would have to be competently busied with.

So, at a cocktail party an analyst searching for a single conversation who, say, doesn't know how to "do" *a* greeting in French when that conversation is going on in French may use something other and different than the work of *just that* company talking conversationally in French, perhaps something inadequate or incongruous to what it takes to be in the specifically unremarkable presence of *just that* company talking *just-this-time-through* conversationally in French.

To find a conversation while disregarding the unique adequacy requirement the analyst might use a procedure for counting turns at talk such as the procedure that Stephan and Mishler (1955, pp. 367-379) designed and administered to describe how frequencies of participation were distributed among members of different sizes of tutorial groups at Princeton. They tape-recorded tutorial meetings of various sizes from two to seven students. Then they decided upon a definition of a tallyable turn at talk: They would *find* parties busied talking in allocated turns of talk by administering a definition of what it was to find *in the tape,* that could be listened to repeatedly, and indefinitely many times, that someone was talking. The analyst listened to and listened for, and for as long as, a same person was heard to be talking, and who continued to talk until that listened for person was no longer heard to be talking; that person was listened for and was heard *not* to be talking. At that point a tally was entered if another person was then heard. After the first person had been correctly tallied, then the next person listened to and listened for was the eligible second. If the person heard to be talking was the same person, then it was listened for and heard that that first person, after the pause, continued to talk.

That is another way to find a conversation. The thing that is gorgeous about it is also what is interestingly cockeyed about it: It's a no news can't lose enterprise. If you start with a careful definition you're halfway home, but only halfway. You still have to make a tape recording. Then, by listening to the taped talk you must listen to it for events provided for in your definition over the vicissitudes of having to find in the *taped* talk such in vivo ordinary *things* as [a person who was talking has stopped talking and a next person is talking after that person has stopped talking]. These are *hearably* lived in vivo ordinary organizational things. In their study of preschoolers at "snack time," Lawrence Wieder and his associates (1988) remind us that these events, *being done by and available to the parties first time through,* are for both lay and professional analysts, at one and the same time *easily* recognized and *intractably* difficult to describe. As they show, it is organizationally the case that they are both. It is incongruous, then, that exactly the phenomena of first time through escape professional analysts. They escape in the very way that analysts administer their definitions over the contingencies that the tapes present to their own search in the tapes for formal descriptive facts of conversation's endogenous achievements. Reflexively, these contingencies compose and assure their work with the tapes' repeated play as just the work that is needed to make their definitions come true.

In contrast, ethnomethodology is concerned to locate and examine the concerted vulgar uniquely adequate competencies of order* production.

About Perspicuous Settings

A perspicuous setting has nothing to do with Webster on perspicacity or with places of geography and architecture. The term collects the policies and methods of EM research for an actual, in vivo occasion of inquiry. We have found it useful to explain the term _perspicuous setting_ by saying ethnomethodology is "embedded" in a local culture—such as law school teaching, mathematics, pickup basketball, the islands of the Pacific Trust Territory—and under that condition the analyst examines various objects in that culture, respectively—classroom cases in civil procedure, Godel's theorem, "following," and how federal programs in medical and mental health fail in Oceania.

When this synopsis is read as instructions it offers this advice to researchers: _Embedded_ is used synonymously and interchangeably with phenomena of order* that are provided for _just in any actual case and only then_ by administering EM's policies, and with the use of EM methods. With these policies and methods our questions are specified: What did we do? What did we learn? A perspicuous setting makes available, in that it consists of, material disclosures of practices of local production and natural accountability in technical details _with which to find, examine, elucidate, learn of, show, and teach the organizational object as an in vivo work site._[10]

Finding Perspicuous Settings by Using Sacks's Gloss

Many procedures have been used to find perspicuous settings. One of them consists of searching for, recognizing, selecting, collecting, and deciding upon a perspicuous setting by using Harvey Sacks's gloss. It can be used repeatedly, and quite deliberately. Its particular virtue is that its use teaches what "embedding" consists of as actual, work-site-specific EM analytic practices.

In 1963 Sacks and Garfinkel were at the Los Angeles Suicide Prevention Center. One day Sacks came into Garfinkel's office: "Harold, I have a distinction." It is relevant to this story that Sacks had finished Yale Law School two years before, because the distinction at first sounds very legalistic. "I have a distinction between 'possessables' and 'possessitives.' By a possessable I'll mean *this*; I might as well mean this; I'll mean this for the time being with which to learn from others, by having them teach me, just what I'm really talking about: You're walking down the street; you see something; it looks attractive; you'd like to have it; and you see of the thing, that you'd like to have, that you can have it. You *see* that of the thing. As compared with: You're in the street; you see something attractive; you'd like to have it, but seeing the thing you'd like to have you see about it that you can't have it. You *see* it belongs to somebody. I'll call that a 'possessitive.'

"Now, Harold, what do I mean by that distinction? That is what I want to *find out*. I don't want you to tell me. I don't want to settle it like that. I *could* go to the UCLA law library; I know how to use it. I could find discussions that would bear on what I might as well mean, but that's not the way I want to learn what I mean." He trusted himself to write definitions, "but I don't want to write definitions; and I don't want to consult authorities. Instead, I want to *find* a work group, somewhere, perhaps in Los Angeles, who, *as their day's work*, and because they know it as their day's work, will be able to teach me what *I* could be talking about as *they* know it as the day's work."

One day he came in with a great grin; he'd found such a group. In the Los Angeles Police Department are police who, in riding around their territories, as part of their work, spot cars that have been abandoned. Other cars look equally bad, but it could be found out that they were not abandoned. You call the tow truck for one of these cars; the other you ticket. As their day's work the police must make this distinction; make it fast; make it subject to supervisory review for the truth, correctness, and other adequacies of the recognition; make it in each particular case; do so within the bureaucratically organized Los Angeles Police Department; and having among its consequences that various parties, who as members of populations that can properly become involved, become forensically interested parties to issues of truth and correctness.

To find a perspicuous setting the EM policy provides that the analyst looks to find, as of the haecceities of some local gang's work affairs, the organizational *thing* that they are up against and that they can be brought to teach the analyst what he needs to learn and to know from them, with which, by learning from them, to teach *them* what their affairs consist of as locally produced, locally occasioned, and locally ordered, locally described, locally questionable, counted, recorded, observed *phenomena of order*, in and as of their in vivo accountably doable coherent and cogent detail for each another next first time.*

The standing task in finding perspicuous settings is to administer Sacks's gloss in and as of the search, doing so over the *in situ* vicissitudes of the search.

A characteristic EM policy consists of administering ethnomethodological indifference over the exigencies of inquiry and argument. From the day it was announced, ethnomethodological indifference was commonly understood as naughty advice. Many persons complain that it is one more inside cheap shot in professional sociology's history of writings that denigrate the skills and achievements of its social science disciplines.

Limits of space will not permit a discussion of the details of administering* that policy. But unless we examine administering's* details the policy merely "evokes" its work-site availability as instructions. As a work-site detail the policy is the first segment of an instructed action.

We insist, the policy has nothing to do with skepticism. It is a procedure of not *needing* to consult the corpus of classic methods and findings with which to carry out the tasks of EM research. For the time being, we will carry out the tasks of our research while abstaining from the use of the classic corpus of findings, policies, methods, and the rest. The policy does not advocate the abandonment of established studies. It is a research practice; one does it as an observance, something like driving in traffic effectively and correctly teaches one to observe it as a skill. Administering ethnomethodological indifference is an instructable way to work in such a fashion as specifically and deliberately, over actual exigencies of the research, to pay no ontological judgmental attention to the established corpus of social science. The policy requires that the tasks of inquiry and argument provide for the practical objectivity and the practical observability of structures of practical action and practical reason in and as of ordinary activities while exercising an indifference to the policies of natural theorizing, withholding the corpus status of formal analytic descriptive facts, avoiding the design and administration of generic representations and their methodized dopes, and in related ways making no use of the methods of constructive analysis.[11]

The Rendering Theorem

Table 10.1 lists several perspicuous settings and their affiliated topics of order* with which to learn about and teach the locally produced, naturally accountable lived orderliness of a phenomenon of order*.

Within the vocabulary and syntax of the rendering theorems, the locally produced, naturally accountable lived phenomenon of order* is referred to with ticked brackets—{ }. While we sometimes use empty ticked brackets, we prefer to write ticked brackets with an enclosed text, for example, {Freeway traveling wave}. With ticked brackets we refer to the lived equipmentally affiliated in vivo in-courseness of the work that is being spoken of, the work *about* which, and of course, at times, *as of* which, the enclosed text is a way to speak. The matter that is being "talked" with a text enclosed in ticked brackets is always a *particular* matter.

An arrow, →, is used to refer to professional social analysts' skilled use of *methodic procedures*. Accounts, ( ), are specified by analysts with →. This specifying is done on the grounds of analysts' careful, technical, skillful administration of →. With →, warrant is provided for accounts of phenomena that → are used to find, collect, specify, make topically reasoned, make observable, and the rest.

These matters, { }, →, and ( ), are written in three positions as in Figure 10.1. Each position marks a column. Matters found in the third position, ( ), are *signed objects*. By a signed object we mean that the object, ( ), consists of a collection of signs.

Perspicuous settings serve as case studies with which we can identify and relate { }, →, and ( ). The availability of { }, →, and ( ) in one or another of several specifying relationships is noted as rendering theorems.

Table 10.1. A Selection from the Em *Corpus* of Perspicuous Settings
and their Affiliated Topics of Order*

For each perspicuous setting the questions are asked: (1) What more, other, different than, depended upon, identifying, but uninteresting and ignored is there to the phenomenon of order* being examined than classic studies, did, ever did, or *can* provide for? (2) What did we do? What did we learn? For each perspicuous setting the setting's affiliated topics of order* are respecified as phenomena of order*.

Chair assembly instructions [Distinctions between instructions read in texts and instructions read as incarnate details of the settings in which they are being "followed"*]

Inverting lenses: "Sit over there" [Synaesthesias of instructed action*]

Inverting lenses: Blackboard writing [Apt and familiar efficacy of trivial but indispensable embodied skills*]

Playing chess while wearing inverting lenses [Accountably and evidently reasoned play in chess*]

Typing and writing thoughtful words [Distinctions between observably transcendent and observably in vivo typing and writing with something in mind*] (Sudnow)

The work of magicians designing tricks [Witnessable and accountable action-as-a-rule*] (Wieder)

Using auditory side-tone delay apparatus to elucidate [The in vivo work of listening to and listening for what is said with which to hear what is meant in and as of the normal sound of one's own voice in detail*]

Listening to and listening for Bach-at-work [Relativized Gurwitschian properties of Bach's figures* provide to phrasing, tempo, rhythm, tonal dynamics, etc., their instructably hearable details* that are both distinctive to his craft and to his corpus, and are omnirelevant to them]

"There's a Gap in the literature" according to the directors of the natural science libraries at UCLA [The unavailability of any materials that are pedagogically relevant to any of teaching's work-sites in a particular natural science that specify the first and second segments of Lebenswelt Pairs]

Heath's visual proof of the Pythagorean theorem [The work of mathematical proving*]

Consulting occasion maps in a way-finding journey [Locally occasioned, locally achieved properties of clarity, consistency, completeness, meaning, method, errors, mistakes, omissions, rational action, logic, order, etc. of occasion maps*]

Galileo's inclined plane demonstration of the motion of bodies in free fall [Provisions for the probativeness of Galileo's demonstration in classic science studies; in contrast are the phenomenal field properties of Galileo's experiment provided for in EM studies.]

Robert Herman's demonstration and specification of freeway traveling waves [Formulating and solving the problem of how to increase the rate of flow posed by the Hudson River Tunnel Authority by finding and operating on indicators*]

Note: In the period June 1987 to August 1989, one or more of these perspicuous settings was reported by Harold Garfinkel and discussed at colloquia at UC San Diego, UC Santa Barbara, Boston University, University of Wisconsin, Écolen des Hautes Études, Western Behavioral Science Institute, Temple University, University of Oklahoma, and University of Calgary.

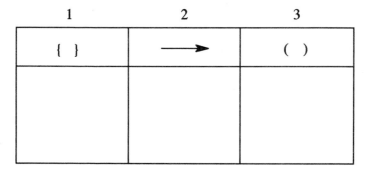

Figure 10.1.

Two Cases

Bill Bryant's Exercise

Let's start with a simple example in which we have the phenomenal field of some human job and a classic account that *some*how accompanies it, respectively { } and ( ). In vivo musical performances offer a gold mine of these pairs.

Bill Bryant demonstrated a pair of these, { } and ( ), and their relationship[12] with some rhythmic clapping. We can sharpen the points to be made by loading his exercise with recording machinery.

Imagine that I have a metronome. I select a tempo and set it going. At the same time I turn on the microphone to an audio recorder, start a video recorder whose camera is focused on the metronome and me, and plug in a digital clock, which enters a visual time signal on the tape. The pieces of apparatus are now furnishing the beats per minute for the metronome; the speed of the tapes; the audible and, separately, the visual elapsed time of travel of the two tapes between record and playback heads; the recorded frames per second of the camera; the speed and detail of the clock display; and so on. I fiddle with the machinery until the recordings are synchronized. To try out the whole thing I clap to the beat of the metronome. When I do I hear the metronome beat, I hear it in the speaker, I see it on the video screen, I see me clapping, I take note of the registered timed values of the metronome arm's travel, and so on.

We'll write → for any or all of the various recording procedures that the equipment provides, ( ) for any or all of the recordings, and { } for any actual episode of clapping, some examples of which would be {′...′...}, {′.′.′.′.}, {″....″....′.′.″}.
Some observations:

(1) Via a particular recording procedure, →, each of the recordings respecifies a performed clapping { } as filmic, or audio, or metronomic details. These details are specific to the recording procedure.

(2) Each and any of the different recordings of {′...′...}, {′.′.′.′.}, (′...′...), and so on can be specified definitely and clearly with the arithmetic properties of clock time.

(3) Each of the different recordings is dense with arithmetic properties to indefinite depths of specifying details.

(4) Each recording of { } respecifies it as a formal scheme of { }'s arithmetic properties, that is, ( ).

(5) The formal scheme of { }'s arithmetic properties, that is, ( ), exhibits the analyzability of { } as formal descriptive facts of { }. Warrant for the formally described facticity of { } is furnished by →.

Of course there are many further observations. Now we ask: If we are playing the piano, or if we are singing, *how* does the beating of the metronome and its arithmetic properties, and *how* do the audio and the video recordings with the arithmetic properties of their filmic and audio details recover the lived phenomenal field properties of our singing? From the question we recognize that something is fishy. If we are busied singing, or if we are playing the piano, then, as David Sudnow knows it and teaches, we are making the time we need. Making the time we need is to be compared with the time that the metronome is marking. The metronome can provide constraints on making the time we need by marking the time that our singing or our playing takes. With the pair we are in the midst of an organizational thing: We can't take all the time in the world to play the prelude.

Now we have two "assemblages" of accountable playing's haecceities: In one case we have playing's in vivo developingly phenomenal details, a locally produced, locally accountable phenomenon of order*, making the time we need—carried on, however, to satisfy, in this example—the beating of the metronome under the piano teacher's complaining instruction, "For crying out loud, you'll never get to be a piano player. You never change from one chord to the next. Don't think a song can be played in any damned time it takes you to go through the piece. You have to get it done from beginning to end, so that others—and even you (Fraise, 1963)—can hear what you're playing, and certainly before everybody dies of boredom."

More: Just in any actual case of an in vivo musical performance we can always find the pair. Whenever we find the pair, but just and only in any actual case, both are available *together* as in vivo, in-course revealed details of a witnessable and examinable demonstration.

With the following demonstration Bryant made observable how the pair can be involved with each other. Set a metronome beating. Then clap to the metronome's beat in such a fashion that you can't hear the metronome. Also make a tape recording so that later you can discriminate the rhythmic clapping from the metronome's beat. Now, if you can't hear the beat from the metronome then it is at least questionable to claim that the metronome is cuing you. So the rhythmic beat is the achievement of another course of work. On these grounds Bryant posed the question: What more does the endogenously achieved coherence of pulsed details consist of if the clapping isn't cued but nevertheless comes out metronomically right? Bryant pointed out that nothing is instructably reproducible by calling the achievement "rhythm." Talk of rhythm only made a vexed problem worse. The mocking question remains unaddressed: What could rhythm possibly be, this "rhythm" that can't be found as locally, endogenously produced orderliness, but neither can it be gotten by allowing, "Some persons have rhythm." Nonetheless the synchronous pulsing is massively and easily done, and easily mimicked and recognized. Withal, as Sudnow points out, pedagogies for musical performances have never lacked analytic descriptions of musical achievements of phrasing, pace, duration, emphasis, rhythms, but in the absence of local apprenticeships these pedagogies remain intractable to instructably reproducible achievement.

That is a first case of a pair. Just in an actual case, by doing it we learn there are two; they are hitched; they have to do with each other, unavoidably and without remedy; and they have to do with each other by way of the locally embodied workplace equipmentally affiliated production of the two. The locally embodied production of the two specifies a chiasmically hearable course of rhythmic pulses as an only developingly coherent "sounded doing." The sounded doing's coherence is found and provided for (a) in an endogenous, followably accountable "making," that is, in an endogenous logic; (b) in its immediately in-hand intelligibility of a world "not yet" reflected upon;

(c) with form emerging endogenously *as contents* rather than form consisting of "pure forms" as an abstraction from contents and then theorized as "imposing order properties" on circumstantial or experiential flux; and (d) nowhere is there relevantly and "with stability of meaning" organizational things "in evidence." Instead, just and only in an actual case and then entirely, there is the organizational thing *evidently, really, actually,* and these *unremarkably and ordinarily.*[13]

Summoning Phones

I'm fond of an exercise that I have used with undergraduates and graduates.[14] I offer you the privilege of hearing the exercise from beginning to end without being required to do it as a condition for hearing more from me beyond my insistence that you do what I ask.

I'll speak to you in the present hypothetical tense. Here's what I *would* ask you to do. Here's what you *would* have done. Here's what we *would* do after you had done what I asked before we came together and as a condition for our coming together. At that time you *would* have brought your tapes and your notes that described what you had done. I too would have done several tapes. From your notes and mine I would show you what we had done and what was to be learned: for your autonomous assessment based on your materials.

The assignment. Here is what I want you to do. After class, and before our next meeting, get the following *things* on tape.

First, tape-record five episodes of a phone that is hearably summoning you, hearably just you, nobody else, and hearably everybody knows it. I'm talking about hearable detail. I'm asking you to get five tape recordings in hearable detail of a phone hearably summoning just you. Get five episodes of that on tape.

With *each* of the five tape-recorded episodes keep notes. For each taped episode write in your notebook just what you had to do: Where did you go? Why there? Who said what? What was easy about it? What was troublesome? Who were you with? When was it done? What was the date? What was the time of day? When did you begin? When did you stop? Be thorough; be good reporters; cover who, what, when, where, what happened then, what happened after that. *For each episode.*

Second, get five tape-recorded episodes of a phone that is hearably summoning someone else, hearably not you, and hearably anybody knows it. Get five episodes on tape. You must get five tape-recorded episodes. And for each episode you must keep notes.

Third, collect five episodes of a phone that is hearably *simulating* a phone hearably summoning you. And for each keep notes. By *simulating* we'll understand that I'm asking for five episodes of a phone that *hearably* deliberately and by your design *resembles* a phone hearably summoning just you. For each episode keep careful notes.

Fourth, tape-record five episodes of a phone that *hearably* deliberately and by your design *resembles* a phone hearably summoning someone else, a phone simulating a phone *certainly not* summoning you, and hearably anyone knows it. For each episode keep careful notes.

Fifth, tape five episodes of a phone hearably ringing. Just ringing. It is hearably *not* summoning, at all. Hearably it's just ringing. For each episode keep notes.

Still speaking in the present hypothetical tense, I would urge that you find time during the next few days to collect those taped episodes and that you keep notes that describe what you did to get each taped episode.

Then we would meet. I would play the tape that *I* had made. I would preface the playback by telling you I thought you'd want to hear a tape recording of a phone hearably summoning me because should you have to recall what it *sounds* like from having heard it so many times that would still leave the remembered and recognized details beyond recovery, but when they were *told* you could be surprised, and you would agree.

You would all know what would be in the record. It would be pretty much as you imagined: br-r-r-r br-r-r-r. That's one *tape recording* of a phone hearably summoning me. Next we have a tape recording of a phone hearably summoning someone else, certainly *not* summoning me. Then we hear a simulation of the phone summoning me. And so on until we hear an episode of a phone hearably just ringing.

Now we need a board display. Let's list the following. In the first column: {A phone summoning me}, 5 episodes, numbered 1-5; {A phone summoning you}, 5 episodes, numbered 6-10; {A simulation of a phone summoning me}, 5 episodes, numbered 11-15; {A simulation of a phone summoning you}, 5 episodes, numbered 16-20; {A ringing phone}, 5 episodes, numbered 21-25.

We'll write in the second column: A methodic procedure with which to specify and analyze the 25 episodes, 5 collections of 5 episodes each, which are the phones in the first column.

In the third column we'll write the account that we get when we administer a methodic procedure to each taped episode of a phone in the first column that is hearably summoning me; to each episode of a phone that is hearably summoning someone else, not me; and so on.

To specify this methodic procedure we'll use a set that consists of a line, ——, and a squiggle, ∿ ; and a collection of rules for administering them as follows: We'll play the tape. As long as we hear a silence we'll continue to draw a line; as long we hear a ringing we'll make and continue a squiggle. Call these the set of rules, (R).

In the third column we'll write the account we get when we administer (——, ∿) according to the set of rules (R), to each of the tape-recorded episodes.

After we had come together for our next meeting I would insert the tape I had made, saying to you, "I made several tapes. Let me play one, since it's possible you have never heard a phone summoning me, but not you." I start the tape, and start drawing a line along the board for the silence. The phone rings and I draw a squiggle. I continue across the board, back and forth several times, for several cycles of silences and rings. The board looks like Figure 10.2.

I ask the class, no one in particular, did any of you get taped calls that sound like mine, and that would look like that? Some students nod. They're wary. They don't see the point. I ask them to consult their ethnographic notes.

Via the ethnographies we come upon some findings in each episode, for each taped collection of five.

The requirement that five episodes be tape-recorded of a phone hearably summoning just you drew complaints, denunciations, refusals, bewilderment. For example:

I really didn't know when I should turn on the tape recorder, because I didn't know what—what you wanted me to do. Was I to simply turn it on until I got an episode of the phone ringing? I went into the living room, from the bedroom. My husband was asleep. I turned on the tape recorder. I turned it off. I didn't know what you wanted. How long was I supposed to wait?! I know I wasn't supposed to call anyone to set it up—to *ask* them—because that wouldn't be the phone that is hearably summoning just me. That would be a phone summoning by arrangement. (SV)

Another student wrote:

Later that day L and I are sitting around in my apartment still thinking about this weird . . . assignment. The phone rings. We scream our delight—another episode, and not a staged one! (LM & BR)

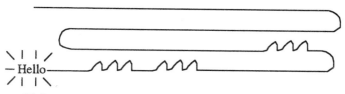

Figure 10.2.

I would then go to the board diagram (Figure 10.2) and point to the first very long line, the line that has coded the first tape-recorded silence. I would call your attention to your bewilderment, your anger, your charges that the assignment is pointless, impossible, I'm stupid, you don't have all the time in the world to get just one of these let alone five, and for what?

Then I would point out this first silence, this long silence for the phone that is hearably summoning you isn't heard until [the first ring] is heard, whereupon [the first ring] is heard [coming out of a silence that just preceded it]. And [the ringing that is now being heard] is [now being heard] in what the phenomenologists call its relationship to the [silence out of which it came] as a dependent contents. By this is meant, not until you hear [the phone ringing] do you hear [the silence out of which it came]. Furthermore, they are so constituently details of that hearably [the first ring] that you can't disengage them without "changing the phenomenon," that is, "losing" [the first ring]-of-the-phone-summoning-just-you, or turning the phone summoning you into another phenomenon, say, the phone ringing in resemblance of a phone summoning you.

At the board I would list other details. I would call them "functional significations," and write each one in square brackets: [The first ring] is hearably [followed by] [an interval] [the interval separates] [the first ring] [from] [a second ring] with [both rings joined] and [therein are hearably directed to timed places ahead] [if they continue] [hearably they will not continue indefinitely].

In the five episodes of the phone that hearably simulates a phone summoning me the functional significations differ dramatically from those of phones hearably summoning me. For several years, each time I needed a tape for a class I would call our departmental secretary. "Linda, I need to make that tape again. Do me the favor. I'll hang up.

Wait for about 15 seconds and then phone me. I'll let it ring four or five time and then answer." "Okay."

While talking to her I've been tape-recording my request. Before I phoned her I turned on my recorder, then I called her, then I was busied arranging with her to call, then I hung up. After about 10 seconds she calls, I answer by thanking her, hang up, and turn off the machine.

When I play the tape for the students I start the tape after I have talked with Linda so they don't hear Linda and me arranging for her to call, and thus I can claim that I taped a phone summoning me. Is that right? Of course not. The students are not brain injured. Those who actually did the exercise had been busied with the trouble of getting even one episode on tape *before* the first ring, without arranging it. They had been *differently* busied, and untroubled, getting tape-recorded resemblances. So for them, "He's up to something. But what?" For my part, I say, "I'm going to play you a phone ringing. I think you might not have listened carefully to what it *sounds* like." Which is tendentiously true.

Now we ask: Just what really, actually, evidently, and these ordinarily distinguishes {the phone hearably summoning me} from {the phone hearably summoning someone else, hearably definitely not me}, from {the phone simulating a phone hearably summoning me} from {a phone hearably just ringing}?

As soon as the students hear that I made an arrangement with Linda, *this* silence in Figure 10.2 from the beginning of the line until the first squiggle becomes [waiting for the first-ring-according-to-the-agreement]. So, *that* phenomenal detail—that functional signification—and its affiliated contexture of phenomenal details—just *that* phenomenal detail, in just how it is locally in and as of an in vivo endogenous coherence of functional significations, that is, of details, just *that* phenomenal field of the concerted human job, {the phone hearably summoning me}, definitely, distinctively, massively, reliably, and validly distinguishes *these* objects, *these* episodes, {Phone summoning me} 1, 2, 3, 4, 5, from each of the other 20 episodes.

More: I would offer to set off the [first silence] of the in vivo silence against the *coded* silence of the taped silence that I had played for you in class. When I played the tape in class *that* silence on the tape is now listened to, and never mind how I got it on tape. Hearably, [it lasts]. Hearably, [it precedes] [the first ring that is listened for], [a ring you are waiting for]. But, in contrast, in your living room *your* phone's silence—the silence you *could* listen to, tonight, *now* that you can listen to hear the phone, [your phone that is silent], a figure on an indefinitely long-lasting silence, you're watching the phone that rings only when your mother calls. And *that* silence lends itself in endless "contextures" of imagined and imaginable details—a-silence-in-and-as-of-objects galore!

Further: The [initial silence] of [first ring] of the phone that is hearably summoning someone else is similar to the [initial silence] of the [first ring] of the phone summoning you. But the first ring of each is differently affiliated to the listened-for direction of the ring. Experimental perception studies are thick with demonstrations that the direction from which a sound is heard is a detail with which the listened to sound is recognized and identified as a sounded doing,[15] that is, the sound-*of-the-coherent-object*; the coherence-of-details-developingly-listened-to-and-listened-for.

In our exercise, although the phone summoning someone else is hearably ringing somewhere, it hearably *need not* be ringing *singularly and distinctly just there*, that is, hearably [in my office]. "Is that my phone?" As compared with the accompanying inquiry of [listening *for* my phone], and [after an intervening interval] [the interval and next ring] is hearably what I'm listening *to*.

What did we learn? If we do the exercise again what *can* we learn? This: We *see*, we *can* see, the following. We offer the following as observably the case:

- In our exercise we have five objects *distinctively*.
- These distinct objects were searched for, located, recognized, and tape-recorded in distinctive collections of five successive episodes each, for 25 distinctive episodes.
- Each episode is given, is only given, and is then entirely available in an "assemblage" of unavoidable haecceities, singular haecceities.
- Each episode in an "assemblage" of singular haecceities is *therein* given and available with full general comparability.
- Each of the foregoing claims is demonstrably the case *but just and only in any actual case that we are present to the lived in vivo coherence of phenomenal details as of which the object in the properties of its local production and natural accountability consists.*

We see that it does not make any difference whether we are talking about *this* object, {   } 1, or *that* one, {   } 12. The same method holds. We use the line for a silence, a squiggle for a ringing, and we administer the set, (line, squiggle) according to a set of rules of procedure (R): Whenever we hear a silence, write a line; when we hear a ringing, write a squiggle. That holds for the roster of objects in Column 1. For each episode in each of five collections of different episodes we get the account depicted in Figure 10.3.

Signed objects. ──◝◜─◝──◝◜─◝── is what I mean by a signed object. It is identical with a collection of signs.

(1) A methodic procedure has rendered the in vivo achieved coherences of objects in Position 3 and warrantably exhibits each of those coherent "assemblage of haecceities" as the details of signed objects.

(2) A signed object is always found in that third position.

(3) That a signed object is always found in the third position has several consequences:

- With *this* collection of indications, (   ), which was obtained with these procedures, →, which thereby gave the collection of indications their warrant and made the warrant secure, one is speaking of *this* phenomenon, {   }.
- With *this* collection of indications, (   ), one is specifying *this* phenomenon, {   }, for its demonstrably essential, real structures; for its demonstrably essential invariant features; for its demonstrably real constituent features; and for its relationship of demonstrable primordiality with respect to {   }.
- The signed objects in Position 3 do not distinguish one recognized object in Position 1 from another. All the tasks above are achieved by giving each of the signed objects an interpreted significance.
- To give each signed object its interpreted significance the analyst must already know what the collection of indications *could* be talking about. I collect the work of specifying the different objects as "the prejudiced analyst." In some of its practices that work consists of (a) administering various theorists' privileges; (b) designing and administering various transcendental analyses with which to find and get rid of otherwise intractable nuisances to the adequacies of the analysis; and (c) wherever studies of practical action are questionable over issues of adequate observability, justifying the interpreted object as essentially unavoidable work of the hermeneutic circle.
- The analyst is *committed* to the *work of interpretation*. I use *committed* to make observable (a) that the analyst's work of interpretation is essentially unavoidable, and essentially without either remedy or alternative; and (b) that the analyst's work of interpretation, that is, of finding and reading signs, contrasts with the incommensurable and irreconcilable alternate of specifying object *production* in and as of the haecceities of the object, which is identical with an in vivo work site.
- The analyst is not committed to the work of interpretation *here*, {   }; the analyst is committed *here*, →(   ).

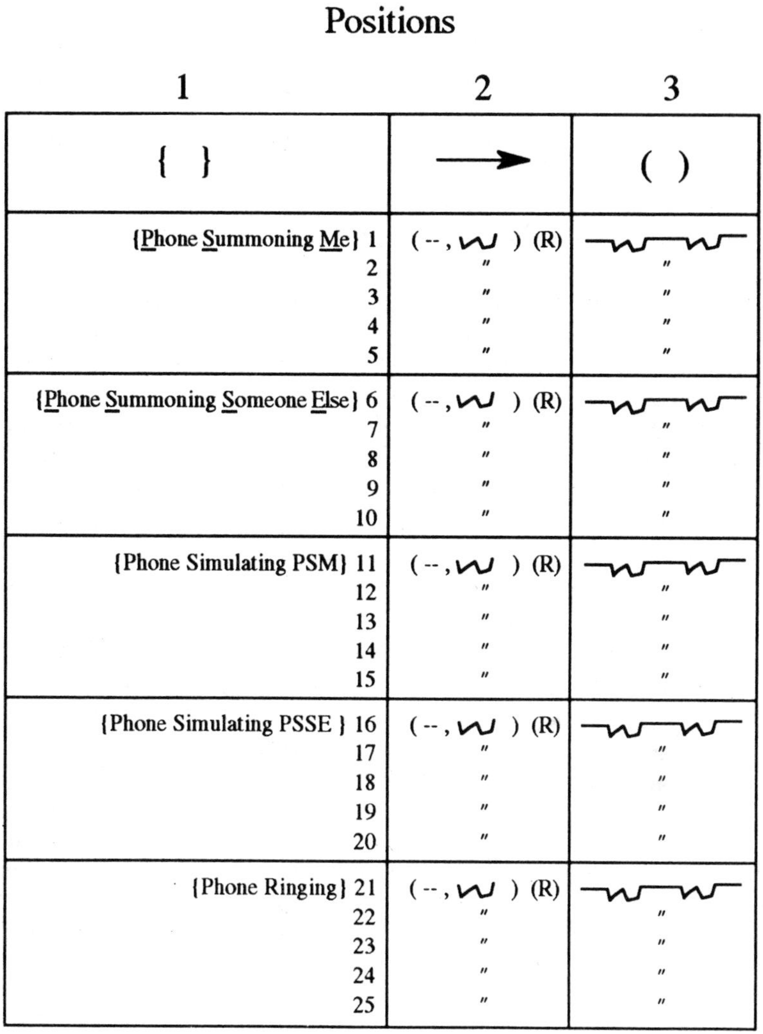

Positions

1 { }	2 →	3 ( )
{Phone Summoning Me} 1	(-- , ⌣) (R)	⌢⌣—⌢⌣
2	"	"
3	"	"
4	"	"
5	"	"
{Phone Summoning Someone Else} 6	(-- , ⌣) (R)	⌢⌣—⌢⌣
7	"	"
8	"	"
9	"	"
10	"	"
{Phone Simulating PSM} 11	(-- , ⌣) (R)	⌢⌣—⌢⌣
12	"	"
13	"	"
14	"	"
15	"	"
{Phone Simulating PSSE } 16	(-- , ⌣) (R)	⌢⌣—⌢⌣
17	"	"
18	"	"
19	"	"
20	"	"
{Phone Ringing} 21	(-- , ⌣) (R)	⌢⌣—⌢⌣
22	"	"
23	"	"
24	"	"
25	"	"

Figure 10.3.

The classical accountability of the summoning phones. The accounts
of each summoning phone in Column 3, ⟶⌣⌢⟶⌣⌢⟶ obtained
with the methodic procedure in Column 2 in the way that it specifies

and warrants these accounts, render the work of each episode of a summoning phone in Column 1 so that in *providing for* the analyzability of each episode in Column 1 the accounts *exhibit* the episode as the analyzable details of a signed object. The signed object, speaking on behalf of the original in Column 1, exhibits the observability of the episode in Column 1; the signed object exhibits the episode as a publicly verifiable object; it exhibits the episode's topical elaboration and exhibits what the episode's proper topics *could* be; it exhibits reasoned discourse about the episode; it exhibits the episode's observable, detectable, demonstrable, discoursable rational properties, that is, its calculability, its strategic efficacy, just what about it is available to the consequences of its occurrence, its predictability, its reproducibility, and so on; it provides for what the episode's topics as matters of rational discourse could consist of; it provides for the episode's topics specified as data; it exhibits in the foregoing practical aspects the episode's transcendental orderliness; and it exhibits the foregoing in established terms for competent members in a natural language.

The signed object provides for very much more than is found in the foregoing list. Just what more, and how much more, and of course just what in large consequentially more the signed object provides can be appreciated if we consider that the signed object exhibits the episode really, actually, and evidently as the signed object's details that are warranted details of corpus membership.

I shall collect these provisions as phenomena of { } that →( ) exhibits as analyzably connected observables of { }, and these are specified as the details of ( ). These analyzably connected observables are the premium achievements of formal analytic social sciences. I shall collect those achievements by using their sense as the data of ( ) to abbreviate them. The matters of { } that are made analyzably observable as the details of ( ) consist of the educated data of formal analytic lingoes.

In contrast are their properties of local production, which include their natural accountability.

Several Issues Summarize What We Have Learned

- *One* of the technologies of social analysis is this: →( ). Here is the other, { }. *This* technology of social analysis, { }, looks like the adequate,

vulgarly competent achievement of the phenomenon as an in vivo endogenously in-course achievement of coherent phenomenal details.

• Just in any actual case of { }, "social analysis" is a collecting gloss for
local production, local and natural accountability, and coherence of phenomenal details, that is, the phenomenal field of the object endogenously
made explicit in equipmentally affiliated concerted practices as of which
its staff come upon, find, and make the organizational object for each
another next first time.

• Nowhere here, { }, are we talking of indications.

• When, in the first rendering theorem, { } →( ), we come upon and
examine *this*, →( ), we see that it consists of a second method of social
analysis. It is not the case, however, that the second method is an ironic
version of the first method, { }. Rather, we see that the second method
→( ) offers a demonstration of what *this* { } consists of, and it does so
by specifying it *here* →( ) as an interpreted, interpretable *collection of
signs*. It makes available to us *this* phenomenon, { }, in *these* established
terms, →( ).

• Afterward, when we ask, "What does the phenomenon of order* consist
of as competent production and recognition?" we look to *this* apparatus,
→( ), to turn the object into the demonstrable aims, tasks, data, findings,
rules, troubles, and other stock-in-trade of the social science movement:
into educated data of, for example, experimental social psychology and
canonical conversational analysis, into teachable achievements, into instructable discourse, into instructions in just what it consists of and just
how it is done to be designing, following, questioning, talking, administering, correcting, demonstrating the production and recognition of these
different phenomena, { }, these concerted achievements of practical action
and practical reason in the world.

• In their studies of structures (on whatever scale) the social sciences have
as their stock-in-trade the design, administration, explication, and interpretation of signed objects.

Concluding Remarks

With their studies of radical phenomena, ethnomethodologists have
come upon the in vivo work of producing the naturally accountable
phenomena of relevance, consistency, coherence, of these two, { },
and →( ).

Viewed in the light of EM studies of radical phenomena, the tasks of
finding and reconciling differences between classic and EM studies can
be endless and can lack probativeness. *Of course* we can study their
differences. But why would we want to? Whereas it *could* be that in the

specified details of two incommensurable technologies that their studies have uncovered ethnomethodologists have come upon an organizational thing in and as of ordinary society, and with it a vast domain of
new organizational phenomena, namely: the design, availability, work-
site administration and presence of careful, skillful, analytic methods—
classic studies—which are organizational details of ordinary society,
furnish members reasoned justifications to dismiss as uninteresting
and pointless the lived, concerted, unavoidably embodied, smoothly
achieved work in content-specific detail that makes up the accomplishment of the most ordinary organizational things in the world. These
achieved most ordinary organizational phenomena in the world are
every possible *topic* of logic, meaning, reason, method, order. All of
them are to be found again and respecified as locally achieved *phenomena* of logic, reason, meaning, method, and so on. As Egon Bittner has
observed, after the Greeks these marvelous topics went to college and
came back educated. Now, all of them are to be found again and
respecified as the workings of the most ordinary organizational *things*
in the world.

It is ethnomethodological about EM studies that they show for ordinary society's substantive events, in material contents, just and only
in any actual case, that and just how vulgarly competent members
concert their activities to produce and show, exhibit, make observably
the case*, demonstrate, and so on, coherence, cogency, analysis, detail,
structure, consistency, order, meaning, mistakes, errors, coincidence,
facticity, reason, methods—locally, reflexively, naturally accountable phenomena—in and as of the haecceities of their ordinary lives together.

We learn from the corpus of EM studies that its radical studies have
begun to reveal immortal ordinary society as a wondrous thing. Its
members, be they "lay analysts" or professionals in the worldwide
social science movement, with straightforward normal thoughtfulness
are able to read it out of relevance, eyeless in Gaza.

Notes

1. Spelled with an asterisk, order* is a collector and a proxy for any and every topic
of logic, meaning, method, reason, and order. It stands in for any and all the marvelous
topics that are available in received lingoes and received topics in intellectual history. Of
course these include the lingoes and studies in the endless arts and sciences of practical
action.

We ask that order* be read as a proxy for any topic of reason, logic, meaning, proof, uniformity, generalization, universal, comparability, clarity, consistency, coherence, objectivity, objective knowledge, observation, detail, structure, and the rest. Topics from any list of these topics will do.

Do not think, however, that ethnomethodology seeks out these creatures in order to settle with them as topics of order*. Nothing of the sort. Rather, EM seeks to respecify them as locally produced, naturally accountable phenomena of order*. In the corpus of EM studies some of these topics are available as phenomena of order* having been respecified in studies that were done with the use of EM's policies and craft. Any and all topics of order* are candidates for EM study and respecification. More pointedly, any and all topics of order* are candidates, ethnomethodologically, for the question: What more, other, different, unavoidable, without remedy, depended upon, ignored, yet identifying of a candidate is there to it as a phenomenon of order* than classic methods do, did, ever did, or can provide?

We shall understand any of the topics of order* as locally produced, naturally accountable phenomena, searched for, findable, found, only discoverably the case, consisting in and as "work of the streets." Some topics of order* have been respecified and are available in the corpus of EM studies. For example, the seminal case by Bjelic and Lynch, in this volume, provides an EM respecification of Goethe's theory of prismatic color. Other topics are available in various "guises" of candidacy. But with whatever "guise" of candidacy a topic of order* is presented, it is respecifiable only as discoverably and inspectably the case. This requirement inhabits EM studies. Its omnirelevance is revealed in our use of the various terms of order* when we say we shall understand them either tendentiously or with strange names for new phenomena.

2. Until recently, Garfinkel spoke of *quiddity*, not *haecceity*. He didn't know that quiddity gave the emphasis to exactly the wrong meaning. When Willard Van Orman Quine (1987) published *Quiddities* it was clear that quiddities had nothing at all to do with what EM had uncovered. Most emphatically, EM studies did not mean essential detail. EM is not interested in essential in any sense of generic provision for a properly formulated propertied class of things. In their corpus the EM company has been looking at something that is other and different than, that is, in contrast to, and is not reconcilable with, established studies of order production, something that is incommensurably an alternate interest in, and an alternate provision for, what technical production of the phenomena of order* *could* be.

EM studies were not looking for *quiddities*. They were looking for haecceities, just thisness: just here, just now, with just what is at hand, with just who is here, in just the time that just this local gang of us have, in and with just what the local gang of us can make of just the time we need, and therein, in, about, as, and over the course of the in vivo work, achieving and exhibiting everything that those great achievements of comparability, universality, transcendentality of results, indifference of methods to local parties who are using them, for what they consisted of, looked like, the "missing what" of formal analytic studies of practical action. For any and all of those achievements there was a local company engaged in and as vulgarly competent practices. It was in and as of a company's smooth concerted doings that those achievements would offer to EM their candidacy for *respecification* from their current, established, availability as received *terms* of order, as received *terms* of logic, as terms of meaning, as terms of reason, as these *terms* of order* are available in received texts of intellectual history.

3. We shall talk about *immortal ordinary society*. Our use of "society" was learned from Edward Rose, who uses "society" in his lectures to collect whatever he needs, at hand, in any witnessable local setting, whose parties are doing some human job. These

jobs can range in scale from an exquisitely transient silence that can precede a refused invitation to the spectacle of a developing freeway jam. The idea is to provide for immortal, ordinary society so as to accord with EM interests in these jobs.

Immortal is borrowed from Durkheim as a metaphor for any of these jobs, where there is *this* to emphasize about them: Their production is staffed by parties to a standing crap game. For whatever is going on the jobs are staffed by parties to a standing crap game. Of course, the jobs are not games, let alone crap games. Think of the flow of freeway traffic in Los Angeles. For the cohort of drivers, there, just this gang of them, driving, making traffic together, are *some*how, *smoothly and unremarkably*, concerting the driving to be *at* the in vivo, lived production of the flow's just thisness: familiar, ordinary, uninteresting, observably-in-and-as-observances-doable-and-done-again, and always, only, entirely in detail for everything that detail could be. In and as of the just thisness of driving's details just this staff are doing again just what, in concert, with vulgar competence, they *can* do, for each another next first time; and it is this of what they are doing, in that that makes up the details of just that traffic flow: that although it is of their doing, and as of the flow they are "witnessably oriented by" and "seeably directed to" the production of it, they treat the organizational *thing* as of their doing, as of their own doing, but *not* of their very own, singular, distinctive authorship. And, further for just this cohort, it will be that after they exit the freeway others will come after them to do again the same, familiar things that they—just they—*just these of us as driving's doings* are in concert doing.

We use *immortal* to speak of Rose's "society" as of which local members, being in the midst of organizational *things*, know, of just these organizational things they are in the midst of, that it preceded them and will be there after they leave, great recurrences of ordinary society, staffed, provided for, produced, observed and observable, locally and accountably, in and as of an "assemblage of haecceities."

4. Part I, "An Announcement of Studies," was first published with the title "A Reflection" in the *Discourse Analysis Research Group Newsletter* (Garfinkel, 1987). After being retitled, it was published in the Spring 1988 issue of *Sociological Theory* (Garfinkel, 1988). Part II, "The Curious Seriousness of Professional Sociology," was presented during 1987 and 1988 in seminars and colloquia at UCLA, Boston University, the Ecole des Hautes Etudes, and the University of Wisconsin. Part III, "Instructed Action," was worked out in classes and seminars at UCLA from 1986 to 1988 and presented at colloquia during 1987 and 1988 at Temple University, the University of Oklahoma, and the Western Behavioral Science Institute.

5. We owe our use of cases to Lois Meyer (1989). With her permission we have borrowed upon the brilliant authority of her dissertation proposal, her prior writings, and her current teaching, research, and writing at the Hawthorne School, San Francisco.

6. The phrase should read, "essentially unavoidable and without remedy or alternative." We must caution the reader, however, that nothing of "essential" or "essence" as these are commonly understood in analytic and phenomenological philosophies is meant. We use "essential" to emphasize that every attempt to remedy or to avoid the haecceity of whatever matters haecceity modifies (e.g., details, immortal society, preserves) in the material practices with which the demonstration assures that the matter has been avoided or remedied, the identical matters that were cause for complaint. Similarly, "constituent" should not be read to mean "constitutive." "Constituent" is a convenient but trivial abbreviation of the phrase "essentially unavoidable and without remedy or alternative."

7. In this discussion of the social sciences we use "descriptive precision" synonymously and interchangeably with "the probativeness of social analysis." We do so with which to recognize a work commitment in the social sciences. The phenomenon of

probativeness is taken from the natural sciences. There a phenomenon of the day's work and a contingency of discovering work in a natural science is that an issue can get settled. For example, Holton (1978) describes the Milliken/Ehrenehaft dispute in physics. For 17 years the two camps mobilized personnel, money, time, laboratory work, reference appearances, and publications, disputing whether the charge on the electron was a unitary or a statistically distributed charge. Milliken reported his oil drop experiment, after which the quarrel could no longer be carried on in its original terms. The phenomenon of probativeness is commonplace in the natural sciences. In the social sciences, however, an actual case of the phenomenon is notably difficult to cite or demonstrate.

8. Cases a and b are discussed at length in Garfinkel and Lynch (n.d.). A discussion of c is found in Garfinkel (n.d.).

9. The following is a note on speaking tendentiously* and using strange names for new phenomena of order* as aims, tasks, methods, and findings of ethnomethodological studies.

EM studies of phenomena of order*—different phenomena—are discussed in two quite different ways. For some "the language of everyday life" is used to speak of them with their familiar names, names found in common vernacular or technical terminologies, but in any actual case as received lingo. Some examples from EM studies are instructions; following instruction; detail, structure; or summoning phones. The point: Their familiar names are used *tendentiously.* Familiar names are used with a deliberately abiding, corrective, but concealed tendency. In speaking tendentiously, a term is written with its asterisked spelling, for example, detail*. In that spelling, we use detail* knowing that by detail* is meant something other than and different from what the reader would explain or *can* explain with any of detail's many vernacular "straightforward" meanings, thus at the same time knowing that detail* is used as a corrective on the reader's understandings. By intent, and at times by reason of achievements of previous EM studies, detail* (or any asterisked term of order* as the case may be) is used as an aim, task, method, or finding according to EM policies and methods, as a radical corrective; knowing, too, that an explanation is being delayed deliberately; doing so on the grounds of later studies; knowing that an explanation will be forthcoming at an appropriate place in the overall argument, although not adequately* particularly in any instant discussion but as the argument develops over actual studies, and not in studies that in the instant volume may be only talked *about*, but studies just and only actually not supposedly doable, and actually not supposedly done, *by the reader* in just and only an actual case. Only and entirely on these grounds, detail* (or any other asterisked phenomenon of order* as the case may be) is used as a radical corrective on the reader's understandings.

Other phenomena of order* are named with strange names and phrases. Examples include lebenswelt pair; signed object; the properties of a phenomenon's local, endogenous production; that the properties of local production include the endogenous achievement's natural accountability; the praxeological validity of instructed action. These phenomena are spoken of with the names by which they are known in EM studies of the radical phenomena of order* production.

These two—that is, speaking in a received, familiar lingo, but speaking tendentiously, and using strange names to speak of new phenomena—are aims, tasks, findings, results (i.e., corpus members) and achievements of EM studies. Caution: These are not somehow aims of EM studies. Nor are they somehow tasks. Nor are they somehow findings. They are just-what-how aims, tasks, results, or achievements. More exactly, they are not some how nor are they just-what-how of classic methods, of any classic methods. Not just any some-how or any just-how are aims, tasks, findings, or achievements, but only radical just-hows. Radical is key.

Perhaps it will clarify the description of radically just how EM studies can hope to speak tendentiously, and radically just how ethnomethodologists in their studies can come to have little choice but to use familiar terms tendentiously or to use strange names for new phenomena as real-worldly aims, tasks, achievements, and so on, if we replace talk of "radical just how" and speak instead of "embedding" ethnomethodology in a setting and from within the setting, and over the exigencies of inquiry and argument, we'll examine some of that setting's objects.

By "embedding ethnomethodology in a setting" we shall understand administering ethnomethodological policies and using ethnomethodological methods over the exigencies of inquiry, in and as a particular, distinctive, real-world setting of human jobs.

10. The reader will find the claim about perspicuous settings and their use observably and examinably provided for by reading by Bjelic and Lynch's chapter in this volume. These claims are discursively provided for in Bjelic's (1989) seminal proposals on logic in his dissertation.

11. Two policies use findings by Gurwitsch (1964) of the functional significations and their properties. These were the results of his transcendental phenomenological examination and respecification of the gestalt theory of form. For ethnomethodology the indispensable achievement of his study consists in his having provided for the achieved coherence of objects with the properties of functional significations. Gurwitsch reported as well *as a finding* the endogenous relevance to a developing contexture of recognizable constituent significations entirely from within the stream of perception.

12. Bill Bryant's demonstration was done (1974) in Sociology 218AB, Methods of Ethnomethodological Research, UCLA.

13. I am indebted to Stacy Burns for her help in working these out as findings from our collaborated studies of formatted queues and R-at-work teaching introductory sociology.

14. For the sake of clarity of exposition, the authors have retained many locutions of Garfinkel's talk in which these arguments were delivered at the Calgary conference.

15. We are indebted to David Sudnow (1972, 1978, 1979, 1984) for sounded doings. We use "sounded doings" as he elucidates them in his work on conversation, talking, typing, gestural improvisation, teaching improvised and classic piano playing, playing jazz piano in professional ensembles, problem solving in video games, and various phenomena of details.

References

Alexander, J. C., & Giesen, B. (1987). From reduction to linkage: The long view of the
micro-macro link. In J. C. Alexander et al. (Eds.), *The micro-macro link* (pp. 1-42).
New York: Columbia University Press.

Alexander, J. C., et al. (Eds.). (1987). *The micro-macro link.* New York: Columbia
University Press.

Anderson, R. J., Hughes, J. A., & Sharrock, W. W. (1985). *The sociology game.* London:
Longman.

Anderson, R. J., & Sharrock, W. W. (1982). Sociological work: Some procedures sociologists use for organizing phenomena. *Social Analysis, 11,* 79-93.

Ardener, E. (Ed.). (1971). *Social anthropology and language.* London: Tavistock.

Atkinson, J. M. (1982). Understanding formality: Notes on the categorization and production of "formal" interaction. *British Journal of Sociology, 33,* 86-117.

Atkinson, J. M., & Heritage, J. (Eds.). (1984). *Structures of social action.* Cambridge,
UK: Cambridge University Press.

Atkinson, M. (1980). Some practical uses of "a natural lifetime." *Human Studies, 1,*
33-46.

Atkinson, P. (1988). Ethnomethodology: A critical review. *Annual Review of Sociology,
14,* 441-465.

Auerbach, E. (1953). *Mimesis: The representation of reality in Western literature.*
Princeton, NJ: Princeton University Press.

Barton, L., & Tomlinson, S. (1981). *Special education: Policy, practices and social issues.*
London: Harper & Row.

Bauman, R., & Sherzer, J. (Eds.). (1974). *Explorations in the ethnography of speaking.*
Cambridge, UK: Cambridge University Press.

207

208   References

Bilmes, J. (1985). Why that now? Two kinds of conversational meaning. *Discourse Processes, 8*, 319-355.

Bilmes, J. (1986). *Discourse and behavior.* New York: Plenum.

Bittner, E. (1965). The concept of organization. *Social Research, 32*, 239-255.

Bittner, E. (1967). The police on skid row: A study of peace keeping. *American Sociological Review, 32*, 699-715.

Bjelic, D. (1989). *The social origin of logic.* Unpublished doctoral dissertation, Boston University.

Blumer, H. (1972). Action versus interaction. *Society, 9*(6), 50-53.

Boden, D., & Zimmerman, H. (Eds.). (in press). *Talk and social structure.* Oxford, UK: Polity.

Boehme, G. (1987). Is Goethe's theory of color science? In F. Amerine, F. J. Zucker, & H. Wheeler (Eds.), *Goethe and the sciences: A reappraisal* (pp. 147-173). Dordrecht, Netherlands: D. Riedel.

Bourdieu, P. (1989). Social space and symbolic power. *Sociological Theory, 7*, 14-24.

Brannigan, A. (1981). *The social basis of scientific discoveries.* Cambridge, UK: Cambridge University Press.

Burke, K. (1954). *Permanence and change.* Indianapolis: Bobbs-Merrill. (Original work published 1935)

Button, G., & Casey, N. (1988-1989). Topic initiation: Business-at-hand. *Research on Language and Social Interaction, 22*, 61-91.

Button, G., & Lee, J. R. E. (Eds.). (1987). *Talk and social organization.* Clevedon, Avon: Multilingual Matters.

Cicourel, A. V. (1968). *The social organization of juvenile justice.* New York: John Wiley.

Cicourel, A. V. (1973). *Cognitive sociology: Language and meaning in social interaction.* Harmondsworth: Penguin.

Collins, H. M. (1985). *Changing order: Replication and induction in scientific practice.* London: Sage.

Coulter, J. (1983). *Rethinking cognitive theory.* New York: St. Martin's.

Crews, F. (1986). In the grand house of theory. In F. Crews (Ed.), *Skeptical engagements* (pp. 159-178). New York: Oxford University Press.

Cuff, E., & Francis, D. W. (1978). Some features of "invited stories" about marriage breakdown. *International Journal of the Sociology of Language, 18*, 111-133.

de Boer, F., & Hak, T. (1986). *Decision-making in emergency psychiatry.* Rotterdam: Erasmus University, Institute for Preventive and Social Psychiatry.

Douglas, J. (1970). *Deviance and respectability.* New York: Basic Books.

Douglas-Steele, D. (1988). *Everyday troubles and their stories: A study in the practices of commonsense reasoning.* Unpublished doctoral dissertation, Boston University.

Drew, P. (1978). Accusations: The occasioned use of members' knowledge of "religious geography" in describing events. *Sociology, 12*, 1-22.

Drew, P., & Wootton, A. (Eds.). (1988). *Erving Goffman: Exploring the interaction order.* Boston: Northeastern University.

Dreyfus, H. L. (1979). *What computers can't do: The limits of artificial intelligence.* New York: Harper & Row.

Eglin, P. (1990). *The everyday life of suicide.* Unpublished manuscript.

Eglin, T. (1986). Introduction to a hermeneutics of the occult: Alchemy. In H. Garfinkel (Ed.), *Ethnomethodological studies of work* (pp. 123-159). London: Routledge & Kegan Paul.

Emerson, R. (1969). *Judging delinquents.* Chicago: Aldine.

Emerson, R., & Pollner, M. (1978). Policies and practices of psychiatric evaluation. *Sociology of Work and Occupations, 5*, 75-96.

Evans-Pritchard, E. E. (1950). *Witchcraft, oracles, and magic among the Azande.* Oxford: Clarendon. (Original work published 1937)

Faris, R. E. L., & Dunham, H. W. (1939). *Mental disorders in urban areas.* Chicago: University of Chicago Press.

Fish, S. (1980). *Is there a text in this class? The authority of interpretive communities.* Cambridge, MA: Harvard University Press.

Ford, J., Mongon, D., & Whelan, M. (1982). *Special education and social control.* London: Routledge & Kegan Paul.

Foucault, M. (1970). *The order of things.* New York: Vintage.

Fraise, P. (1963). *The psychology of time.* New York: Harper & Row.

Frank, A. W. (1988). Garfinkel's deconstruction of Parson's plenum. *Discourse Analysis Research Group Newsletter, 4*(1), 5-8.

Frank, A. W. (1990). Getting help for bodies at risk: A comment on Zimmerman, ethnomethodology, and current social theory. *Discourse Analysis Research Group Newsletter, 6*(3), 6-10.

Garfinkel, H. (n.d.). *Ethnomethodological studies with which to respecify the logic of non-inductive inference*.* Unpublished manuscript, University of California, Los Angeles.

Garfinkel, H. (1963). A conception of, and experiments with, "trust" as a condition of stable concerned actions. In D. J. Harvey (Ed.), *Motivation and social interaction* (pp. 187-238). New York: Ronald.

Garfinkel, H. (1984). *Studies in ethnomethodology.* Cambridge, UK: Polity. (Original work published 1967)

Garfinkel, H. (1987). A reflection. *Discourse Analysis Research Group Newsletter, 5*(2), 5-9.

Garfinkel, H. (1988). Evidence for locally produced, naturally accountable phenomena of order, logic, reason, meaning, method, etc., in and as of the essential quiddity of immortal ordinary society (I of IV): An announcement of studies. *Sociological Theory, 6*, 103-106.

Garfinkel, H., & Bittner, E. (1967a). Good organizational reasons for "bad" clinic records. In H. Garfinkel, *Studies in ethnomethodology* (pp. 186-207). Englewood Cliffs, NJ: Prentice-Hall.

Garfinkel, H., & Bittner, E. (1967b). Methodological adequacy in the quantitative study of selection practices in psychiatric outpatient clinics. In H. Garfinkel, *Studies in ethnomethodology* (pp. 208-261). Englewood Cliffs, NJ: Prentice-Hall.

Garfinkel, H., Livingston, E., Lynch, M., Macbeth, D., & Robillard, A. B. (1989). *Respecifying the natural sciences as discovering sciences of practical action (I and II): Doing so ethnographically by administering a schedule of contingencies in discussions with laboratory scientists and by hanging around their laboratories.* Unpublished manuscript, University of California, Los Angeles, Department of Sociology.

Garfinkel, H., & Lynch, M. (n.d.). *A comparison of classic and ethnomethodological studies of work.* Unpublished manuscript, University of California, Los Angeles.

Garfinkel, H., Lynch, M., & Livingston, E. (1981). The work of a discovering science construed with materials from the optically discovered pulsar. *Philosophy of the Social Sciences, 11*, 131-158.

Garfinkel, H., & Sacks, H. (1970). On formal structures of practical actions. In J. C. McKinney & E. A. Tiryakian (Eds.), *Theoretical sociology: Perspectives and developments* (pp. 338-366). New York: Appleton-Century-Crofts.

Gluckman, M. (1955). *The judicial process among the Barotse of Northern Rhodesia.* Manchester: University of Manchester Press.

Goethe, J. W. von. (1970). *Theory of colors.* Cambridge: MIT Press. (Original work published 1840)

Goethe, J. W. von. (1971). *Farbenlehre* (G. Ott & H. O. Proskauer, Eds.). Stuttgart: Verlag Freies Geisteleben.

Goethe, J. W. von. (1982). *Naturwissenschaftliche Schriften* (R. Steiner, Ed.). Dornach: Rudolph Steiner Verlag.

Goffman, E. (1959). *The presentation of self in everyday life.* Garden City, NY: Doubleday.

Goffman, E. (1961). *Asylums.* Garden City, NY: Doubleday.

Goffman, E. (1983). Felicity's condition. *American Journal of Sociology, 89,* 1-53.

Goffman, E. (1984a). *Forms of talk.* Philadelphia: University of Pennsylvania Press.

Goffman, E. (1984b). Response cries. In E. Goffman, *Forms of talk* (pp. 78-123). Philadelphia: University of Pennsylvania Press. (Reprinted from *Language,* 1978, *54,* 787-815)

Goldman, L. (1983). *Talk never dies: The language of Huli disputes.* London: Tavistock.

Goodman, N. (1954). *Fact, fiction, and forecast.* London: Athlone.

Grillo, R. (Ed.). (1989). *Social anthropology and the politics of language.* London: Routledge & Kegan Paul.

Gumpertz, J. J., & Hymes, D. (Eds.). (1972). *Directions in sociolinguistics: The ethnography of communication.* New York: Holt, Rinehart & Winston.

Gurwitsch, A. (1964). *Field of consciousness.* Pittsburgh: Duquesne University Press.

Hak, T. (1989a). Developing a text-sociological analysis. *Semiotica, 75,* 25-42.

Hak, T. (1989b). Constructing a psychiatric case. In B. Torode (Ed.), *Text and talk as social practice* (pp. 72-92). Dordrecht, Netherlands: Foris.

Halfpenny, P. (1988). Talking of talking, writing of writing: Some reflections on Gilbert and Mulkay's discourse analysis. *Social Studies of Science, 18,* 169-182.

Hargreaves, D., Hester, S., & Mellor, F. (1975). *Deviance in classrooms.* London: Routledge & Kegan Paul.

Harper, R. R. (1989). *An ethnographic examination of accountancy.* Unpublished doctoral dissertation, University of Manchester.

Havelock, E. A. (1963). *Preface to Plato.* Cambridge, MA: Harvard University Press.

Hayes, P. J., & Reddy, D. R. (1983). Steps toward graceful interaction in spoken and written man-machine communication. *International Journal of Man-Machine Studies, 19,* 231-284.

Heap, J. L. (1980). What counts as reading: Limits to certainty in assessment. *Curriculum Inquiry, 10,* 265-292.

Helm, D. T. (1982). Talk's form: Comments on Goffman's *Forms of talk. Human Studies, 5,* 147-157.

Heritage, J. (1984a). *Garfinkel and ethnomethodology.* Oxford, UK: Polity.

Heritage, J. (1984b). A change-of-state token and aspects of its sequential organization. In J. M. Atkinson & J. Heritage (Eds.), *Structures of social action* (pp. 299-345). Cambridge, UK: Cambridge University Press.

Heritage, J., & Watson, D. R. (1979). Formulations as conversational objects. In G. Psathas (Ed.), *Everyday language: Studies in ethnomethodology* (pp. 123-162). New York: Irvington.

Hester, S. (1985). Ethnomethodology and the study of deviance in schools. In R. Burgess (Ed.), *Strategies of educational research: Qualitative methods* (pp. 243-264). London: Falmer.

Hester, S. (in press). *Making sense of deviance in school.* London: Falmer.

Heyman, R. (1986). Formulating topic in the classroom. *Discourse Processes, 9,* 37-55.

Hodge, B. (1989). Discourse in time: Some notes on method. In B. Torode (Ed.), *Text and talk as social practice* (pp. 93-112). Dordrecht, Netherlands: Foris.

Holton, G. (1978). Subelectrons, presuppositions, and the Millikan-Ehrenhaft dispute. In *The scientific imagination.* Cambridge, UK: Cambridge University Press.

Husserl, E. (1970). *The crisis of European sciences and transcendental phenomenology* (D. Carr, Trans.). Evanston, IL: Northwestern University Press.

Jary, D., & Smith, G. W. H. (1976). Extended review of Goffman's frame analysis. *Sociological Review, 24,* 917-927.

Jayyusi, L. (1984). *Categorization and the moral order.* London: Routledge & Kegan Paul.

Jefferson, G. (1972). Side sequences. In D. Sudnow (Ed.), *Studies in social interaction* (pp. 294-338). New York: Free Press.

Jefferson, G. (1980). *The analysis of conversations in which "troubles" and "anxieties" are expressed: Final report.* London: Social Science Research Council.

Jefferson, G. (1985). On the interactional unpackaging of a "gloss." *Language in Society, 14,* 435-466.

Jefferson, G., & Lee, J. R. E. (1981). The rejection of advice: Managing the problematic convergence of a "troubles-telling" and a "service encounter." *Journal of Pragmatics, 5,* 399-422.

Jeffery, R. (1979). Rubbish: Deviant patients in casualty departments. *Sociology of Health and Illness, 1,* 90-107.

Jones, J. (1962). *On Aristotle and Greek tragedy.* New York: Oxford University Press.

Kitamura, K. (1990). Interactional synchrony: A fundamental condition for communication. In M. Moerman & M. Nomura (Eds.), *Culture embodied* (Senri Ethnological Studies, No. 27) (pp. 123-140). Osaka: National Museum of Ethnology.

Knorr-Cetina, K. D., & Cicourel, A. V. (Eds.). (1981). *Advances in social theory and methodology: Toward an integration of micro- and macro-sociologies.* Boston: Routledge & Kegan Paul.

LaFleur, W. R. (1983). *The karma of words: Buddhism and the literary arts in medieval Japan.* Berkeley: University of California Press.

Lee, J. (1987). Innocent victims and evil doers. *Women's Studies International Forum, 7,* 69-73.

Livingston, E. (1986). *The ethnomethodological foundations of mathematics.* London: Routledge & Kegan Paul.

Long, N. E. (1958). The local community as an ecology of games. *American Journal of Sociology, 64,* 251-255.

Louch, A. R. (1966). *Explanation and human action.* Berkeley: University of California Press.

Lounsbury, F. G. (1951). A semantic analysis of the Pawnee kinship usage. *Language, 32,* 158-194.

Lynch, M. (1982). Technical work and critical inquiry: Investigations in a scientific laboratory. *Social Studies of Science, 12*, 499-533.

Lynch, M. (1983). Accommodation practices: Vernacular treatments of madness. *Social Problems, 31*, 152-164.

Lynch, M. (1985a). *Art and artifact in laboratory science: A study of shop work and shop talk in a research laboratory.* London: Routledge & Kegan Paul.

Lynch, M. (1985b). Discipline and the material form of images: An analysis of scientific visibility. *Social Studies of Science, 15*, 37-66.

Lynch, M. (in press). Extending Wittgenstein: The pivotal move from epistemology to the sociology of science. In A. Pickering (Ed.), *Science as practice and culture.* Chicago: University of Chicago Press.

Lynch, M., Livingston, E., & Garfinkel, H. (1983). Temporal order in laboratory work. In K. D. Knorr-Cetina & M. Mulkay (Eds.), *Science observed: Perspectives on the social study of science* (pp. 204-238). London: Sage.

Macbeth, D. (1989). Basketball notes: Finding the sense and relevance of detail. In H. Garfinkel, E. Livingston, M. Lynch, D. Macbeth, & A. B. Robillard, *Respecifying the natural sciences as discovering sciences of practical action (I and II): Doing so ethnographically by administering a schedule of contingencies in discussions with laboratory scientists and by hanging around their laboratories* (pp. 73-90). Unpublished manuscript, University of California, Los Angeles, Department of Sociology.

MacKinnon, R. (1980). Psychiatric history and mental status examination. In H. Kaplan, A. Freedman, & B. Sadock (Eds.), *Comprehensive textbook of psychiatry* (3rd ed., pp. 906-920). Baltimore: Williams & Wilkins.

Manning, P. (1989). Ritual talk. *Sociology, 23*, 365-385.

Matthaei, R. (Ed.). (1971). *Goethe's theory of color.* New York: Van Nostrand.

Maynard, D. W., & Wilson, T. P. (1980). On the reification of social structure. In S. G. McNall & G. N. Howe (Eds.), *Current perspectives on social theory* (Vol. 1, pp. 287-322). Greenwich, CT: JAI.

Maynard, D. W., & Zimmerman, D. H. (1984). Topical talk, ritual, and the social organization of relationships. *Social Psychology Quarterly, 47*, 301-316.

McHoul, A. (1982). *Telling how texts talk: Essays in reading and ethnomethodology.* London: Routledge & Kegan Paul.

Mehan, H. (1979). *Learning lessons: Social organization in the classroom.* Cambridge, MA: Harvard University Press.

Mercer, J. (1973). *Labelling the mentally retarded.* Berkeley: University of California Press.

Messenger, S., with Sampson, H., & Towne, T. (1962). Life as theater: Some comments on the sociology of Erving Goffman. *Sociometry, 25*, 98-110.

Meyer, L. (1989). *The language circle: Inside the teaching and learning of language in an inner city elementary school.* Unpublished doctoral dissertation, University of California, Los Angeles.

Miner, H. (1956). Body ritual among the Nacirema. *American Anthropologist, 58*, 503-507.

Moerman, M. (1965). Ethnic identification in a complex civilization: Who are the Lue? *American Anthropologist, 67*, 1215-1230.

Moerman, M. (1966a). Ban Ping's temple: The center of a "loosely structured" society. In *Anthropological studies of Theravada Buddhism* (pp. 137-174). New Haven, CT: Yale University, Southeast Asia Studies Department.

Moerman, M. (1966b). Kinship and commerce in a Thai-Lue village. *Ethnology, 5*, 360-364.

Moerman, M. (1968a). Being Lue: Uses and abuses of ethnicity. In J. Helm (Ed.), *Essays on the problem of tribe* (pp. 153-169). Seattle: University of Washington Press.

Moerman, M. (1968b). *Agricultural change and peasant choice in a Thai village.* Berkeley: University of California Press.

Moerman, M. (1972). Analysis of Tai conversation: I. In D. Sudnow (Ed.), *Studies in social interaction* (pp. 170-228). New York: Free Press.

Moerman, M. (1973). The use of precedent in natural conversation. *Semiotica, 9*(3), 193-218.

Moerman, M. (1988). *Talking culture: Ethnography and conversation analysis.* Philadelphia: University of Pennsylvania Press.

Moerman, M. (1990). Studying gestures in their social context. In M. Moerman & M. Nomura (Eds.), *Culture embodied* (Senri Ethnological Studies, No. 27) (pp. 5-52). Osaka: National Museum of Ethnology.

Morrison, K. L. (1990). Some researchable recurrences in disciplinary-specific inquiry. In D. T. Helm et al. (Eds.), *The interaction order: New directions in the study of social order* (pp. 141-157). New York: Irvington.

Murdock, G. P. (1949). *Social structure.* New York: Macmillan.

Newton, I. (1952). *Opticks.* New York: Dover. (Original work published 1704)

Nomura, M. (1990). Remodelling the Japanese body. In M. Moerman & M. Nomura (Eds.), *Culture embodied* (Senri Ethnological Studies, No. 27) (pp. 259-274). Osaka: National Museum of Ethnology.

Parsons, T. (1937). *The structure of social action.* New York: McGraw-Hill.

Payne, G. (1976). Making a lesson happen: An ethnomethodological analysis. In M. Hammersley & P. Woods (Eds.), *The process of schooling* (pp. 33-40). London: Routledge & Kegan Paul.

Pickering, A. (1984). Against putting the phenomena first: The discovery of the weak neutral current. *Studies in the History and Philosophy of Science, 15*(2), 85-117.

Pollner, M. (1979). Explicative transactions: Making and managing meaning in traffic court. In G. Psathas (Ed.), *Everyday language: Studies in ethnomethodology* (pp. 227-255). New York: Irvington.

Preston, D. L. (1988). *The social organization of Zen practice.* Cambridge, UK: Cambridge University Press.

Proskauer, H. O. (1986). *The rediscovery of color: Goethe versus Newton today.* Spring Valley, NY: Anthroposophic Press.

Psathas, G. (1986a). The organization of directions in interaction. *Word, 37*, 83-91.

Psathas, G. (1986b). Some sequential structures in direction giving. *Human Studies, 9*, 231-245.

Psathas, G. (in press). The structure of direction-giving in interaction. In D. Boden & H. Zimmerman (Eds.), *Talk and social structure.* Oxford, UK: Polity.

Psathas, G., & Anderson, T. (1990). The "practices" of transcription in conversation analysis. *Semiotica, 78*, 75-99.

Psathas, G., & Kozloff, M. (1976). The structure of directions. *Semiotica, 17*, 111-130.

Quine, W. V. O. (1987). *Quiddities.* Cambridge, MA: Harvard University Press.

Rabinow, P. (1977). *Reflections on fieldwork in Morocco.* Berkeley: University of California Press.

Ronchi, V. (1970). *The nature of color.* Cambridge, MA: Harvard University Press.

Rosenhan, D. L. (1973). On being sane in insane places. *Science, 179*, 250-258.

Ryle, G. (1966). *The concept of mind.* Harmondsworth: Peregrine.

Sacks, H. (1963). Sociological description. *Berkeley Journal of Sociology, 8*, 1-16.

Sacks, H. (1965-1972). [Unpublished lectures on conversation]. Irvine: University of California, School of Social Science.

Sacks, H. (1967). The search for help: No one to turn to. In E. Schneidman (Ed.), *Essays in self destruction* (pp. 203-223). New York: Aronson.

Sacks, H. (1970, March-April). [Lectures]. University of California, Irvine.

Sacks, H. (1972a). An initial investigation of the usability of conversational data for doing sociology. In D. Sudnow (Ed.), *Studies in social interaction* (pp. 31-74). New York: Free Press.

Sacks, H. (1972b). On the analyzability of stories by children. In J. Gumpertz & D. Hymes (Eds.), *Directions in sociolinguistics: The ethnography of communication* (pp. 325-345). New York: Holt, Rinehart & Winston.

Sacks, H. (1973). On some puns with some intimations. In *Report of the 23rd Annual Round Table Meeting on Linguistics and Language Studies* (pp. 135-144). Washington, DC: Georgetown University Press.

Sacks, H. (1974). An analysis of the course of a joke's telling in conversation. In R. Bauman & J. Sherzer (Eds.), *Explorations in the ethnography of speaking* (pp. 337-353). Cambridge, UK: Cambridge University Press.

Sacks, H. (1984). Notes on methodology. In J. M. Atkinson & J. Heritage (Eds.), *Structures of social action* (pp. 21-27). Cambridge, UK: Cambridge University Press. (Original work published 1967)

Sacks, H. (1987). You want to find out if anybody really does care (Lectures delivered in Fall 1964 and Spring 1965; G. Jefferson, Comp.). In G. Button & J. R. E. Lee (Eds.), *Talk and social organization.* Clevedon, Avon: Multilingual Matters.

Sacks, H., Schegloff, E. A., & Jefferson, G. (1974). A simplest systematics for the organization of turn-taking in conversation. *Language, 50*, 696-735.

Schaffer, S. (1989). Glass works: Newton's prisms and the uses of experiment. In D. Gooding, T. Pinch, & S. Schaffer (Eds.), *The uses of experiment* (pp. 67-104). Cambridge: Cambridge University Press.

Schaller, G. B. (1963). *The mountain gorilla.* Chicago: University of Chicago Press.

Scheff, T. J. (1966). *Being mentally ill.* Chicago: Aldine.

Schegloff, E. A. (1963). Toward a reading of psychiatric theory. *Berkeley Journal of Sociology, 8*, 61-91.

Schegloff, E. A. (1968). Sequencing in conversational openings. *American Anthropologist, 70*, 1075-1095.

Schegloff, E. A. (1978). On some questions and ambiguities in conversation. In W. U. Dressler (Ed.), *Current trends in text linguistics* (pp. 81-102). Berlin: Walter de Gruyter.

Schegloff, E. A. (1979). Identification and recognition in telephone conversation openings. In G. Psathas (Ed.), *Everyday language: Studies in ethnomethodology* (pp. 23-78). New York: Irvington.

Schegloff, E. A. (1986). The routine as achievement. *Human Studies, 9*, 111-51.

Schegloff, E. A. (1987a). Between macro and micro: Contexts and other connections. In J. C. Alexander et al. (Eds.), *The micro-macro link* (pp. 207-234). New York: Columbia University Press.

Schegloff, E. A. (1987b). Some sources of misunderstanding in talk-in-interaction. *Linguistics, 25*, 201-218.

Schegloff, E. A. (1988a). From interview to confrontation: Observations of the Bush/ Rather encounter. *Research on Language and Social Interaction, 22*, 215-240.

Schegloff, E. A. (1988b). Goffman and the analysis of conversation. In P. Drew & A. Wootton (Eds.), *Erving Goffman: Exploring the interaction order* (pp. 89-135). Boston: Northeastern University.

Schegloff, E. A. (in press). Reflections on talk and social structure. In D. Boden & H. Zimmerman (Eds.), *Talk and social structure*. Oxford, UK: Polity.

Schegloff, E. A., Jefferson, G., & Sacks, H. (1977). The preference for self-correction in the organization of repair in conversation. *Language, 53*, 361-382.

Schegloff, E. A., & Sacks, H. (1973). Opening up closings. *Semiotica, 8*, 289-327.

Schiffrin, D. (1977). Opening encounters. *American Sociological Review, 44*, 679-691.

Schwartz, H. (n.d.). *The "what's new" problem: Or, why are sociologists so interested in deviance?* Paper presented at a seminar at the University of California, Santa Barbara.

Searle, J. R. (1969). *Speech acts: An essay in the philosophy of language*. Cambridge, UK: Cambridge University Press.

Shapin, S. (1984). Pump and circumstance: Robert Boyle's literary technology. *Social Studies of Science, 14*, 481-520.

Shapin, S., & Schaffer, S. (1985). *Leviathan and the air pump: Hobbes, Boyle, and the experimental life*. Princeton, NJ: Princeton University Press.

Sharrock, W. (1974). On owning knowledge. In R. Turner (Ed.), *Ethnomethodology* (pp. 45-53). Harmondsworth: Penguin.

Sharrock, W., & Watson, R. (1988). Autonomy among social theories. In N. Fielding (Ed.), *Actions and structure* (pp. 56-77). London: Sage.

Shimanoff, S. (1980). *Communication rules: Theory and research*. Beverly Hills, CA: Sage.

Smith, D. (1978). K is mentally ill: The anatomy of a factual account. *Sociology, 12*, 23-53.

Smith, G. W. H. (1989a). *A Simmelian reading of Goffman*. Unpublished doctoral dissertation, University of Salford.

Smith, G. W. H. (1989b). Snapshots *sub specie aeternatis*: Simmel, Goffman, and sociology. *Human Studies, 12*, 21-59.

Steenstra-Houtkoop, H. (in press). Opening sequences in Dutch telephone conversations. In D. Boden & H. Zimmerman (Eds.), *Talk and social structure*. Oxford, UK: Polity.

Stephan, F. F., & Mishler, E. G. (1955). The distribution of participation in small groups: An exponential approximation. In A. P. Hare, E. F. Borgatta, & R. F. Bales (Eds.), *Small groups: Studies in social interaction* (pp. 367-379). New York: Knopf.

Sudnow, D. (1965). Normal crimes. *Social Problems, 12*, 255-276.

Sudnow, D. (Ed.). (1972). *Studies in social interaction*. New York: Free Press.

Sudnow, D. (1978). *Ways of the hand*. Cambridge, MA: Harvard University Press.

Sudnow, D. (1979). *Talk's body: A meditation between two keyboards*. New York: Knopf.

Sudnow, D. (1984). *Pilgrim in the microworld*. New York: Warner Bros.

Tomlinson, S. (1981). *Educational subnormality*. London: Routledge & Kegan Paul.

Torode, B. (1989). Discourse analysis and everyday life. In B. Torode (Ed.), *Text and talk as social practice* (pp. xi-xvii). Dordrecht, Netherlands: Foris.

Tur-Sinai, N. H. (1957). *The book of Job*. Jerusalem: Kiryath Sepher.

Vaida, C. (1989, August). *The messy middle chapters of Austin's* How to do things with words. Paper presented at the First International Conference on Understanding Language in Everyday Life, Calgary, Alberta.

Watson, G. (1984). The social construction of boundaries between social and cultural anthropology in Britain and North America. *Journal of Anthropological Research, 40*, 351-366.

Watson, R. (1976). Some conceptual issues in the social identification of victims and offenders. In E. Viano (Ed.), *Victims and society* (pp. 60-71). Washington, DC: Vintage.

Watson, R. (1978). Categorization, authorization and blame-negotiation in conversation. *Sociology, 12*, 105-114.

Watson, R. (1983). The presentation of victim and motive in discourse: The case of police interrogations and interviews. *Victimology: An International Journal, 8*, 31-52.

Watson, R., & Sharrock, W. W. (in press). Something on accounts. *Discourse Analysis Research Group Newsletter.*

Watson, R., & Weinberg, M. (1982). Interviews and the interactional construction of accounts of homosexual identity. *Social Analysis, 11*, 56-78.

Weber, M. (1968). *Economy and society* (Vol. 1). New York: Bedminster.

Whalen, J., Zimmerman, D. H., & Whalen, M. R. (1988). When words fail: A single case analysis. *Social Problems, 35*, 335-362.

Whalen, M. R., & Zimmerman, D. H. (1987). Sequential and institutional contexts in calls for help. *Social Psychology Quarterly, 50*, 172-185.

Whittaker, E. T. (1952). Introduction. In I. Newton, *Opticks* (pp. lxi-lxxvii). New York: Dover.

Wieder, D. L. (1974a). *Language and social reality: The telling of the convict code.* The Hague: Mouton.

Wieder, D. L. (1974b). Telling the code. In R. Turner (Ed.), *Ethnomethodology* (pp. 144-172). Harmondsworth: Penguin.

Wieder, D. L., Friederich, G., Chatham, A. D., Prusahk, D. T., Stearns, S., & Frazer, P. (1988, November). *Some forms and sources of disorder and order in children's snack time conversation.* Paper presented at the annual meeting of the Speech Communication Association, New Orleans.

Williams, P., et al. (Eds.). (1989). *The scope of epidemiological psychiatry.* London: Routledge & Kegan Paul.

Wilson, T. P. (1970). Normative and interpretive paradigms in sociology. In J. Douglas (Ed.), *Understanding everyday life: Toward the reconstruction of sociological knowledge* (pp. 57-79). Chicago: Aldine.

Wilson, T. P. (in press). Social structure and the sequential organization of interaction. In D. Boden & H. Zimmerman (Eds.), *Talk and social structure.* Oxford, UK: Polity.

Wittgenstein, L. (1958). *Philosophical investigations* (G. E. M. Anscombe, Trans.). Oxford, UK: Basil Blackwell.

Wittgenstein, L. (1977). *Remarks on color* (G. E. M. Anscombe, Ed.). Berkeley: University of California Press.

Woolgar, S. (Ed.). (1988). *Knowledge and reflexivity: New frontiers in the sociology of knowledge.* London: Sage.

Zimmerman, D. H. (1970). The practicalities of rule use. In J. Douglas (Ed.), *Understanding everyday life: Toward the reconstruction of sociological knowledge* (pp. 221-238). Chicago: Aldine.

Zimmerman, D. H. (1984). Talk and its occasion: The case of calling the police. In D. Schiffrin (Ed.), *Meaning, form, and use in context: Linguistic applications* (George Washington University Round Table on Language and Linguistics). Washington, DC: Georgetown University Press.

Zimmerman, D. H. (1990). Prendre position. In *Le Parler frais d'Erving Goffman: Arguments* (pp. 218-230). Paris: Les Éditions de Minuit.

Zimmerman, D. H. (in press). The interpersonal organization of calls for emergency assistance. In J. Heritage & P. Drew (Eds.), *Talk at work.* Cambridge, UK: Cambridge University Press.

Zimmerman, D. H., & Boden, D. (1985, May). *Service calls as interpersonal achievements of impersonal ends.* Paper presented at the annual meeting of the International Communication Association, Honolulu.

Zimmerman, D. H., & Boden, D. (in press). Structure-in-action. In D. Boden & H. Zimmerman (Eds.), *Talk and social structure.* Oxford, UK: Polity.

Zimmerman, D. H., & Pollner, M. (1970). The everyday world as a phenomenon. In J. Douglas (Ed.), *Understanding everyday life: Toward the reconstruction of sociological knowledge* (pp. 80-103). Chicago: Aldine.

Zimmerman, D. H., & Wieder, D. L. (1970). Ethnomethodology and the problem of order: Comment on Denzin. In J. Douglas (Ed.), *Understanding everyday life: Toward the reconstruction of sociological knowledge* (pp. 285-298). Chicago: Aldine.

Index

About the Contributors

Jack Bilmes, Ph.D. (Stanford), is Associate Professor of Anthropology, University of Hawaii. He has done fieldwork in Thailand and at the U.S. Federal Trade Commission. He is author of *Discourse and Behavior* (1986) and has published in *Language and Society, Semiotica,* and the *Journal of Anthropological Research.*

Dusan Bjelic, Ph.D. (Boston), is Assistant Professor of Sociology at the University of Southern Maine. He has recently published papers in sociology and theology journals on the practical and social accomplishment of suicide and the logical organization of dialogue in different social settings.

Harold Garfinkel, Ph.D. (Harvard), is Visiting Professor of Sociology at Boston University. He is author of *Studies in Ethnomethodology* (1967) and is currently studying work in the natural sciences.

Tony Hak, Ph.D. (Amsterdam), is Lecturer in Medical Sociology at the School of Medicine, Erasmus University. He is author of *Tekstsociologische Analyse* (1988). He has published in *Semiotica* and has a chapter in Brian Torode's *Text and Talk as Social Practice* (1989).

James L. Heap, Ph.D. (British Columbia), is Associate Professor in the Department of Sociology in Education at the Ontario Institute for Studies in Education. His principal research interests are in the social organization of reading activities, computers in language arts, and classroom discourse. He has published in *Human Studies* and in various education journals.

Stephen Hester, Ph.D. (Kent), is Associate Professor of Anthropology and Sociology at Wilfred Laurier University, Ontario. His recent publications include articles on methodological issues in ethnomethodological research, mundane reason and talk about discourse, and negotiation and membership categorization.

Michael Lynch, Ph.D. (UC Irvine), is Assistant Professor of Sociology at Boston University. He is author of *Art and Artifact in Laboratory Science* (1985) and coeditor (with Steve Woolgar) of *Representation in Scientific Practice* (1990). He is currently working on books on ethnomethodology and the sociology of science, and (coauthored with David Bogen) the testimony at the Iran-Contra hearings.

Michael Moerman, Ph.D. (Yale), is Professor of Anthropology, University of California, Los Angeles. Among his principal publications are *Agricultural Change and Peasant Choice in a Thai Village* (1968), *Talking Culture: Ethnography and Conversation Analysis* (1988), *Culture Embodied* (with Nomura Masaichi) and papers on Thai ethnicity, interaction, and social organization.

George Psathas, Ph.D. (Yale), is Professor of Sociology at Boston University, where he teaches ethnomethodology and conversation analysis. His most recent works are *Interaction Competence* (1990) and *Phenomenology and Sociology: Theory and Research* (1989). He is the founder and Editor-in-Chief of *Human Studies*.

Robert M. Seiler, (Ph.D., Liverpool) is Professor of General Studies at the University of Calgary. His research interests have included the expository prose of 19th-century England, theories of communication, word-and-image relations, and conversation analysis, with a focus on naturally occurring talk in institutional settings. He published two books on Walter Pater, the critic of fine arts. Since 1985 he has edited *The D.A.R.G. Newsletter.* He was William Noble Fellow from 1973 to 1975 at Liverpool University.

Graham Watson, Ph.D. (Simon Fraser), is Associate Professor of Anthropology at the University of Calgary. He is author of *Passing for White: A Study of Racial Assimilation in a South African School* (1970). Research in race relations in South Africa and Canada has led him into the field of language-oriented constructivism.

Rodney Watson, Ph.D. (Warwick), is Senior Lecturer in Sociology at the University of Manchester. He has numerous publications in ethnomethodology, conversation analysis, and related approaches, focusing on deviance, education, racial and ethnic relations, textual analysis, and sociological theory pertaining to language and practical reasoning.

D. Lawrence Wieder, Ph.D. (UCLA), is Associate Professor in the Department of Communication at the University of Oklahoma. He is the author of *Language and Social Reality: The Case of Telling the Convict Code* (1974). His recent publications are in the areas of ethnomethodology, intercultural communication, and language and social interaction.

Don H. Zimmerman, Ph.D. (UCLA), is Professor of Sociology at the University of California, Santa Barbara. His current work analyzes audio- and videotape recordings of the operation of several emergency dispatch centers.

NOTES

NOTES

NOTES

NOTES

NOTES

ACA - 3265